MINISTERING TO THE DIVORCED CATHOLIC

MINISTERING
TO THE
DIVORCED CATHOLIC

Edited by
James J. Young, C.S.P.

PAULIST PRESS
New York/Ramsey/Toronto

Library of Congress
Catalog Card Number: 78-61731

ISBN: 0-8091-2142-5

Published by Paulist Press
Editorial Office: 1865 Broadway, New York, N.Y. 10023
Business Office: 545 Island Road, Ramsey, N.J. 07446

Printed and bound in the
United States of America

ACKNOWLEDGEMENTS

The article "A New Marital Form: The Marriage of Uncertain Duration" © 1978 by Robert S. Weiss is a revision of an article which appeared in *On the Making of Americans: Essays in Honor of David Riesman,* edited by Herbert J. Gans, Nathan Glazer, Joseph R. Gusfield, and Christopher S. Jencks, and is reprinted by permission of the University of Pennsylvania Press. "Canonical-Pastoral Reflections on Divorce" by Thomas J. Green and "The Religious Educator and the Children of Divorce" by James J. Young are taken from the Winter, 1976 edition of *The Living Light* and are reprinted by permission of Our Sunday Visitor. "The Orthodox Position on Divorce" by Lewis J. Patsavos is reprinted by permission of *Diakonia.* Karl Lehmann's "Indissolubility of Marriage, and Pastoral Care of the Divorced Who Remarry" is reprinted by permission of *Communio.* "A Demographer Looks at American Families" by Paul C. Glick, which appeared earlier in the *Journal of Marriage and the Family,* is reprinted by permission of the author. "The Family Today: A Sociological Perspective" by John L. Thomas and "The Gospel and Culture: Christian Marriage and Divorce Today" by Charles E. Curran are reprinted by permission of *Social Thought,* copyright © 1977 by the National Conference of Catholic Charities, 1346 Connecticut Avenue, N.W., Washington, D.C.

2061062

Contents

PART IV

SOCIOLOGICAL ISSUES

PART V

DOCUMENTATION

Introduction:
The Divorced Catholics Movement

James J. Young, C.S.P.

Divorce has now touched almost every American Catholic family somewhere in its immediate family network. It is no longer a remote or theoretical problem for American Catholics, but a deeply personal one. Beyond the pain and anxiety marital break-down causes individuals and families, it is raising complex problems for the whole Church community, problems we are just beginning to face and understand. It's not hard to understand why this problem has shaken the American Catholic community so badly. It came upon us so quickly, so unexpectedly. There had always been an occasional marriage that did not work, and we all knew neighbors or distant friends who became divorced; but in recent years it had begun to seem that every other couple in some parishes were splitting up.

Although we have no accurate information on the relationship between religious affiliation and divorce, our best estimates, borrowing from the pollsters and the government, indicate that there are presently at least six million divorced Catholics in the United States, of whom at least half have remarried. Divorce among observant Catholics was surely a major ingredient in the accelerated divorce rates of the 60's and 70's.

How could this have happened? The American Church over the past century invested vast resources in helping dislocated immigrant families find new life and new stability in a foreign land, and could look back on a record of real achievement. The Church sponsored an enormous network of parishes, schools, hospitals and social agencies to help families in trouble. In the

1

years of the post-World War II boom and on into the 50's, it seemed that for many children of immigrant Catholic parents the American dream had come true. Catholics were emerging into the middle and upper middle classes; as the first persons ever to graduate from college in their family histories; they were moving into the professions; they were having large families and providing their children with advantages they had been denied in the depression years. It was a time of budding lay movements in the Church dedicated to building up the Catholic family; a time when the Catholic population almost doubled.

Then the cracks began to appear. In the early 60's, the divorce rate in the country as a whole began to climb. At first slowly and then with increasing acceleration more and more marriages began to come apart. Researchers began to point out that Catholics, who had once trailed behind the population at large in the incidence of divorce, were now contributing their full share to the rising divorce rate. By the early 70's some observers began to wonder aloud whether Catholics were experiencing a kind of catchup phenomenon and divorcing ahead of their place in the population.

Strangely, it may have been because the Church had succeeded so well in helping Catholics become assimilated into American life that the divorce rate began to rise. Social observers concluded by the late 60's that Catholics had, for better or worse, become "mainstream"; they no longer differed significantly from the population at large on most major life indices. As they became as "American as apple pie," they began to absorb new aspirations abroad in the culture. Older values about marriage and family gave way among many Catholic groups to new expectations about personal fulfillment in marriage, friendship, and greater sexual satisfaction; new concerns about raising children and providing for their emotional nurture and education raised questions about large families; new appetites for leisure, a freer role for women, and higher education—all had dramatic impact upon the Catholic family as well as upon the American family at large.

The Catholic community began to respond in a pattern often associated with the victims of a natural disaster, such as flood or fire. At first there was shock, numbness and even denial that Catholics were divorcing. Then came a period of recoil, a negative time when divorced Catholics often found themselves with rectory doors shut in their faces or sentences of excommunication laid upon them. Then came a frantic time of new efforts to set things right, a time of busy new programs to bolster family life, all the while carefully avoiding the alarming implications of such widespread divorce. Finally, and this is the phase we seem to be entering now, a period of coming to terms with our irremediable losses—a time of facing the problem squarely—of coming to terms with the need for new ministry—a period of reshaping our Catholic life and attitudes—a time of recognizing that a great amount of divorce will be a sad constant of Catholic lives for some time to come.

Over recent years a vital, growing ministry by and to separated, divorced and remarried Catholics has begun to take inventive shape in the American Church. Over 500 support groups, official diocesan ministries, and a national organization have given structure and momentum to this new ministry.

One of the first organizations for divorced Catholics was put together in Boston in the Fall of 1971. The divorced Catholics we began to meet there had experienced personal failure and social disruption at the time of divorce, for which they were totally unprepared; on top of that they felt that they had been made to feel like outcasts in the Church community. They saw the Church's refusal to permit remarriage as a punishment for having failed in a first marriage. They felt at the time when they needed support from the Church they usually got stony silence. They were disappointed in their Church, but they were not leaving. They were Catholics in their bones and wanted to remain Catholics. They didn't hate the Church for having failed them, but still loved it and wanted to work to change it.

What we began to discover from the start was the enormous strengths of Catholic identity and belonging, and the strong communitarian character which American Catholicism nurtured in its parishes, schools and ethnic communities. Many of these people insisted that their Catholic faith was a great resource when it came to coping with the pain of divorce. Some even said that they made the decision to divorce only after intense personal prayer. "I knew God didn't mean for me and my children to live in this destructive atmosphere," one woman said. We saw men and women who had poured out the last drop trying to make a marriage work before sadly admitting it was impossible. We saw those who never seemed to have a chance—economic, emotional and even accidental forces beyond their control seemed to destroy the marriage. We saw those who simply made a mistake—they chose the wrong person. We saw those who had a good marriage for a time, much like their friends, but then something happened—the relationship fell apart—it couldn't be put back together. These hundreds of poignant stories gave the divorce debate real flesh and blood for us.

These spunky, articulate divorced Catholics who began to pour into the Paulist Center in 1972, were the products of American Catholicism of the 50's and 60's. They were not going to drift away, feeling unwanted; they were intent on making a place for themselves in the Church. They were not children looking for approval, but rather adults looking for acceptance. They were men and women who knew what it was to belong to a faith community, and they wanted to maintain that identity even though they were divorced. They decided to call their group the "Divorced Catholics Group," because there was something shocking about the title for some, and more importantly, something hopeful about the title for others. Significantly, they did not see themselves as change-agents or a political vanguard in the Church, rather they mainly wanted to help others going through the same transition and wanted us to find ways to make it easier for them.

The shape of the group we put together in Boston over the next few years has become an important model for some 500 Divorced Catholics Groups in the United States and Canada. There are some consistent features of these groups:

1. *The groups are self-help groups.* Divorced Catholics Groups see divorced people themselves as the primary helping agents with one another. Like Alcoholics Anonymous or weight loss groups, they challenge the participants to take responsibility for themselves and for one another. This personal responsibility

for oneself and others has always been a part of Catholic ethics. We begin with a theoretical assumption that divorced people are basically healthy, but might be exhibiting some transitory signs of distress while negotiating a difficult adjustment. Experience over five years has borne out how effective this group support can be for the separating and recently divorced. We have found group members most insightful about the needs of one another and most inventive in finding sensitive ways to help. From the beginning we saw the groups surrounding those going through the worst pain, and offering them a cushion to help them through the up's and down's of the transition.

2. *The format of meetings.* Most groups have at least one monthly meeting which features a speaker, panel, or taped lecture. This educational model has proved to be effective for two reasons: First, divorced people need a lot of information (single parenting, religious questions, community resources, law, taxes), and second, an educational program provides a fairly non-threatening base at which newcomers can easily touch down. Most groups go on to provide "rap groups" on other evenings; these groups usually bring together 6-8 recently divorced people in a closed group which meets over a limited span of time (usually 6-8 weeks) with a veteran member or professional serving as facilitator. Some groups have enhanced the leadership capacities of veteran group members by providing them with communications skills training.

3. *More specialized resources are needed.* Most groups have developed relationships with more professional helping resources. The groups seem to be realistic about referring people for more individualized attention when this is indicated; yet they are well aware that these special helping resources are either too expensive or not available at all in many places. In many informal, caring ways the groups seem to absorb and support the troubled. Some groups offer special programs such as the Seminar for the Separated, an eight-week group model for those going through separation, developed by Dr. Bob Weiss and his colleagues at Harvard's Laboratory for Community Psychiatry. We have taken this eight-week group model and fashioned new seminars around special issues such as single-parenting and growth

issues after recovery. A group for men only has recently been most successful. These seminars bring together a professional who offers input with about 15-20 people in an educational format.

4. *Those who attend.* Divorced Catholics Groups seem to be most effective with those who are recently separated or those who are still working through divorce adjustment. The group leaders are becoming more aware recently of the need to support the personal growth of the single parent and the divorced person who has not remarried. We like to feel that the groups provide space and support for people to grow so that they do not get drawn into a hasty remarriage. We see very few remarried people in the groups since marriage usually means that they've resolved their need for support; some remarrieds come with religious questions about their place in the Catholic community, but these usually can be cleared up in several private counseling sessions. Recently some people on the West coast and in Canada have started support groups for remarried Catholics; they want to find ways to help one another in working through growth issues in their new marriages.

5. *The groups have a strong religious identity.* The groups usually call themselves Divorced Catholics Groups, not out of a desire to exclude non-Catholics, but because being divorced and Catholic presents a special set of problems and opportunities. (In most areas non-Catholics are most welcome.) We are learning that separation and divorce is more than a disciplinary problem for Catholics; it is a wrenching experience which touches the depths of one's religious identity. Divorce challenges a person's whole value system about fidelity and commitment. After attending the national Divorced Catholics conference last year at the University of Notre Dame, Mel Krantzler, author of *Creative Divorce,* told me how deeply impressed he was by the divorced Catholics he met. He said he felt spiritually re-energized by being with them. He said that all professionals who work with divorced people know that they can offer them some knowledge and skills, but the most crucial question is how to get them to believe in themselves again. How do divorced people get "turned on" again to themselves, their world, and other people? "I see that

happening in Divorced Catholics Groups,'' Krantzler said. That is the deeply religious nature of this ministry: helping women and men confront failures and death and grow through them to new life. As a psychiatrist friend once said, ''Anyone who is dealing with grief work is dealing with resurrection.'' That is why divorced Catholics pray and worship together, go on retreats, and become involved in courses to develop their religious understanding. The groups lead people to that most basic of all levels where they can make an act of faith in themselves and in their God.

Father Jerry Brown, S.S., recently finished a doctoral dissertation at Temple University's School of Communications, which focused on the Divorced Catholics Movement. Father Brown sought to analyze the major themes that have characterized the development of the movement over the past five years. The first message he felt captured the attention of divorced Catholics and the Church community was a message of hope. For divorced Catholics who had felt that there was no place for them in the Church community, or no one cared about them, the early voices insisted that there was a reservoir of genuine concern for them in the Church. These early leaders pleaded that divorced people not be treated like outcasts, called for the Church to offer them pastoral care in their time of need, and held out hope that their new marriages might be accepted. As the movement developed, the second message which gained momentum was a message of reconciliation. Divorced Catholics were told to approach the growing numbers of sympathetic priests who want to help; and to contact the increasingly helpful staffs of the marriage tribunals. Even where annulments and the blessing of second marriages were not possible, divorced Catholics were told that many pastors would reconcile them privately to the Church. The third message was a challenge to divorced people to minister to one another. An awareness began to surface that divorced people themselves were the best Church helpers for other divorced people.

In the past five years divorce ministry has won a growing degree of acceptance in the Catholic community, and the process seems to have been accelerated by the highly symbolic removal of the penalty of automatic excommunication by Pope Paul in

November 1977. The Church seems to be admitting that it was un-Christian in denying divorced people pastoral care, and now wants them to feel very much part of the Catholic community. There is a stereotype abroad in the Catholic community that divorced Catholics are men and women who have rejected the Church's teachings on the permanence and indissolubility of marriage, and are a growing pressure group seeking to change the laws of the Church prohibiting second marriage. There is little evidence that this is true. This false impression may get a start from the Catholic penchant to intellectualize behavior, i.e., when we see someone who has chosen to end a marriage, we tend to assume that he or she does not really believe in permanent marriage. Yet most behavioral scientists tell us that very often people in crisis do not work out clear intellectual positions before they act, but rather usually act on impulse or out of fear. This seems to be the case with most divorced Catholics. They tell us that they hid for years from the signs of marital failure, reluctant even to entertain the thought of ending a marriage. It had never occurred to them that their marriage might not work; no one in their family had ever been divorced; but then they began to find life around deteriorating. They found themselves in deep conflict with the values of their Catholic upbringing, but on a deep emotional level they were feeling that there was no hope for their marriage. Nowhere in this process was there a denial of the Church's teaching on lasting marriage; rather there was a painful yearning that some solution might be found to help restore this ideal in their lives. Then a step was taken, sometimes impulsively, even unconciously, and the die was cast. After the decision to end a marriage, then separation and divorce, the typical person found himself/herself in a deep conflict over values. On the one side were concrete reasons calling for the end of this downward marriage spiral, while on the other hand the inherited values of one's life were a taunting contradiction. For they regretted the divorce greatly and were having a very hard time justifying their actions—they knew what they had done could not be approved by the Church. Yet they hungered for understanding and acceptance. All they wanted was for family, friends, and especially a priest, to say, "I understand what you had to do; I know how hard it must have been."

We are beginning to learn that divorced Catholics are not asking the Church to abandon its traditional teaching—their experience, most of all, has taught them the power and the attractiveness of that ideal; they wished they had achieved it. They feel like failures; they worry about themselves, their children, and even at times, about their former spouse. Their self-esteem has plummeted and they have lost confidence. It is a time when they need the Church community.

Last year Msgr. Stephen J. Kelleher conducted a thoughtful survey of Divorced Catholics Groups in the United States and Canada; he asked the leadership of these groups whether they saw the change of the Church's discipline on second marriage as one of their goals. With responses from about one hundred groups, he found little interest in changing Church law. Again, there is a stereotype that all Catholics contemplating second marriage want the Church to change its discipline to provide the blessing of this new marriage. One conclusion is that they are not so much concerned about the canonical regularity of this new marriage, as they are about continuing to belong to the Catholic community. The issue isn't the blessing of a marriage, but rather being able to receive Communion. These men and women know that much of what has happened in their lives cannot be approved, yet they feel that they have acted sincerely; they want the Church to understand and accept them. They have been raised to believe that the consequences of a second marriage is excommunication from the Catholic people, if no longer in law, surely in fact, for they have been told that if they remarry, they can no longer take Communion. They dread this prospect for they love being Catholic; they have been born and raised in the Catholic community and their lives have been enriched by a unique sense of Catholic belonging. Father Richard McCormick has said that the most painful aspect of the divorce remarriage issue presently for Catholics is the issue of the Eucharist.

We forget sometimes that Catholics are a deeply Eucharist people—that reception of Communion at Sunday Mass has been the powerful sign of Catholic belonging and acceptance. This is why the removal of the American law of excommunication by the bishops was such an important step toward reconciliation. Catholics certainly desire to be in good standing with the Church community; and most second married Catholics do want to have their new marriages recognized. The number of Catholics pursuing annulments testifies to this desire to be in good standing. The newer pastoral theology of the Eucharist which welcomes those who have not achieved Gospel perfection to the banquet of reconciliation, along with the development of approved pastoral solutions in the internal forum have been two of the most important pastoral developments for remarried Catholics.

We may be fortunate at this time in the Catholic community that we cannot offer a blessing for a second marriage. This past year I participated in two workshops for Protestant clergy, at which they all raised serious questions about their own practice regarding solemnizing second marriages. They agreed that all too often they have remarried people who were unprepared, and too often they saw the doubly tragic situation of a second failed marriage. They, like ourselves, are appreciating anew the need to give public witness to the Lord's teaching on permanent marriage while recognizing the need to help those whose marriages have failed find recovery. The researchers sadly admit that second marriages are not doing as well in American society as first marriages, and one of the obvious causes is hasty marriage. I have become convinced that the discussion of a change in Church discipline, must be deferred until we have developed the pastoral skills necessary to help the divorced rebuild their lives.

Another stereotype suggests that most divorced and second married Catholics are angry at the Church and want nothing to do with it. It is true that we find a great deal of anger in them; yet, whenever any invitation to reconciliation is offered, even just a talk on the subject, these people come pouring out. Their hunger to be reunited to the Catholic community is far deeper than we ever suspected.

We Catholics have been conditioned by our moral training to look upon divorce all too often as a sign of personal failure and weakness. Hence the familial rejection, the stigmatization, and the outright discrimination in the Church community toward the divorced. Obviously personal characteristics enter into the breakdown of every marriage, but we seem inattentive to the changing social conditions which make lasting marriage difficult

We are caught in a crisis of rising expectations in marriage, given impetus by the convenant imagery of *Gaudium et Spes,* which creates enormous new appetites for satisfaction and personal happiness in marriage. Gone is the dominant male/submissive female image of marriage. Greater financial security for many, longer life, better health, and leisure, to mention but a few significant factors, have given couples much more time and energy to invest in developing a marriage relationship marked by friendship and intimacy. Where the poor are denied these advantages their frustration in marriage can be most severe.

We know that almost every American marriage can expect to face severe crisis. The Census Bureau reports that of all Americans marrying this year fully 40% can expect to have their marriages end in divorce, unless the divorce rate declines precipitously, and there is no reason to believe that that is going to happen. Of the remaining 60% half of them can expect to experience marital separation ending up in reconciliation or severe marital problems which will lead them into counseling. Where once divorce was seen as an extreme solution to be considered only when things had reached unbearable proportions, it seems that over the past decade it has become accepted as a reasonable solution to an unworkable marriage. Increased yearning for satisfaction in marriage leads the unsatisfied to leave unhappy unions in search of a new, more satisfactory marriage. Even though increased divorce has brought with it a host of new problems, it has not been without its element of social gain—men and women, who in the past would have been condemned to blighted lives, now can free themselves from such destructive unions and possibly make a new life.

Further, we Catholics could be more attentive to the social contagion that often wounds the fragile relationship of husband and wife. Divorced people tell us of marriages wounded irreparably by long periods of unemployment, unexpected and chronic illness, the dislocation of Vietnam and its aftereffects, the death of children, the onset of personality disorders, and relocations which separated partners from kinship supports. In recent weeks the Carnegie Council on Children, under the chairmanship of Dr. Kenneth Keniston, has documented in a new study how hostile the climate of American life can be for millions of married couples and their children. It is estimated that at least a quarter of American Catholic families fall within the threatened social circumstances that Keniston's committee describes. Too often in stigmatizing the divorced as moral failures, we may well have fallen into the old trap of blaming the victims.

In conclusion, the divorce situation among American Catholics is revealing to us the pervasive pressures that affect American marriage as an institution. All the experienced observers see no indication that things will change dramatically in the near future. Divorced Catholics can sketch for us the human dimensions of those pressures and can help us shape realistic family life programs. Divorced Catholics can also give us confidence to face this most complex task, for they reveal to us some of the most enduring strengths of being Catholic. We find in their stories the spiritual resources which come from being raised in the Faith. They exhibit a strong sense of Catholic belonging and a prayerfulness developed over long years of pain and rejection.

Father John Haughey, S.J. writes in a recent article that "new things do not become part of the behavior of Christians unless they are seen in the behavior of Jesus after whom devoted Christians pattern themselves." I like to sketch for audiences whenever I can the beautiful portrait we have of Jesus in conversation with the divorced woman at Jacob's well. Here we find the same Lord who presented such a powerful call to permanent and lasting marriage revealing himself gently and compassionately to this woman who had been divorced by five men. The strength of his position did not distance him from those who had not been able to achieve the ideal. We find in his behavior a kind of balance between the service of permanence and the service of the failed which we need to imitate in our marriage ministry today. I like to suggest that the key scriptural message which shapes this ministry for us comes from Paul in his second letter to the Corinthians: "It is all God's work. For it was God who was in Christ reconciling the world to himself and gave us the ministry of reconciliation; that is, God was in Christ reconciling the world to himself, not counting their trespasses against them, and entrusting to us the message of reconciliation." (2 Cor 5:19-20)

Part I
Theological Issues

The Gospel and Culture: Christian Marriage and Divorce Today

Charles E. Curran

Within the last few years, there have been growing discussions within the Roman Catholic Church about changing the discipline that excludes divorced and remarried Catholics from participation in the Eucharist and changing the teaching on the indissolubility of marriage.[1] The call for change recognizes developments in contemporary culture and society which are different today from what they have been in the past. Thus, the particular question of the proper understanding of Christian marriage and divorce today raises the broader question of the relationship between the gospel message and contemporary culture—a perennial question for Christianity.

I
GOSPEL AND CULTURE

Many times it seems that Christianity in general has seen too close an accord between the gospel and culture. Were not Christians apparently too ready to accept the reality of slavery for many years and too slow in the last few centuries to denounce the evils of colonialism?[2] Today, many people point a finger at the Christian Church and accuse the Church of not standing up against the prevailing opinion and fighting for the rights of the poor, the underprivileged, and the outcasts.[3] History presents other examples of how the Christian Church may have too easily accommodated the gospel message to the culture of the time.

American Catholic Experience

In the United States, historical circumstances have focused the problem even more acutely for the Roman Catholic Church. As an immigrant church in the nineteenth and early twentieth centuries, the Roman Catholic Church in the United States naturally evoked suspicion on the part of many Americans outside the church membership because of its allegiance to Rome and its immigrant constituents. In many ways, the dominant motif of the American Catholic Church was to prove both to Americans and to other Catholics that one could be both Catholic and American at one and the same time. The Catholic Church in this country set out to prove that there was no basic incompatibility between Roman Catholic faith and the American culture. Signs of this approach are evident in the encouragement shown by the mainstream of American Catholicism to the immigrants to become acclimated to the new culture, and to adopt the American language, customs, and mores, despite the persistent appeal of some church people that Catholics would lose their faith if they became Americanized.[4] In earlier times, the small Catholic minority in the United States also adopted a conformist attitude toward the prevailing cultural and social attitudes.[5]

One very significant event in which Cardinal Gibbons, who was the leader of the American Church for many years, played a prominent role illustrates such an approach. The Catholic Church in the United States, unlike the Catholic Church in many other parts of the world, has not lost the support of the workers, and much credit here is due to Gibbons and the leadership of the American Church. In the 1880's, the Catholic Church in this country was faced with the question of Catholic membership in the Knights of Labor. The Archbishop of Quebec had already condemned the organization and forbidden Catholics to belong. Although the Holy See had twice upheld the condemnation of the Knights of Labor by the Archbishop of Quebec, Gibbons believed the condemnation was imprudent and unnecessary. He presented his case in favor of the Knights of Labor when he was in Rome in 1887 to receive the red hat of the Cardinalate. His case was so convincingly presented that ultimately his opinion prevailed.[6]

In his written presentation to Rome, Gibbons listed some of the consequences that would follow from a condemnation of the Knights. The Catholic Church would lose her reputation as a friend of the working person. There would be a great danger of pitting the Church against the political powers of the country which were defending the workers and their right to organize. One sentence in his memorandum is most revealing: "The accusation of being un-American—that is to say, alien to our national spirit—is the most powerful weapon which the enemies of the Church can employ against her."[7]

Those who espoused the cause of a basic compatibility between being Catholic and being American had to respond to attacks from two sides. On the one hand, many people in the United States, as illustrated in the Know Nothing persecutions, were suspicious and hostile to the immigrant Roman Catholic Church.[8] This hostility was still prevalent well into the twentieth century and was apparently put to rest only with the election of a Catholic as President of the United States in 1960.

There was also opposition from Rome. In 1899, Pope Leo XIII condemned "Americanism," which called for the Church to accommodate itself not only in discipline but also in dogma to the new conditions of the times, and stressed the natural and active virtues over the supernatural and passive virtues. The American bishops often pointed out that the condemnation was based primarily on a poor French translation of the life of Isaac Hecker and that the condemned attitudes and teachings did not really exist in the United States.[9] However, the condemnation underlined the tension that Rome felt in fully reconciling political freedom, especially in the form of religious liberty, with the self-understanding of the Catholic Church. The problem of religious liberty was to continue being a difficult point for Roman Catholics in the United States well into the twentieth century. It was only at the Second Vatican Council with the Declaration on Religious Liberty, which had been heavily influenced by the theological work of the American Jesuit, John Courtney Murray, and fervently supported by the American bishops, that the Roman Catholic Church officially accepted the concept of religious liberty.[10]

In social ethics, there emerged at the time of Gibbons and continued in the mainstream of American Catholicism the policy often called Catholic Social Liberalism. In the twentieth century, it took the form of the Catholic Church's being identified with the moderately progressive forces working for the rights of workers, for their right to organize, for a living wage, social security, and the legitimacy of strikes under certain circumstances. Problems and difficulties were recognized with the American system, but the belief in a basic compatibility between Christian teaching and the American spirit indicated that the existing inequities and injustices could be overcome if all people of good will would cooperate.[11]

After the Second World War, as more Catholics entered the mainstream of American life and, as Catholics became generally accepted, the basic compatibility between American culture and the Catholic faith became even more solidified. Catholics proudly boasted of the vitality of the Catholic Church in this country. Catholics and Americans were of one mind in fighting the evils of Communism. As individual Catholics climbed up the economic ladder, and the Church in general grew in influence, it seems that, to a degree at least, the reforming aspect of the earlier part of the century became lost. Economically, with the assimilation of Catholics into the middle class of American society, politically, with the acceptance that came in the wake of the election and presidency of John F. Kennedy, and theologically, with the acceptance of the American issue of religious liberty at the Second Vatican Council, there was an even greater stress on compatibility between Catholicism and Americanism.

The Vietnam War and the opposition to it by a number of Catholic priests, sisters, and laity made many Catholic conscious of another approach to the question of the relationship between the gospel and American society.[12] Movements in opposition to the prevailing culture, such as the Catholic Worker Movement which began in the 1930's,[13] had been present and quite meaningful in Roman Catholicism, but their effect on the American Church as a whole was limited. The Vietnam War, urban riots, revolutionary movements at home and abroad, Watergate, and other realities made many Catholics aware of the fact that there might be something other than a basic compatibility between American culture and the gospel. The shock for Roman Catholicism as a whole was even more rude because in the years immediately prior to the Vietnam involvement, the accepted compatibility of Catholicism and Americanism had actually reached its highest point.

It would be wrong and quite inaccurate to think that American Catholics alone made this mistake. In fact, Protestant liberalism in general and liberal Protestant thought in the United States had succumbed to the same danger. In the minds of some social gospelers there was an identity between the Kingdom of God and American culture and society.[14] Aspects of the theology of secularity in the 1960's suffered from the same defect.[15]

Later attempts within the Catholic and other Christian Churches at developing a theology of hope and a recognition of the role of the crucifixion and of the paschal mystery have tried to overcome the defects of the too easy identification between culture and Christianity which characterized quite a bit of Christian thought in the early part of the 1960's,[16] and to reassert the areas of difference.

On the other hand, both Catholic theory and historical indications show that it would be equally wrong to assert *only* a basic incompatibility between culture and the gospel. Vatican Council II stressed the need for dialogue with culture and with the entire world. In many areas, the Catholic Chruch must acknowledge what it has learned from others concerning many important moral realities. In our contemporary world, for example, the Church has learned from others the value and importance of freedom. In our day, the Church has often been taught by others the need for equality and justice for women, for blacks, and for other minority groups in our society. One might object that, in this case, the Christian Church had already accommodated itself to the prevailing cultural ethos and had truly forgotten the gospel. Such an explanation is not inaccurate, but in the culture the Church has also found aspects of the gospel which it had forgotten.

The Catholic theological tradition in theory has shown a basic openness to culture, although in practice this has not always been true. The natural law tradition, from the theological perspective, acknowledged the fact that creation was good and that human reason, on the basis of creation, could arrive at ethical wisdom and knowledge. The Roman Catholic theological tradition never disparaged the human but saw it as positively related to the gospel. In the now obsolete terminology of the manuals of theology, "nature" and "supernature," or faith and reason, were not opposed, but there were continuities between them. Grace did not destroy nature but rather built on nature.[17] So great an appreciation did Catholic thought show for the natural, the created, and the human that it could rightly be accused, in part, of not giving enough importance to the gospel, redemption, and faith—especially in its ethical methodology and teaching. Likewise, sacramental theory in Roman Catholicism shows that the basic human elements of bread, wine, and oil are not denied but, rather, are accepted, integrated, and transformed.

The theology of Christian marriage well illustrates that the Catholic theological tradition was open to the true and the good found in culture and did not see a basic incompatibility between the gospel and culture. The principal thesis of Edward Schillebeeckx's volume on Christian marriage views Christian marriage as a secular reality that becomes a saving mystery.[18] Rather than deny or contradict what was found in culture, the Catholic Church has accepted it and transformed it into a saving mystery. Schillebeeckx in his historical section has probably not given enough importance to the sacred character of marriage in Greek and Roman culture,[19] but one can still accept the soundness of his conclusion. According to Schillebeeckx, it is impossible for the Christian view of human marriage and the family to be a pure datum of revelation; it is more the result of a reflective human existence illuminated by revelation. Marriage as a human commission is always closely linked to the prevailing historical realities and is subject to development. God's offer of salvation to human persons follows this human history and assumes certain characteristics which become increasingly clear with the passage of time.[20]

The history of the sacrament of marriage illustrates perhaps better than any other aspect of Catholic life how the developing human culture influenced the Christian reality of marriage. Sacramental theology itself developed over time and in dialogue with the culture. The first time that a document of the Church referred to marriage as a sacrament was at a synod in Verona in 1184.[21] It was only in the second half of the thirteenth century that theologians asserted that marriage gives a grace which positively aids in doing good. By the middle of the sixteenth century when the Council of Trent was convened, it was a commonly held teaching, and universally accepted by the theologians, that marriage was a sacrament which gave grace and was in no way different on this point from the other sacraments.[22]

Many historical changes have occurred in the Christian understanding of marriage, based on changes and developments in the culture. The essence of marriage was understood to be the contract or the consent of the spouses, which was borrowed from Roman law, and which differed from seeing the essence of marriage in the handing over of the daughter by the father to her husband or the sexual relationship (which was, however, recognized as being essential for the consummation of marriage).[23] Today, theologians are rightly trying to see marriage primarily in terms of a covenant relationship and not as a contract.[24] The requirement that for a valid marriage Catholics must be married before a priest and two witnesses was introduced into the Church by the Council of Trent in the sixteenth century as a means to prevent the abuses of clandestine marriages.[25] The unfolding understanding of Christian marriage thus shows the influence of historical and cultural circumstances.

A Proposed Solution

Illustrations have been proposed showing there are many things in culture which are compatible with Christianity but also many things in culture which contradict the Christian gospel. The above statement seems in keeping with the historical evidence, but in my judgment it rests primarily on strong theological justification. The relationship between the gospel and culture has been a perennial question in Christian thought and a most difficult problem in practice. H. Richard Niebuhr describes five different models in Christian ethics for understanding the relationship between Christ and culture.[26] Niebuhr describes the two extreme positions as Christ against culture, which sees the relationship in terms of incompatibility, and the opposite extreme as the Christ of culture, which sees only continuity and even identification between the two. In the middle ground, where most Christians find themselves, there are three mediating positions—Christ above culture, Christ and culture in paradox, Christ the transformer of culture.

I approach the Christ and culture question on the basis of the stance proposed for moral theology—the basic perspective or horizon with which Christian ethics and the Christian understand reality. The Christian stance is structured by the fivefold Christian mysteries of creation, sin, incarnation, redemption, and resurrection destiny.[27] This stance, applied to the question of the gospel and culture, results in a nuanced approach.

Since all things are created by God, the goodness of creation is present in culture. Sin, however, affects not only the hearts of human beings but also has social and cosmic dimensions which affect culture. The incarnation indicates that in the plan of God everything truly human is to be brought into the divine plan. Redemption for the Christian has already occurred and affects all reality, but redemption does not totally eradicate the presence of sin which will continue until the end of time. Resurrection destiny, or, the fullness of the eschaton, lies in the future, so that the fullness of gospel perfection will never be obtained in this world. Such a stance presents a framework within which one can approach the general question of the gospel and culture. Culture shares in the goodness of creation, the call to participation in the divine plan, the reality of redemption, and the hope of resurrection destiny. But culture also knows the finitude and limitations of created reality, the effects of sin, and the limitations coming from the fact that the fullness of the eschaton is not yet here. Such an approach cannot accept either a dogmatic incompatibility between Christ and culture nor an absolute compatibility and identification between the two. The primary task for the Christian Church and the individual Christian remains the critical function of continually discerning what is compatible with the gospel in the contemporary culture. In general, such a discerning process of the contemporary culture must be done in the light of the scriptural witness, the historical tradition, and the eschatological pull of the future. The examples given in the first part of this paper can be understood as illustrations of the stance and methodology just proposed.

II
CHRISTIAN MARRIAGE AND DIVORCE TODAY

In the light of the proposed stance and methodology, how does one evaluate the question involving Christian marriage and divorce today? Statistics show the great number of Christian marriages which are ending in divorce. Surveys and polls indicate that increasing numbers of Roman Catholics do not accept the Church's teaching on the indissolubility of marriage. In general, my stance would tend to avoid the extreme opinions that the breakdown of many Catholic marriages is due only to weakness, sinfulness, and selfishness, or only to positive or neutral factors.

Need for Divorce

In two previous studies, I have developed in great detail the reasons why the Roman Catholic Church should change its teaching on indissolubility and acknowledge the possibility of divorce and remarriage.[28] In the context of the present study, it is neither necessary nor possible to repeat all the reasons which were proposed in the earlier articles. The following paragraphs will point out only the aspects in the contemporary culture and in present-day theological method which call for a change in the older teaching of the Catholic Church.

Moral theology today employs a more historically conscious approach which gives greater importance to historicity, process, and change, and follows a more inductive methodology. The *Pastoral Constitution on the Church in the Modern World* employed such a methodology by beginning its consideration of different topics with a reading of the signs of the times. Christian marriage today has evolved to a personal love relationship between spouses as opposed to the arranged marriages in older cultures which were often supported by political and economic considerations. Marriage based primarily on the love of the spouses and not arranged by parents represents a positive development, but at the same time such marriages are more fragile. Marriage can no longer be considered as the making of a contract which lasts forever but as a commitment made by two individuals to each other to grow in their union of love. Growth, dynamism, and development of the spouses are necessary aspects of Christian marriage today. Here, again, one must accept the fact that such an understanding of marriage leads to the recognition that such growth might not always occur. Roman Catholic theology has traditionally acknowledged that vows are no longer obliging if the matter of the vow or the person making the vow undergoes substantial changes. The possibility of such change is much more prevalent today.

The emphasis on personalism and its effects on marriage constitute a significant moral development, but at the same time indicate that marriages might break down when that loving relationship is no longer present or possible. Influenced by personalism, contemporary moral theology recognizes that no one individual choice, no matter how important, can ever be totally identified with the person who remains even to himself or herself a mystery. The solemn commitment of marriage requires a most mature and well thought out decision, but there still exists the possibility of a mistake which might only become apparent in the years ahead.

Other sociological changes are of great importance. The single person in contemporary society often feels alone and adrift. In an older society, within the extended family, there was always a place for an aunt or an uncle, but this is not the case today. In our present American culture, a twenty-five-year-old single person looking for a marriage partner meets divorced persons more often than those who have never married.

Contemporary experience argues strongly against the validity of the rational or natural law arguments proposed against divorce—the good of the spouses, the good of the children, and the good of society. These reasons cannot prove the absolute indissolubility of all marriages. Historical studies have also shown a curious development in the arguments proposed by the Roman Catholic Church for the indissolubility of marriage. Before the nineteenth century, the great canonists and theologians of the Church generally acknowledged that reason and the natural law did not prove the absolute indissolubility of marriage.

Roman Catholic Scripture scholars are no longer in agreement that the Scriptures forbid the possibility of divorce and remarriage. The famous exception clauses in *Matthew 19:19* and *5:32* (whoever divorces his wife except for the case of *porneia*) might very well refer to some exceptions made in the early Christian community to the absolute teaching against divorce. Paul's famous exception (often interpreted by Catholics as the basis for the Pauline privilege) can be interpreted in the same way. Contemporary theology has given great attention to eschatology. Scripture scholars and theologians today recognize the influence of eschatology on the ethical teaching of Jesus. I opt for the opinion that one can partially understand some of the strenuous ethical teachings of Jesus in the Sermon on the Mount as a goal or ideal towards which the Christian must strive without always being able to attain the ideal. In the light of these and other reasons, I propose that indissolubility remains a goal and ideal for Christian marriage; but Christians, sometimes without any personal fault, are not always able to live up to that ideal. Thus the Roman Catholic Church should change its teaching on divorce.

The emphasis on historicity has occasioned a greater interest in and understanding of the historical teaching on divorce and indissolubility. Experts disagree about the historical evidence and its interpretation, but at least in some places in the early Church divorce and remarriage were allowed and tolerated, although from the tenth century onwards there has been a solid tradition in the Roman Catholic Church in favor of the indissolubility of consummated, sacramental marriages between two baptized persons. However, there have been many other developments affecting the dissolution and invalidity of marriages.

Finally, it should be pointed out that a most significant change has already occurred in the question of divorce. In prac-

tice, many divorced and remarried Catholics are now fully participating in the Eucharistic celebration. Some argue that the
Church should not change its teaching on divorce but only change
the pastoral practice which until just recently called for divorced
and remarried Catholics not to participate fully in the Eucharist.
In my judgment, such an approach does not go far enough. A
change in the teaching on indissolubility is demanded by a proper
theological interpretation of the Scriptural evidence, the historical development, the contemporary experience, and the eschatological pull of the future.

Even if the cultural and theological factors mentioned above
present a total picture, the acceptance of divorce cannot be
viewed as the only response or the totally adequate response of the
Church. More important in the long run is the need for the Church
to bring all its people to a better understanding of Christian marriage and to equip them with what is necessary for trying to live out
Christian marriage in our culture. Dynamic, personalistic, and
more historically conscious understandings indicate that marriage
requires a constant effort for spouses to deepen and grow in their
loving commitment. The fragility of marriage argues not only for
the acceptance of divorce in some circumstances but also calls for
the Church to do everything possible to strengthen Christian marriages.

However, the factors briefly mentioned above which call for
a change in the Roman Catholic Church's teaching on the indissolubility of marriage are not the only cultural factors affecting
Christian marriage today. As should be expected in the light of
the proposed stance, there are also elements in the culture inimi-
cal to the ideal of Christian marriage. Human shortcomings and
sinfulness together with the incarnations of sin in our culture and
in our societal structures also influence the breakup of many marriages. This paper will now examine some areas in which contemporary culture stands in opposition to the ideal of Christian marriage. In the light of these factors, it becomes even more necessary for the Church to realize the great pastoral need to create an
ethos within which the living out of the reality of Christian mar-
riae can take place.

The Marriage Vow

The heart of Christian marriage and the basis of indissolubility as an ideal toward which it is incumbent for spouses to strive come from the covenant commitment of wives and husbands. Our culture and civilization have been obviously influenced by Christianity; and the traditional marriage vow or promise often used in our society well illustrates the meaning of the covenant commitment of husband and wife one to the other—"I take you for my lawful wife or husband, to have and to hold, from this day forward, for better, for worse, for richer, for poorer, in sickness and in health, until death do us part."

A moment's reflection reveals how this vow flies in the face of some contemporary understandings. The commitment of the spouses is a commitment based on the love of each for the other as other. If the commitment were based on things which can be here today and gone tomorrow, there would be no basis for the ideal of indissolubility. Excluded as the basis for the commitment are some things which are considered of primary importance by many in our contemporary culture—wealth, health, and success. In so many ways, the accumulation of wealth and power seems to be the driving force in a consumption-oriented society, but the simple marriage vow refuses to make this the most important reality. Health is certainly a significant value, and people go to great lengths to protect and preserve their health; but the marriage promises do not depend on the health of the other. Success has become all-important with many Americans, and there is great anguish in families when children of successful people seem to fail or even turn their backs on the success achieved by parents; but the marriage promise does not depend upon earthly success as it is generally understood. The marriage promise is made with the realization that all these things might change without ever changing the basic commitment which is deeper than all these realities. One should never romanticize the harshness of poverty, sickness, and hard times, for these are dehumanizing social conditions. But the vow of Christian marriage bears witness to the fact that these significant realities are not the most important aspects of human existence. The personal love of the spouses is stronger, deeper, and more transcendent than all these other realities.

The Christian marriage vow remains a strong witness to a Christian view which recognizes that ultimate happiness is not to be found merely in the possession and acquisition of things. In our society, people often feel the need for a new car every other year. It is not fashionable to dress in last year's styles. Consumerism has affected our cultural attitudes towards human sexuality which so often becomes a quest for one conquest after another and a source of exploitation. In so many ways, we are constantly striving after more and newer things, but the Christian marriage promise points to a different understanding of human beings. How often does the thirst and drive for possessions—be they material or spiritual goods—bring about a frantic and anxious groping that of necessity is bound to remain unfulfilled no matter how much is acquired. The basic human desire is for something deeper and more profound—a personal union of love.

There is a more fundamental objection that must be discussed. Does the marriage commitment, in the last analysis, involve a confining limitation on the human person? The transcendence and greatness of the human person seem to chafe at the limitation of an exclusive and life-long partnership. Do not all the boring marriages and loveless marriages that continue to exist for other reasons also indicate the limiting aspect of marriage? Intimately connected with this is the objection based on the understanding of human freedom. If freedom is the greatness of the human person and the distinguishing aspect of human existence, then should not the person be free to enter into new relationships which might bring about greater personal development? The marriage vow can often be felt as a limitation and restriction on the freedom of the person.

Different responses to this question point to fundamental differences in the basic understanding of the human person and of human freedom. The possibility of making such a life-long commitment of love testifies, in my judgment, to the greatness and transcendence of the human person and does not constitute an undue limitation and restriction. Part of the limitation of the human comes from the fact that he or she lives his or her existence stretched out in space and time, although this limitation should not be considered only as something negative, or space and time dismissed as not being important. Space and time, however, participate in a very fundamental limitation of the human. Our existence is lived out in different moments of time and disparate spaces. We cannot physically be in two places at one time. We live in one culture, in one historical moment, in one given time—all of which are limiting factors. As people existing in time and space, we are not even sure what the morrow will bring, for it lies to a great extent beyond our control. The marriage commitment involves a sign of human transcendence because, through the marital vow, wife and husband overcome the limitations of time and space. One can never even be sure that the morrow will come, but the marriage commitment remains a promise that no matter what happens, for better, for worse, for richer, for poorer, in sickness and in health, one thing will remain constant—the loving commitment of one for the other. The marriage promises, thus, do not constitute a limitation of human greatness nor a restriction on human freedom but, rather, significantly witness to human transcendence because of which the restrictions of time and space can be overcome.

In this perspective, the reality of freedom does not consist in the ability to make different choices and decisions at any moment in time. Paul Ramsey, the Methodist theologian from Princeton, insists that Christian love does not consist primarily in doing good but in being faithful, as God was faithful to his promise. Ramsey chides John A. T. Robinson, who, as an Anglican, believes in the sacramentality of marriage. If Robinson understands freedom to mean that, at any given moment, the individual is free to make a new and different choice, then, claims Ramsey, it is divorce that should logically be the sacrament and not marriage.[29] The binding commitment of love ultimately shows forth the transcendence of the human and is not a restriction of basic human freedom. Nonetheless, there are many in our contemporary culture who tend to see such a commitment as a restriction of human freedom.

The Marriage Covenant

The Judaeo-Christian tradition has often seen the married love of husband and wife in the context of the covenant love of Yahweh for the people of Israel and Jesus for the Church. In the Old Testament, there exists a reciprocal relationship between the marital union and the covenant union of Yahweh and the people. The covenant is often described and understood in terms of the marital relationship. Yahweh is considered as the spouse of Israel in many of the prophetic writings (e.g., *Is. 54:5; 50, 1ff; Jer. 2; Ez. 16*) and especially in the *Canticle of Canticles*. The infidelity of the people to the covenant is described as adultery (*Ez. 16:8, Os. 4:13, 14*). Reciprocally, marriage is looked upon as a covenant or alliance. Adultery and mixed marriages are contrasted with the covenant of God with his people *(Mal. 2:10-16)*. In the New Testament, the unconditional love of Jesus for the Church by which the Church is constituted is even given by Paul as an example to those who are married in the Lord *(1 Cor. 7:39* and *Eph. 5:21-32)*.

By the covenant promise, God chose a people: I will be your God and you will be my people. The life of Israel found ultimate meaning in terms of this alliance. The covenant reaches its zenith in the love of Jesus for the Church because of which he gave himself so that we might share in the fullness of the love and life of God. The covenant love of Yahweh for Israel and Jesus for the Church has four important characteristics which should also be present in the Christian marital love of wives and husbands.

First, God's covenant love is the source of life and joy for the people. The people of Israel and the Church come into existence because God in goodness chose them and gave them life—not because of any merits, accomplishments, or works of their own but only because of God's graciousness. Truly, the gift of covenant love is the good news, and the first response of the people is marked by thanksgiving, praise, and worship for the gift of the covenant. The covenant meal of the New Testament which is the heart and center of the sacramental life of the Church is called the Eucharist—the prayer of thanksgiving and praise. So, too, for Christian spouses, their gift of love is the source of their life and their joy. Experience tells of the need to continually recognize how the married love of the spouses gives life and joy one to the other, for all too often the joy which is present at the celebration of the marriage tends to become less as time goes on.

Second, God's love is a source of hope for the people. The life of the people of the covenant in the Old Testament was not easy. The people of Israel knew slavery, wandering, deportation, and imprisonment, but the faithful people never despaired because of their hope in the covenant. Even in the midst of oppression, bewilderment, and exile, they never lost hope because of the promise. In the new covenant, the power of God's love is so strong that ultimately it overcame all obstacles, even death itself. The death of Jesus, can be looked upon from one viewpoint as the triumph and victory of his enemies and of the powers of darkness and sin; but can be looked upon from another perspective as the ultimate conquest of death, evil, and sin through the transforming power of the resurrection and of God's love. The resurrection of Jesus stands as the source of our hope that the love of God will ultimately triumph over all obstacles, sin, and even death itself.

There is a danger in theoretical considerations of marriage to romanticize and forget about many of the realities involved in Christian marriage. Experience reminds us all of the problems, difficulties, and heartaches which are part and parcel of every marriage. No Christian should ever think that marriage exists without its exasperations and sorrows, but the covenant promise of the spouses remains the source of their mutual hope. In the midst of reverses, setbacks, sorrow, and tears, there always remains a hope based on the faithful love of each for the other. Marriage truly involves a great act of faith and of hope on the part of the spouses. The future is unknown. Obviously, the future will include not only joys and laughter but also sorrows and tears; but on the basis of their mutual love spouses give each other the support and the hope necessary to face the future. Sharing in the love of Jesus for the Church, they believe that the power of their love can ultimately overcome all obstacles. Their love and their hope can transcend the problems of any present moment. Such is the meaning of the marital love of Christians as the source of their hope so that even in the midst of sorrow there is joy, in the midst of weakness there is power, in the midst of sickness there is healing, in the midst of darkness there is light.

Third, the faithful love of Yahweh for Israel and Jesus for the Church was also a source of forgiveness. The great characteristic of Yahweh's love is its constancy and faithfulness. No matter how often Israel refused Yahweh's love and turned its back, God was always faithful to the promise that he had made. In the New Testament, the parable of the prodigal son (*Lk. 15*), which might more properly be called the parable of the merciful father, highlights once again the mercy and forgiveness of the Father, which is always present no matter how heinous the crime, provided there is now a movement toward conversion. So, too, in marriage, the love of husband and wife must always contain a willingness to forgive. Human frailty and weakness mean that there will always be some misunderstandings, mistakes, and even offenses; but, in a willingness to forgive, the marital love of spouses share and participate in one of the most outstanding characteristics of God's love for Israel and for the Church.

As a fourth characteristic, the love of Yahweh and of Jesus always became a source of challenge to the people of Israel and the Church. We are called to love others as God has first loved us. How often in the Scriptures are we reminded that we are to forgive others as God has first forgiven us. The love of God, with its sheer willingness to give and to share, is a challenge for those who receive it to show the same kind of love toward others. So, too, the love of husband and wife must accept the challenge of God's love. They must challenge one another to grow in love and deepen their marriage commitment, but, above all, their love must extend beyond themselves and their families to embrace those who are most in need—the poor, the outcast, and the oppressed. In the light of these four characteristics, marking the love of God's covenant and called for in Christian married love, one can understand better how the marriage vow came into existence.

All Christians must admit that to put Christian love into practice is not easy. Likewise, Christian marital love calls for spouses to come out of the slavery and selfishness of Egypt and walk towards the promised land. In the imperfect world in which we live, Christian spouses will not always be able to live out the reality of their marital love. For this reason, the Catholic Church must accept divorce, but in the very acceptance of divorce as a possible alternative, the Church must strive in every way possible to make the ideal of sustaining every Christian marriage a reality for Christian people today.

In implementing this ideal, even on the level of theory and understanding, the idea of Christian love as the base of marriage also raises some problems. In the New Testament, love or *agape* does not have a univocal meaning. The synoptic gospels often stress love of enemies, whereas John emphasizes love of the brethren. The synoptic gospels speak of a twofold commandment of the love of God and the love of neighbor, whereas Saint Paul tends to avoid speaking of our love for God. These different uses of the term indicate different characteristics associated with *agape* or love.[30]

In our culture, the meaning of love has often become trivialized, but there is a temptation for some theologians to so exalt the meaning of love that it seems to be opposed to, or even go beyond, the human. Some theologians, especially in the Lutheran and classical Protestant tradition, understand *agape* as a pure, disinterested giving which does not involve mutuality, reciprocity, or the union of friendship, to say nothing of a proper love of self. Such an understanding of love from the theological perspective takes as its model God's love for the sinner, which involves the sheer gratuity of God's gracious gift and is totally independent of the attributes, characteristics, or qualities of the sinner. Such an understanding of love stresses love as faithfulness and forgiveness but does not include elements of friendship, mutuality, and reciprocity.[31]

The Roman Catholic theological tradition has always emphasized that God's love for human beings brings about a real change in the person and creates a true communion so that the person now begins to share in the love and life of God. The primary model of love is not that of God for the sinner but of God calling us to friendship which mirrors the very life of the Trinitarian Godhead with its emphasis on communion, mutuality, and reciprocity. The Catholic tradition has attempted, not always successfully, to unite in Christian love a love for self, a love for neighbor, and a love for God. Christian love includes a proper love of self and an aspect of mutuality as well as the willingness to give and sacrifice for others.[32] It is necessary to mention this theological dispute to avoid the danger of overly simplistic understandings of Christian love. Interestingly, the traditional Catholic approach of not denying a place to love of self and to sharing in love is more open in theory to recognize at times the need for divorce and remarriage.

This paper has looked at the question of Christian marriage and divorce in the context of the broader question of the relationship between the gospel and culture. In culture, over the long run, one can expect to find elements that are both supportive of the gospel message and other elements that are opposed to it. Reasons were briefly recalled for justifying the need for divorce and therefore for recognizing remarriage within the Church. But the major thrust of the paper was to show that the mission and responsibility of the Church go beyond concern for the individual marriage. It was to emphasize that there are also many elements in the contemporary culture which stand in opposition to the Christian understanding of marriage. In the light of this situation, the Church must expand its pastoral efforts to create an ethos somewhat opposed to the prevailing cultural ethos so that the ideal of Christian marriage remains a possibility. Yes, Christian theory and practice must accept the possibility of divorce, but an even greater source of challenge focuses on the need to create an atmosphere in which Christian marriage may be both understood in theory and lived in practice.

Notes

1. For an overview of this question in different parts of the world, see two issues of the *Recherches de Science Religieuse* devoted exclusively to the question of marriage and divorce—*Recherches de Science Religieuse*, LXI (1973) 483-624; LXII (1974), 7-116. Significant recent books on the American scene include: Dennis H. Doherty, *Divorce and Remarriage: Resolving a Catholic Dilemma* (St. Meinrad, Indiana: Abbey Press, 1974); Stephen J. Kelleher, *Divorce and Remarriage for Catholics?* (Garden City, N.Y.: Doubleday, 1973); *Divorce and Remar-*

riage in the Catholic Church, ed. Lawrence G. Wrenn (N.Y.: Newman Press, 1973).

2. Christian Duquoc, *L'Eglise et le progres* (Paris: Cerf, 1964), 68-84.

3. Juan Luis Segundo, in collaboration with the staff of the Peter Faber Center in Montevideo, Uruguay, *The Community Called Church* (Maryknoll, New York: Orbis Books, 1973). Segundo and collaborators have published a five-volume contemporary Catholic theology under the general title of *A Theology for Artisans of a New Humanity.*

4. "Conditions of Catholic Growth" in *American Catholic Thought on Social Questions,* ed. Aaron I. Abell (Indianapolis: Bobbs-Merrill Co., 1968), pp. 3-140.

5. C. Joseph Nuesse, *The Social Thought of American Catholics, 1634-1829* (Westminster, Maryland: Newman, 1945).

6. Henry J. Browne, *The Catholic Church and the Knights of Labor* (Washington: Catholic University of America Press, 1949).

7. James Cardinal Gibbons, *A Retrospect of Fifty Years* (Baltimore: John Murphy Co., 1916), I, pp. 186-209.

8. Ray Allen Billington, *The Protestant Crusade, 1800-1860: A Study of the Origins of American Nativism* (Chicago: Quadrangle Books, 1964).

9. Thomas T. McAvoy, *The Americanist Heresy in Roman Catholicism, 1895-1900* (Notre Dame, Ind.: University of Notre Dame Press, 1963).

10. John Courtney Murray, *The Problem of Religious Freedom* (Westminster, Md.: Newman, 1965); Richard J. Regan, *Conflict and Consensus: Religious Freedom and the Second Vatican Council* (New York: Macmillan, 1967).

11. Aaron I. Abell, *American Catholicism and Social Action: A Search for Social Justice, 1865-1950* (Notre Dame, Ind.: University of Notre Dame Press, 1963), pp. 90-285. For the rise of Catholic social liberalism, see Robert D. Cross, *The Emergence of Liberal Catholicism in America* (Cambridge: Harvard University Press, 1958).

12. *American Catholics and Vietnam,* ed. Thomas E. Quigley (Grand Rapids, Mich.: W. B. Eerdmans, 1968).

13. William D. Miller, *A Harsh and Dreadful Love: Dorothy Day and the Catholic Worker Movement* (Garden City, N.Y.: Doubleday Image Books, 1974).

14. Lloyd J. Averill, *American Theology in the Liberal Tradition* (Philadelphia: Westminster Press, 1967).

15. David Little, "The Social Gospel Revisited," in *The Secular City Debate,* ed. Daniel Callahan (New York: Macmillan, 1966), pp. 69-76.

16. Note the progression in the thought of Jurgen Moltmann in his two important works—*The Theology of Hope* (New York: Harper and Row, 1967); *The Crucified God* (New York: Harper and Row, 1974).

17. Josef Fuchs, *Natural Law: A Theological Investigation* (New

MINISTERING TO THE DIVORCED CATHOLIC

York: Sheed and Ward, 1965).

18. E. Schillebeeckx, *Marriage: Human Reality and Saving Mystery* (New York: Sheed and Ward, 1965).

19. Paul F. Palmer, "Christian Marriage: Contract or Covenant?" *Theological Studies,* XXXIII (1972) 628-629.

20. Schillebeeckx, pp. 384-385.

21. *Enchiridion Symbolorum Definitionum et Declarationum de Rebus Fidei et Morum,* ed. H. Denzinger, A Schonmetzer (32nd ed.; Herder: Barcelona, 1963), n. 761.

22. Pierre Adnes, *Le Mariage* (Tournai: Desclee, 1963), pp. 91-93.

23. Adnes, pp. 76-82.

24. See Theodore Mackin, "Consummation: Of Contract or of Covenant?" *The Jurist,* XXXII (1972), 213-223; 330-354; also Palmer, *Theological Studies,* XXXIII (1972), 617-665.

25. Schillebeeckx, p. 365.

26. H. Richard Niebuhr, *Christ and Culture* (New York: Harper Torchbook, 1956).

27. Charles E. Curran, *New Perspectives in Moral Theology* (Notre Dame, Ind.: Fides, 1974), pp. 47-86.

28. Charles E. Curran, "Divorce—From the Perspective of Moral Theology," *Canon Law Society of America: Proceedings of the Thirty-Sixth Annual Convention* (1975), pp. 1-24. See also an earlier article reviewing the literature on divorce, "Divorce: Catholic Theory and Practice in the United States," *The American Ecclesiastical Review,* CLXVIII (1974), 3-34; 75-95.

29. Paul Ramsey, *Deeds and Rules in Christian Ethics* (New York: Charles Scribner's Sons, 1967), p. 46.

30. Ceslaus Spicq, *Agape in the New Testament,* 3 vols. (St. Louis: B. Herder, 1963, 1965, 1966); Victor Paul Furnish, *The Love Command in the New Testament* (Nashville: Abingdon, 1972).

31. Anders Nygren, *Agape and Eros* (New York: Harper Torchbook, 1969).

32. Martin C. D'Arcy, *The Mind and Heart of Love* (New York: Meridian Books, 1956); Jules Toner, *The Experience of Love* (Washington/Cleveland: Corpus Books, 1968).

New Testament Perspectives on Marriage and Divorce

George W. MacRae, S.J.

No reader will expect to find in the New Testament a justification for or a critique of the institution of marriage tribunals. To seek one would be an exercise in anachronism, if not wrongheadedness. In addition, however, it would be theologically naive to conclude that therefore the tribunals have no justification in the life of the Church. For just as a good deal of recent theological literature has reminded us that we cannot expect to find the institution of priesthood in the New Testament and yet should not therefore regard priesthood as itself in question,[1] there is an analogy with many other features of the Church's structure, thought and practice. The Church must be constantly aware of its "home" in the New Testament communities and the teaching of Jesus; it must indeed be subject to the judgment of Scripture in all that it says and does. But even the Church "can't go home again." It cannot solve problems of its own time and culture by a flight into the past of its beginnings, which are often rather romantically portrayed.[2]

In fact, there is a surprising amount of material in the New Testament, especially in the Pauline correspondence, which indirectly supports the development of such institutions as the marriage tribunal. St. Paul urged the Corinthian community more than once to regulate its own affairs. In the case of the incestuous man (1 Cor 5) he ordered the Corinthians uncompromisingly to take drastic action to protect the integrity—including the moral integrity—of the community by "excommunicating" the offender. In the next chapter of the same epistle he rebuked the community for its failure to deal with lawsuits in "courts" of its own makings: "Do you not know that the saints will judge the world?"

The case of the lawsuits is an interesting analogy for the business of marriage tribunals, although traditionally Catholic theology has been reluctant to seek analogies to its teaching on marriage and divorce. In 1 Corinthians 6:1-11 the genuine Christian stance is not to have lawsuits with one another in the first place. But when they exist—and Paul is no less a realist than Canon Law—the community has the competence to deal with them. It is true that in the same epistle Paul also discusses marriage and divorce—and we must return to the passage presently—but in that context he makes no provision for any quasi-juridical determinations on the part of the Church. The point here is not really whether one can find some biblical precedent for the marriage tribunal, nor whether Paul would have felt more or less at home with our modern tribunals, but rather that the Pauline "Church order" allows for the Church taking the responsibility, even formally and almost institutionally, for the management of its own affairs. I should like later to suggest an analogous function for the marriage tribunals, which I do not think they now feel empowered to perform.

But the main issue I wish to raise in these pages is not whether we look to the New Testament when examining our modern ecclesiastical life. One may hope we will do so increasingly as a theology and an ecclesiastical "life-style" for our age continue to be elaborated. Rather, the issue is: What do we look for when we turn to the New Testament and the teaching of Jesus? Do we seek the formulation of an absolute, divinely revealed law or model, or do we seek a process of understanding and adaptation with which the modern Church can identify only by entering into the process and furthering it? I believe it is the latter that is the more appropriate by virtue of the nature of the New Testament materials themselves. I should like to illustrate this choice and develop the principles involved by examining the New Testament statements on the indissolubility of marriage. Obviously the example chosen is one that is of considerable concern to the marriage tribunals, though it does not directly determine their propriety or utility. As much as possible, these pages will deal with the New Testament question and the issues to which it gives rise, avoiding facile comparisons and contrasts with later Church practice. On the other hand, we will try to avoid becoming mired in exegetical detail and conjecture; in this question more than many others exegetical ingenuity has obscured what is really present in the New Testament itself.

What God Has Joined Together

Information about Jesus' teaching on the indissolubility of marriage comes to us from three main sources: (1) the Gospel of Mark, which I take to be the earliest extant example of the genre Gospel;[3] (2) Q, the sayings collection drawn upon apparently independently by both Matthew and Luke; and (3) Paul's tradition about the sayings of the Lord. These sources are preserved for us in the five New Testament passages (Mk 10:2-12 and Mt 19:3-12; Lk 16:18 and Mt 5:32; 1 Cor 7:10-16) which have always been the object of intense study on the part of theologians and biblical scholars but which lately have unleashed a flood of literature.[4] It is remarkable that no single interpretation of these passages has ever won what could be called the general consent of interpreters, at least of Catholic ones, and the Church has reflected this hesitancy by never attempting to define their sense. It is not the intention of these pages to survey this mass of scholarship or to build upon any argument from consensus. Instead, the very diversity of interpretation suggests a tendency to resist the obvious implications of these passages. Let us examine them in succession.

1. The Markan version of the saying of Jesus places it in the context of a challenge from the Pharisees (10:2), though a somewhat obscure one, since in asking whether divorce was allowed, they were supposedly ignoring the explicit provision of the Torah (Dt 24:1). Jesus makes them cite the Torah passage and then he interprets it as a concession to hardheartedness. Jesus' own reflections center on the order of creation: he cites Genesis 1:27 and 2:24 and comments: "What therefore God has joined together, let not man put asunder" (10:9). Privately, as elsewhere

in the Gospel,[5] his disciples question him about his statement and Jesus replies: "Whoever divorces his wife and marries another, commits adultery against her; and if she divorces her husband and marries another, she commits adultery" (10:11-12).

The original force of Jesus' encounter with the Pharisees is lost in Mark's version, and the whole passage is very typical of that Gospel in structure. Moreover, the form of Jesus' interpretation of his own words is difficult to imagine in a Palestinian-Jewish (in contrast to a Roman) setting where the concept of a woman divorcing her husband was unheard of—unless we are to imagine that Jesus consciously wished to extend the individual responsibility in marriage to the wife as well.[6] In any event, the point of the saying is clear: Jesus unequivocally and unconditionally rules out divorce.

The Matthean version of this incident is much more coherent, but in view of Matthew's habitual treatment of his Markan source, it is not therefore more original, as has sometimes been alleged.[7] In Matthew the Pharisees put Jesus to the test by inviting him to take sides in a famous Jewish legal dispute; "Is it lawful to divorce one's wife *for any cause?*" (19:3). The issue is that between the school of Shammai, for whom divorce was permissible only on the grounds of adultery, and the school of Hillel, for whom divorce was permissible on many grounds. The surprising thing is that at least at first sight, after resisting the trap with his interpretation of Genesis, Jesus then seems to fall into it, for his saying on divorce is addressed to the Pharisees, not to the disciples, and it contains the famous exceptive clause: "And I say to you: whoever divorces his wife, *except for unchastity (mē epi porneia)*, and marries another, commits adultery" (19:9). Perhaps it is only Matthew's concern for interpreting the teaching of Jesus within his own community that leads him to make Jesus' position seem not sufficiently distinct from that of Shammai. That is to say, the dynamic of the encounter with the Pharisees is less important to Matthew than the practical implementation of Jesus' teaching in the community. More on this in a moment. Let us forego, at least for the present, all the philological discussion which centuries of exegetes have found irresistible. It is enough to note that no matter how the exceptive clause is to be interpreted,[8] it seems to reflect a modification within the Matthean community of the absoluteness of Jesus' prohibition.

2. The Lukan witness to the saying (16:18) is completely independent of the discussion with the Pharisees in which Matthew and Mark place it. For convenience we regard the Lukan verse as derived from the Q source, conscious that this derivation could be challenged since the Matthean parallel in the Sermon on the Mount is not a close one. In Luke, the context contributes almost nothing to the understanding of the saying; it is best treated as an isolated element of Jesus' teaching and is often regarded as the clearest and most "primitive" form of the tradition: "Everyone who divorces his wife and marries another commits adultery, and he who marries a woman divorced from her husband commits adultery."

Another Matthean witness to the saying (5:32)—whether derived from Q or a Matthean reworking of the Markan story—presents the same problem as Matthew 19:9. Here the context is the Sermon on the Mount and specifically the list of antitheses between what was said in the Torah and the demands of Christian righteousness. In contrast to the law in Deuteronomy 24:1 Jesus says: "But I say to you that everyone who divorces his wife, *except on the ground of unchastity (parektos logou porneias).* makes her an adulteress; and whoever marries a divorced woman commits adultery."

3. For a number of reasons it may be suggested that the most important New Testament passage on the indissolubility of marriage is Paul's discussion of it in 1 Corinthians 7. This is chronologically the earliest witness both to a traditional saying of the Lord and to the practice of the early Christian communities. And like Matthew, Paul too both reiterates an absolute doctrine and introduces a qualification. And like Mark, Paul expresses the prohibition in terms of the mutual obligations of husband and wife, though without implying complete equality. In fact, in Paul's statement there is no linguistic allusion whatever to the Synoptic sayings, but this is not surprising when we note that Paul gives this teaching as his own even though he understands it to coincide with that of Jesus: "To the married I give charge, not I but the Lord, that the wife should not separate from her husband

(but if she does, let her remain single or else be reconciled to her husband)—and that the husband should not divorce[9] his wife" (7:10-11).

Having addressed "the married (Christians)," Paul immediately turns to "the rest," i.e., those in "mixed marriages," presumably marriages in which one partner has subsequently become Christian. In this instance, Paul speaks on his own authority: "To the rest I say, not the Lord . . ." (7:12); but there is no indication that his strictures are less authoritative here. First, he forbids the Christian partner in such a union to initiate divorce, "for the unbelieving husband is consecrated through his wife, and the unbelieving wife is consecrated through her husband" (7:14). But secondly, he asserts the freedom of the Christian partner in cases where the non-Christian partner initiates divorce: "But if the unbelieving partner desires to separate, let it be so; in such a case the brother or sister is not bound.[10] For God has called us to peace" (7:15). This is the precedent for what became the classic case of the "Pauline privilege" in later Church practice. For our purposes it is enough to note at present that Paul on his own authority admits an "exception" to the indissolubility of marriage—which, to be sure, he understands as primarily applicable to the Christian situation, but also to the mixed as far as the Christian's initiative is concerned.

Let Not Man Put Asunder

What is the total impact of the New Testament evidence about the absolute indissolubility of marriage? First, all three of our sources (Mark, Q and Paul) report an unqualified prohibition of divorce as a saying of Jesus. The only reasonable conclusion is that this is what Jesus really taught. It could not reasonably be accounted for as an invention of the early Church because it so radically runs counter to the accepted practice of both Jewish and Greco-Roman society. One should note that the method underlying this conclusion is not the mathematical analogy of the least common denominator but the careful analysis of the development of the forms of dominical sayings in the Synoptic tradition.[11] In the overall context of the preaching of Jesus this radical and uncompromising assertion must be seen in relation to the eschatological urgency of his preaching: the kingdom of God is at hand!

Our second observation on the basis of the above survey of passages is that, of the four New Testament authors who deal with the teaching of Jesus about marriage and divorce, two of them make exceptions to the absolute statement. It is this fact which must be reckoned with, not by any exegetical legerdemain, but by attempting to understand the process by which the sayings of Jesus were evaluated and transmitted in the New Testament itself. That we are really dealing with exceptions on the part of Matthew (or his community) and Paul becomes clear if we allow the texts to say what they most obviously seem to say. Let us first eliminate some unsuccessful attempts to avoid this conclusion.

One cannot introduce into the New Testament the distinction between a sacramental marriage and a non-sacramental marriage. In the Synoptic passages there is no hint of the possible sacramentality of marriage. On the contrary, the argument for the indissolubility of marriage in the Markan source is derived from the order of creation and thus makes no special provision for the Christian believer at all. Paul, on the other hand, seems at first sight to place Christian marriage in a separate category, but this is not really so, for the point of his concentration is the attitude of the Christian partner, not the nature of the marriage itself. From the point of view of the Christian, a marriage entered into before conversion is as "permanent" as one between Christians. It is not the nature of the marriage which determines its permanence, but the commitment of the partners. The Christian partner who is "deserted," i.e., divorced, is "not bound." It is important to emphasize the fact that it is reading Christian history backward to argue that the New Testament is even "implicitly" talking about the distinction between sacramental and non-sacramental marriage which the later Church articulated. What is most significant is that the later Church is responsible for this distinction, not any revealed divine law. And if the Church is responsible, it is our suggestion here that the Church is empowered to modify the distinction if it should see fit to do so. The nature of marriage as derived from the early Church's understanding of the order of creation is apparently not so absolute as to exclude all exceptions.

Again, one cannot argue that the exceptive clauses of Matthew or the Pauline exception have to do with separation without the right to remarry. If the context of Matthew is a Jewish (-Christian) one, such an arrangement is simply meaningless. As for the situation of 1 Corinthians 7, it is true that Paul explicitly rules out remarriage in the first case that he deals with, that of Christian partners initiating separation. It is probably also true that, given his eschatological perspective, Paul would dissuade the divorced Christian partner of a mixed marriage from remarrying (cf. 1 Cor 7:8, 27). But he makes it unequivocally clear in the same context that those who are free, i.e., widows and those who have never been married, do no wrong, even in the situation of a proximate eschatological expectation, if they choose to marry (cf. 1 Cor 7:9, 28, 39). It is very difficult to imagine him holding an unexpressed reservation for the victims of a broken marriage whom he expressly calls "not bound."

One could continue to list and criticize attempts to read the New Testament passages in such a way that they do not conflict with traditional Church practice. But the longer the list, the more uncomfortable we become about the very presuppositions of such attempts. Instead, we should perhaps look to the larger contexts of the preaching of Jesus, Paul and Matthew and seek to identify the factors which the early Christians understood to authorize them to interpret the teaching of Jesus without abandoning it.

It has already been pointed out that the context of Jesus' radical reinterpretation of the law was an eschatological one. Paul had certainly not lost that sense of eschatological urgency when writing 1 Corinthians 7, but Paul confronted a new situation which had not been part of Jesus' experience. He is conscious of the newness of the situation and of the lack of direct guidance from the Lord when he points out that the instruction on mixed marriages is his own. A few verses later this consciousness is even more emphatic: "Now concerning the unmarried, I have no command of the Lord, but I give my opinion as one who by the Lord's mercy is trustworthy" (7:25). The new situation is the missionary one in which Christians are confronted with working out a way to live in the midst of pagan society. Paul does not abandon the lofty ideal of the dominical teaching about marriage; he repeats it (7:10-11). But he accommodates it to the new situation of mixed marriages, in effect introducing an exception to the absolute indissolubility of marriage. By what authority? He ends the discussion of marriage and celibacy with the remark, "And I think that I have the Spirit of God" (7:40b).

Matthew too faces a new situation with respect to the teaching of Jesus, which he too first reaffirms (19:6). The eschatological message of the pressing kingdom of heaven has now to be related to the on-going life of a Jewish-Christian Church, a Church which is confronted with solving the daily problems of its existence by exercising the powers of binding and loosing.[12] In this context Matthew — or the community he represents — is empowered by his understanding of Jesus' intentions to adapt his teaching on marriage to a situation in which a marriage broken by "unchastity" can no longer be understood as a marriage. It is of course *possible* that *porneia* in the Matthean exceptive clauses refers to a marriage within degrees of kindred which Gentiles might tolerate but Jews (i.e., Jewish Christians) would regard as incestuous (Lev 18: 7-18).[13] Such a marriage would be intolerable in the eyes of Matthew's community. But that is by no means the obvious meaning of the passage since it is not clear that such a union would be regarded as a marriage in the first place. It is at least equally understandable in a Jewish-Christian context that adultery would in fact establish the situation of a ruptured marital union that was once genuine.[14]

What we must suppose in the Matthean Church is a conflict of values that has to be resolved in the on-going life of the Church and for which the tradition about Jesus' sayings provides no immediately applicable solution. The confrontation is between the principle of the indissolubility of marriage which is the tradition of Jesus' teaching and the "right" to a genuine integral marriage. The latter would no doubt be more deeply felt in a community of Jewish background where marriage was regarded as a duty.[15] If Matthew's solution falls into something like the Shammaite interpretation of the Torah which Jesus had avoided in the controversy story, we must allow that the inconsistency may mean much more to the modern interpreter than to a Jewish-Christian community of the late first century.[16] The interpretation of Shammai was not a rabbinic innovation, after all, but a strict construction of the law itself in Deuteronomy 24:1.

God Has Called Us to Peace

It is time to draw some conclusions and formulate some suggestions regarding the status of New Testament teaching on the indissolubility of marriage and the status of contemporary Church practice.

First, regarding the teaching of Jesus. We have indicated above that we can with some confidence identify what was Jesus' attitude toward divorce and what was that of some of the New Testament writers, and these are not identical. It would be false to conclude that theological judgment must rest on our ability, through historical and literary means, to isolate Jesus' teaching at the expense of that of his followers. In the light of modern New Testament scholarship, especially the methods of source, form and redaction criticism applied to the Gospels, there is widespread agreement among interpreters that we have access to the mind of Jesus primarily—indeed only—through the interpretation of the early Christian communities and their theologians. The authority of Jesus' teaching does not reach us independently of the Church. Consequently we cannot assume, in view of the role of Scripture in the life of the Church, that what scholarly research points to as Jesus' own utterance is necessarily any more determinative for the Church than what are apparently the interpretations of him by his followers. This means that we cannot regard as more authoritative for Church life the apparently "primitive" Lukan form of the divorce statement rather than the qualified Matthean form.

On another level, this observation means that we cannot rest Church practice regarding marriage and divorce upon a supposedly divine revealed law—to the extent that the New Testament serves as the vehicle of that revelation. Instead we must discern the process by which the teaching of Jesus was remembered, communicated, interpreted, adapted and enshrined in the practice of the early Christian communities. That process, we have seen, is one of accommodation to circumstances that were not the context of the preaching of Jesus himself. The Church of today must relate, not to an absolute divine law which is in practice inaccessible to our scholarly research, but to the process of identifying what is of Christ and what is Christian and entering into that discerning process for our own day. The matrix of modern discernment is, as it was in the churches of Paul or Matthew, the dwelling of the Holy Spirit among God's people.

But Jesus did teach the absolute indissolubility of marriage (note that the New Testament does not authorize us to say "of *Christian* marriage"). Was his teaching then merely an ideal from which the "realist" perceives an inevitable decline? There are modern authors who stress the nature of Jesus' matrimonial teaching as an ideal.[17] If we have in mind the formulation of Matthew 5:32, especially in the context of the antitheses of the Sermon on the Mount, there are good grounds for this view.[18] Nor does this mean the "reduction" of the Sermon on the Mount to a mere statement of an impossible ideal over against a serious program for a Christian morality.[19] The alternative of law vs. ideal is not a complete disjunction; there is also what some theologians call "Gospel," the genuine and specifically Christian challenge that can only be met by the fusion of free will and grace. But perhaps one can and even must go a step further and argue that the very preservation of the teaching of Jesus in all its eschatological and challenging purity *requires* the kind of adaptation the early Christians made.[20] The paradox is not meant to be a logical statement but an existential one. What prevents Jesus' teaching from becoming a chimera is the willingness to interpret it anew in each generation. And in this respect, is there not a serious danger that an intransigent interpretation of the indissolubility of marriage in the Catholic Church today is rapidly approaching the point of disdain for the ideal itself as a utopian one?

But are there in fact grounds for the discernment of new situations in the life of modern Christians which require new interpretation and new adaptation of the New Testament teaching on marriage? An ever growing number of serious theologians and

Christian social scientists believe that there are. It would far out-strip the present writer's competence to attempt to describe these factors, but the reader may simply be referred to the other chapters in this book. What is emerging is a new perception of values, and every age of creative thought must perceive its own values anew. There is a growing consciousness of the conflict of values in our Christian society over the issue of marriage, the conflict between a clear but inflexible matrimonial legislation which does indeed express an important part of the Christian ethical ideal, and a way of life that must reflect Christian love, pardon, dedication and self-giving in a world of loveless technocracy and existential depression.

The marriage tribunal was our starting point. What are we to conclude about it? If its principal function is a judicial one, modeled on the kind of civil judiciary that St. Paul excoriated the Corinthians for having recourse to, then it has no place in the life of the Church. The Church is a human society and its agencies are human agencies, but it is not a civil society and its courts are not civil courts. But if the tribunal can be modified so that it really enters into the process of discerning values and narrowing the perennial gap between Christian ideals and the practice of Christians, then it has an important role to play. It must arbitrate a conflict of values, not a conflict of laws. But the courts are interpreters of the law. In that case, the Church's tribunals have but one law to serve, what St. Paul calls the "law of Christ": "If a man is overtaken in any trespass, you who are spiritual should restore him in a spirit of gentleness. . . . Bear one another's burdens, and so fulfill the law of Christ" (Gal 6:1-2).

Notes

1. See, e.g., R. E. Brown, *Priest and Bishop, Biblical Reflections* (New York: Paulist Press, 1970); H. Küng, *Why Priests?* (Garden City: Doubleday, 1972).

2. Only after writing the above paragraph did I read R. L. Wilken, *The Myth of Christian Beginnings* (Garden City: Doubleday, 1971), which develops eloquently the argument implied in the adoption of Thomas Wolfe's title.

3. It would not be appropriate here to substantiate the use of the so-called two-source theory of Synoptic relationships, which a majority of Catholic scholars now seem to accept. For a recent discussion, see J. A. Fitzmyer, "The Priority of Mark and the 'Q' Source in Luke," in *Jesus and Man's Hope* I (Pittsburgh: Pittsburgh Theological Seminary, 1970), pp. 131-170.

4. Much of it quite independent of the recent divorce question in Italian civil law. For bibliography see J. Dupont, *Mariage et Divorce dans l'Évangile* (Bruges: Desclée de Brouwer, 1959); B. Vawter, "The Divorce Clauses in Mt 5, 32 and 19, 9," in *Catholic Biblical Quarterly* 16 (1954), pp. 155-167; D. L. Dungan, *The Sayings of Jesus in the Churches of Paul* (Philadelphia: Fortress Press, 1971), pp. 83-131; and for some suggestions on the most recent literature, cf. L. Sabourin, "The Divorce Clauses (Mt 5:32, 19:9)," in *Biblical Theology Bulletin* 2 (1972), pp. 80-86.

5. Notably in the interpretation of parables: 4:10; 7:17.

6. Contrast Paul's conscious insistence on the equal rights of husband and wife in marriage in 1 Corinthians 7:2-4. For Paul's reciprocal formulation of the prohibition of divorce, see below.

7. See, e.g., D. L. Dunga, *op. cit.*, pp. 102ff.

8. Except of course in the so-called "preteritive" interpretation, i.e., in the sense of an allusion to Deuteronomy 24:1 "notwithstanding"; this view has been most ably defended by Vawter, *art, cit.*, but few interpreters have found it a satisfactory explanation of the text. One would also have to except those interpretations which understand *porneia* to refer to concubinage, incestuous relationships and the like; see below.

9. The word for "divorce" is *apolienai*, not *apolyein* as in the Synoptics. It might be rendered "dismiss" or "put away," but the RSV (which we are citing here) is correct, since the sense is technical.

10. Literally, the brother or sister, i.e., the Christian partner, "is not enslaved," *ou dedoulōtai*. This is generally interpreted to mean that remarriage is allowed; see below.

11. See R. Bultmann, *The History of the Synoptic Tradition*, rev. ed. (New York: Harper & Row, 1968), pp. 132-136. We cannot of course repeat the details of such an analysis in this brief chapter.

12. Cf. Matthew's "ecclesiological" transformation of the confession of Peter at Caesarea Philippi (16:13-19) as well as of other Markan passages such as the storm on the lake (Mt 8:23-27); for the problem-solving concern of the Church, see also Matthew 18:15-20.

13. The principal exponent of this view as J. Bonsirven, *Le divorce dans le Nouveau Testament* (Tournai: Desclée, 1948).

14. It is true that *porneia* is not the ordinary word for adultery, as the very context shows. But it is quite possible that *porneia* was chosen precisely to generalize the concept of the unchastity that can break a

marriage. In any case, Matthew does not use the language of Deuteronomy 24:1 (LXX). On this interpretation of the exceptive clauses, see among Catholic authors K. Haacker, "Ehescheidung und Wiederverheiratung im Neuen Testament," in *Theologische Quartalschrift* 151 (1971), pp. 28-38, and the survey of L. Sabourin, *art. cit.*, pp. 83-84.

15. Q. Quesnell has very ably argued, taking up a suggestion of J. Dupont, that the eunuch saying in Matthew 19:12 refers to those who accept the separation of a broken marriage without the right to remarry: " 'Made Themselves Eunuchs for the Kingdom of Heaven' (Mt 19, 12)," in *Catholic Biblical Quarterly* 30 (1968), pp. 335-358. But if this is correct, the real innovation in Jesus' teaching is the notion of separation without remarriage, and this seems only very obliquely stated in the various sayings of this pericope.

16. One must understand such a statement in the context of Matthew's presentation of the on-going validity of the law in the Jewish-Christian community even though Jesus has radicalized it; see the sayings in Matthew 5:17-20 and the essay of G. Barth in G. Bornkamm *et al.*, *Tradition and Interpretation in Matthew* (Philadelphia: Westminster Press, 1963).

17. Cf., e.g., W. J. O'Shea, "Marriage and Divorce: The Biblical Evidence," in *Australasian Catholic Record* 47 (1970), pp. 89-109; J. A. Grispino, *The Bible Now!* (Notre Dame: Fides, 1971), pp. 95-107.

18. One should compare carefully and objectively the antitheses in Matthew 5:21-48: "You, therefore, must be perfect, as your heavenly Father is perfect." In the immediate context of the divorce saying, the Church has long recognized idealistic hyperbole in the saying: "If your right hand causes you to sin, cut if off and throw it away," and Jesus' absolute prohibition of oaths has not only not been taken literally as law, but has been formally contravened even by ecclesiastical practice. It is difficult to refrain from exploiting this and other examples from Jesus' teaching when discussing the divorce statements. See J.A. Grispino, *op. cit.*, pp. 98-100 (references).

19. For discussion of the alternatives, see J. Jeremias, *The Sermon on the Mount* (Philadelphia: Fortress Press, 1963).

20. Cf., e.g., G. Schneider, "Jesu Wort über die Ehescheidung in der Überlieferung des Neuen Testaments," in *Trierer Theologische Zeitschrift* 80 (1971), pp. 65-87.

The Orthodox Position on Divorce

Lewis J. Patsavos

In an article entitled "Divorce and Remarriage: East and West,"[1] Father O. Rousseau correctly observes: "In this matter (of divorce and remarriage) as in many others, nothing will be done as long as Christians do not think in terms of "East and West" instead of thinking of one against the other." With this in mind I offer the present article in the hope that it may contribute to a better understanding of divorce and remarriage as practiced in the Orthodox Church. It is not intended to be a defense, but rather an informative account of the position regarding the practice adhered to by our Church. Furthermore, it attempts to establish the continuity of this practice in the East and the conviction that no scriptural law has thereby been disregarded.

The Practice of the Orthodox Church

The teaching of the Orthodox Church concerning marriage is a constant affirmation of scriptural pronouncements relative to this subject. The ideal marital relationship to which it ascribes is reflected in St. Paul's exhortation: "Art thou bound unto a wife? Seek not to be loosed" (I Cor. 7, 27). With exception of St. Matthew's gospel, the remaining scriptural references stress the positive indissolubility of marriage.[2] Matthew, undoubtedly influenced by the predominantly Jewish community to which his gospel was addressed, permits divorce only upon grounds of unchastity.[3]

The principle of indissolubility is reiterated three centuries later in no uncertain terms by St. John Chrysostom.[4] This reaffirmation of earlier scriptural teaching reflects unequivocally the sentiments of the Eastern Church towards divorce. It follows that under ordinary circumstances a validly contracted marriage is dissolved only by physical death.

Nevertheless, owing to the frailties of human nature the Church recognizes divorce in the case of unbearable marital relationships, which she equates with physical death. Such intervention in the seemingly indissoluble bond of marriage is regarded as transitory leniency,[5] in no way contradictory to scriptural law. Furthermore, it is the exception rather than the rule, exercised as a preventive of more severe consequences. Indeed, marriage is held in such an exalted degree that a deterioration of its sanctifying quality is regarded as intolerable. The moral disintegration caused thereby thus warrants the means of arresting the spread of spiritual decay.

At first the practice of the Orthodox Church which tolerates divorce under certain conditions might appear to contradict the aforementioned definitive teaching on this issue. These conditions correspond to provisions outlined by Roman law and are the result of carefully articulated legal relations. Especially noteworthy is the fact that the Eastern Church rejected, modified or approved such provisions as she saw fit. In the case of approval, the cause of divorce is regarded as revoking the ecclesiastical concept of marriage by negating its religious and moral foundation. In other words, it effects spiritual death.

Divorce consequential to spiritual death emerges by itself as soon as the foundation of marriage disappears and the purpose of conjugal union is frustrated. The competent ecclesiastical authority does not dissolve the marriage, but rather formally acknowledges that the legitimate marriage is without foundation and has been dissolved "ipso facto."

The Influence of Roman Law

In a broad sense the causes of divorce were carried over from Roman law to Byzantine law, which in turn was under the incontestable influence of the Church. Whenever necessary, the Church availed herself of the state's law to solve the problems arising from the existing gaps in her own legislation. Oftentimes these laws were totally rejected or modified to coincide with ecclesiastical doctrine.

Justinian law distinguished between "divortium ex consensus" and "divortium ex rationali causa,"[6] otherwise known as "repudium." By the former heading was understood the mutual agreement of both spouses to sever their marital bond, while, according to the latter category, the behavior of one of the spouses effected a cessation of the marital relationship.

Regarding the application of civil laws to regulate problems left unsolved by the ecclesiastical canons, it must not be thought that the laws of the state were always rigorously upheld. Indeed, when the Church felt her rights infringed upon, her voice was raised in protest. This is especially evident in the long struggle undertaken to abolish the notorious "divortium ex consensus" which was a constant plague to the life of the Church. It was no easy task, since the legislation of the emperors up to the reign of Justinian silently acquiesced to the moral decadence of Roman society by retaining this means of divorce.

Among those violently opposed to the abuses of the "divortium ex consensu," or "divorce by mutual consent," is Clement of Alexandria (+c.217). In his "Stromata"[7] he stresses that a husband may dismiss his wife on the grounds of adultery alone; furthermore, that conjugal union with one of the spouses during the lifetime of the other is equivalent to adultery. Of a similar opinion is Theophilus of Antioch, (an apologist of the latter 2nd century), who considers such a practice improper for Christians.[8]

Two centuries later St. Gregory of Nazianzus (325-389) reflects the same view in an epistle addressed to the monk Olympius.[9] Making mention of the antithesis between the Church's law and Roman law, he bids Olympius to exercise all possible means to prevent the daughter of Verianus from receiving an "apostasion."[10]

No less ill-disposed to Roman law, which he considers responsible for distorting the law of the Church in its development is St. John Chrysostom (347-407). In one of his homilies,[11] he reminds his listeners that they will not be judged according to Roman law, which permits the "apostasion," but according to the law of God.

A contemporary of Chrysostom, St. Asterius of Amasea,

having in mind the moral degradation of his time, sharply rebukes those who take marriage lightly. In his opinion there are those who marry wealth and change wives as if they were merchandise; others send a writ of divorce for any insignificant cause; and still others, who are yet alive, leave behind many "widows," indifferent to the fact that marriage is dissolved only by death or adultery.[12] The sentiments of these Church fathers should suffice to indicate the strong disapproval of an abhorrent practice with which they wished to disassociate themselves and the Church.

At first, Justinian, too, accorded his subjects the "divorce by mutual consent," but later paved the way for its eventual abolition by limiting the dissolution of marriage to causes determined by court order. These causes were set forth in his Novel 117 of the year 541. Due to the fact that this canon was issued with the collaboration and consent of the *Church,* it was included in the fundamental canonical collection of the Eastern Church, the Nomocanon in XIV titles.[13]

Accordingly, the basic causes for granting divorce are:[14]

1. Crimes carrying with them the death penalty;
2. Events, the results of which are equivalent to natural death;
3. Adultery, or an act giving rise to suspicion of it;
4. Absence of the essential natural presupposition for the realization of marriage;
5. Election of the monastic life by one of the spouses.

Owing to the circumstances by which this canon was adopted, its provisions were far-reaching, serving as a model for the later application and expansion of the causes for divorce. Consequently it is no wonder that these very same provisions constitute the basis of the divorce laws as applied today in the Orthodox Church.

Subsequent centuries saw the recurrence of pre-Justinian legislation favorable to "divorce by mutual consent"; however the persistent attempts by the Church to bring the laws of the state into harmony with her own moral teachings on divorce finally prevailed. From the 9th century marriage could be dissolved

only by the competent authority, providing certain pre-
determined causes had taken place. "Divorce by mutual consent" was now limited to a justifiable cause alone, such as the
desire of one or both spouses to enter the monastic life. Although
the Church originally undertook to change the divorce laws, the
distinction of having ultimately reconciled the civil provisions
regulating divorce to the principle of indissolubility belongs
paradoxically enough to the State.

Testimony of the Fathers and Councils

It now remains to be examined whether the Orthodox
Church is justified in her practice of divorce and remarriage. Is
there anything in the Scriptures or writings of the Church Fathers
to support her practice, or has she arbitrarily usurped authority
with which she was never invested? Pertinent to this question is
the fact that the Church always considered the scriptural references regarding the indissolubility of marriage prohibitive of
"divorce by mutual consent." Applying this same premise later,
both the holy canons and the writings of the Church Fathers
upheld the integrity of marriage. Nevertheless, although not
openly sanctioning divorce and remarriage, the Church Fathers
nowhere indicate their opposition to this practice in principle,
when governed by a legitimate cause.

Once Church and State were of one accord concerning the
illegality of "divorce by mutual consent," there was no longer
dissension between them regarding the justifiable reasons for
divorce.

The Orthodox Church bases her right to acknowledge the
dissolubility of marriage for certain justifiable causes upon Holy
Scripture. These causes are death, as evidenced in I Cor. 7, 39,
and adultery, in Matt. 5, 32 and 19, 9. That adultery was universally not considered the sole grounds for divorce is attested by the
numerous requests submitted to councils concerning the dissolubility of marriage. Similarly, other evidences of the same fact
include the following:[15]

1. Uninterrupted legislation by the State[16] from the earliest
years up to the present regarding the causes of divorce;

2. Justinian's high regard for ecclesiastical practice would

certainly not have permitted him to promulgate his Novel 117 if it were contrary to ecclesiastical law;

3. Fear of repercussions from the Church would have prevented emperors from increasing the causes of divorce if this meant disregard for ecclesiastical practice;

4. The clergy would certainly have opposed state legislation offensive to the Church, as in the tetragamy of Leo the Wise;

5. No voice of protest was raised by either Pope Vigilius (538-555) or Patriarch Menas (536-552) in opposition to Justinian's Novel 117 in 541;

6. Divorce was never an issue of contention between the Eastern and Western Churches prior to their separation. In fact those who favored an austere interpretation of the law on divorce did not prevail until the Gregorian reform in the 11th century. By the 12th century both the tradition of the ancient Church and the practice of the Eastern Church were ignored in the West, due both to the now accomplished schism and the lack of accessible patristic documents.[17]

As has already been established, besides the scriptural basis for the conditional dissolubility of certain marriages, the Orthodox Church recognizes this possibility expanded to include a number of additional grounds.[18] Since the results of these expanded grounds correspond in essence to physical death and adultery, they have the same effect upon marriage as do the latter causes. In support of their viewpoint, the canonists of the Orthodox Church call upon ancient custom as reflected in the words of one of Christianity's earliest teachers—St. Justin the Martyr (c. 165). In his second apology he bears witness to the fact that due to the prodigal life of a certain husband, a bill of divorce was sent by his wife and forthwith their marriage was dissolved.[19]

Likewise, the great doctor of the primitive Church, Origen (183-254), although reluctant to commit himself unequivocally, nevertheless admits the dilemma that a certain canonical problem poses for him. The problem involves the question whether a husband is justified in dismissing a wife guilty of serious offenses other than fornication. The offenses named include witchcraft, infanticide and breaking up one's home.[20] From his cautious reply one readily discerns his leaning towards an affirmative stand. Accordingly, our Lord did not exclude the possibility of divorce in such an instance, but rather stressed the complicity of a husband whose wife, divorced for reasons other than fornication, is considered an adulteress.

St. Basil (c. 330-379), bishop of Caesarea in Cappadocia, also knew and approved of remarriage while the first spouse was still living. By consenting in some instances to divorce and subsequent remarriage, although he might have wished otherwise, he was following contemporary ecclesiastical practice. Owing to the great authority of St. Basil, several canons originating from his correspondence with Amphilochius, bishop of Iconium, were also adopted by the Quinisext Ecumenical Council held in 691-692. Mention here is made of those canons alone which have direct bearing on our topics. Of the 85 canons attributed to St. Basil these include especially canons 9, 31, 35, 36 and 48.[21]

Canon 9 states that a husband abandoned by his wife can remarry, whereas according to canon 48 an innocent wife abandoned by her husband cannot. Unfair as this treatment appears today, such was the custom accepted at that time. The remaining three canons, of which canons 31 and 36 partially constitute canon 93 of the Quinisext Council, concern a woman who without cause abandons her husband and conversely, also the status of a woman whose husband disappears in bottle. The consensus of opinion either implied or expressly stated is that such unions can be dissolved.

From a careful scrutiny of the writing of St. Gregory of Nazianzus (325-389), it would seem that he tolerates only adultery as a legitimate cause for divorce.[22] In such a case, he permits the "apostasion" taken from Roman law and permitting remarriage. In all other circumstances he recommends a conciliatory approach.

Writing at the end of the 4th century, St. Epiphanius, archbishop of Salamis, mentions the numerous causes of divorce. He observes that the spouse whose marriage was dissolved because of fornication, adultery, or other justifiable cause can remarry upon the death of the partner without the Church's censure.[23]

The great teacher and orator, St. John Chrysostom (347-407), joins ranks with those who consider adultery the primary cause of divorce. One occasionally detects a tendency, however; to expand the causes in order to justify divorcing a woman filled with wickedness.[24] Elsewhere, sins against the husband other than adultery which may effect a divorce are listed.[25] In yet one more statement from the writings of this illustrious father, we learn of his opposition to the remarriage of a divorced woman. The reason for this prohibition is to discourage further possible attempts at divorce in a subsequent marriage.[26]

Besides the testimony of these Church Fathers, there are the canons themselves which have always been understood by the canonists of the Eastern Church as lending support to the practice of divorce in certain defined instances. Noteworthy is the 48th Apostolic Canon[27] which prohibits remarriage to one who divorces his lawful wife in order to marry another unmarried woman, or a woman who has been unlawfully divorced from her husband. By employing the term "apolelymene," used to denote an unlawfully divorced woman, the opposite, i.e. a lawfully divorced woman, is implied. Although not mentioning the particular causes, the canon nevertheless conveys its recognition of the possibility of divorce.[28]

From the Church's practice is seen her view which considers the husband of an immoral woman himself guilty of a grave offense. As a reinforcement of this practice, the local council of Neocaesarea held about 315 prohibits through its 8th canon[29] the ordination of a layman whose wife is guilty of adultery. The alternatives left to a cleric whose wife committed adultery after his ordination is her dismissal[30] or, in the case of a continued marriage relationship, the cessation of his sacerdotal functions. The reason for this austerity is the firmly held conviction that the sanctity of the functions performed by a cleric automatically rule out his affinity to impurity.

Another canon worthy of mention here is the 102nd[31] of Carthage dating from a collection compiled in 419. In accordance with the stricter tendencies of the African Church, it prohibits divorced husbands and wives from remarrying. The only alternative left to them is either reconciliation or separation. The canon ends by stating the intention of the council fathers to request imperial intervention in this matter. Certainly such a request would not be made if divorce and remarriage were limited to the undisputed cause of adultery alone. As observed by the commentator Balsamon,[32] not until Justinian's Novel 117 regulating precisely all causes for divorce and subsequent remarriage was an end put to the ambivalent practice prevalent up to then.

Together with Zonaras, the other renowned commentator of the 12th century, Balsamon lists still other causes of divorce. In his interpretation of the 48th Apostolic Canon he expresses the opinion that remarriage is barred only to that husband, who without reasonable cause ("paralogos") dismisses his wife. This obviously implies the opposite, i.e., that one's wife can be dismissed with reasonable cause ("eulogos"). This same view is reiterated in his interpretation of the 87th canon of the Quinisext Council. Here the distinction is made between an arbitrary departure of a woman from her husband without judicial pronouncement and a legal divorce.

In his interpretation of yet another canon, the 9th of St. Basil, Balsamon once again has occasion to repeat the significance of Justinian's Novel 117 and to stress its being the guideline for the causes of divorce.[33] The other commentators of this period express similar views on the same subject.[34]

Conclusion

The mention of these sources dating from the early centuries of the Church, together with the elucidating remarks of the commentators from a later period, should suffice to show the uninterrupted practice of the Orthodox Church regarding divorce and remarriage. Accordingly, the marital bond can be broken for reasons other than natural death. Such a dissolution takes place of course with much pain and sadness to the Church. It is only after all attempts at reconciliation have proved futile that the marriage is recognized as having ceased "eo ipso."

Although there may exist several causes justifying divorce, their application ought not to be looked upon as inconsequential to the principles of indissolubility. On the contrary, they are evidences of leniency and sympathy which recognize the frailties of human nature. They in no way abolish the rule, but, as the exception, illustrate the mercy and understanding exercised so profusely by our Lord during His life. Finally, as evidenced by a verse of Origen,[35] one of the most illustrious of all Christian writers of the ancient Church, it is to prevent greater harm that divorce is granted as an ultimate solution.

Notes

1. O. Rousseau, "Divorce and Remarriage: East and West," in *Concilium*, 24, 1967.

2. Mk. 10, 4; Lk. 16, 18; I Cor. 7, 10 fol.

3. Mt. 5, 31-32; 19, 4 fol.

4. Homily 62 on Mt. 19.

5. As a dispenser of divine mercy, the Church possesses the indispensable right of employing "economy," a principle whereby deficiencies in extreme instances are supplied by the powers which the Church received from Christ.

6. In its desire to reconcile civil laws on divorce to her own decrees the Eastern Church eventually accepted the legitimacy of the "divortium ex rationali cause" (divorce for a reasonable cause). Provisional to its application, however, was a penalty to be imposed upon the guilty partner. Cf. Joseph Zhishman, *The Law of Marriage of the Eastern Orthodox Church*, (Gr. transl.), vol. I, (Athens, 1912) p. 205.

7. Stromata 2, 23.

8. Theophilus, *To Autolycus*, 3, 13.

9. Epist. 176.

10. As understood in the civil law of the time, "apostasion" meant total divorce with permission to remarry.

11. Homily 19 on I. Cor. 7.

12. Homily on Mt. 19, 3.

13. This collection originally appeared in the first half of the 7th century and acquired canonical status throughout the entire Eastern Church.

14. See Nicodemus Milasch, *Ecclesiastical Law of the Orthodox Eastern Church*, (Gr. transl.), (Athens, 1906) p. 901.

15. See J. Zhishman, op. cit., p. 211 fol.

16. This, of course, refers to a state which recognizes Orthodoxy as its official religion.

17. See Victor Pospishil, *Divorce and Remarriage*, (New York, 1967) p. 48.

18. It is the opinion of some non-Orthodox that the addition of these causes of divorce constitute a flagrant offense. To those the words of a Catholic theologian best answer these charges levied against her: "The

Greeks on their side have multiplied the case of divorce with remarriage by applying the law far beyond the Matthean exception. . . . We on our part have an equivalent today, a phenomenon of which we have no right to be proud: the increasing number of requests for annulment to the Roman Rota. . . .'', O. Rousseau, art. cit., p. 136. See also A. Kokkinakis, Bishop of Elaia, *Parents and Priests as Servants of Redemption,* (New York, 1958) pp. 48-54.

19. Apology II, 2.

20. Commentary on Mt. 14, 24.

21. For the text of these canons, see Hamilcar Alivizatos, *The Holy Canons* (in Greek), 2nd edition, (Athens, 1949) pp. 361, 371, 372 and 374.

22. Homily 31.

23. Contra haereses II, haer. 69, 4.

24. Homily 62 on Mt. 19, 1.

25. Homily 26 on Gen. 8.

26. Homily 17 on Mt. 5, 27.

27. Text in Alivizatos, op. cit., p. 147. The Apostolic Canons do not, as their name implies, come from the Apostles, but are statutes dating from the 4th century.

28. See Balsamon's commentary to this canon in G. A. Rhalles and M. Potles, *Syntagma ton Theion kai Hieron Kanonon,* vol. II, (Athens, 1852) p. 64.

29. Alivizatos, op. cit., p. 167.

30. The ''Shepherd'' of Hermas, an early writing which originates from the 2nd century, had already called for the expulsion of an adulterous wife (Mandatum IV, 1).

31. Alivizatos, op. cit., p. 279.

32. Rhalles and Potles, op. cit., vol. III, p. 549.

33. Rhalles and Potles, op. cit., vol. IV, p. 122.

34. J. Zhishman, op. cit., pp. 204-205.

35. Commentary on Mt. 14, 23.

Part II
Divorced Catholics and the Eucharist

Indissolubility and the Right to the Eucharist: Separate Issues or One?

Richard A. McCormick, S.J.

This is the issue I have been asked to address. In the words of your chairman of Research and Discussion, Rev. John A. Alesandro, my mandate is as follows: "We would foresee such a talk as dealing with both sides of the issue, trying to present a balanced picture of moral theologians and their arguments and then offering the speaker's own evaluation of the situation today. We are not looking for a solution to the dilemma in one talk but at least a clarified expression of the question. . . ." In attempting to respond to this mandate I shall proceed in four steps: 1) the issue, 2) the cons, 3) the pros, 4) my own evaluation of the situation.

Before proceeding into the problem, two caveats are in order. First, I cannot speak for moral theologians in general, a fact of which you are well aware but could possibly forget in the course of this study. *Quot capita tot sententiae* is, sometimes regrettably, the state of affairs in moral theology these days. Another moral theologian would approach the matter quite differently, I am sure. Indeed, this occurred at your last annual convention as I recall. Second, even within the above qualifications, I feel compelled to underline the tentative and probing character of this presentation. For the issue is many-sided and complex; it is thoroughly steeped in biblical, historical and systematic considerations which remain incomplete and problematic. Furthermore, my own limitations have led in the past to several changes of opinion on this entire matter. Such chastening experiences suggest appropriate reserve and heavy doses of self-doubt.

1. *The Issue*. In order to clarify the exact question we want to discuss, I must say a word about both indissolubility and reception of the sacraments. By indissolubility I mean the doctrine *in se* and its pastoral implications. The term *in se* is used to distinguish the notion from any prevailing understanding of it at a particular time. In all matters doctrinal and moral we must always distinguish the substance of a teaching from its formulation at a particular point in history. That is a burden I wish the term "indissolubility *in se*" to carry. Concretely, one particular understanding of indissolubility might join it inseparably with reception of the Eucharist by the divorced and force the conclusion that the two are but one issue. Another understanding might yield a different conclusion. To make the distinction between substance and formulation where indissolubility is concerned will, of course, clearly require an attempt on my part to state what I believe to be the substance of that teaching. That I hope to do, delicate and even arrogant as the attempt may appear.

As for reception of the Eucharist I wish to understand a reception warranted by Church policy, a policy stated in and controlled by public norms whereby at least some divorced-remarried persons can be allowed to receive the Eucharist. I put the matter this way, not because it is desirable or even tolerable that there be a policy of exceptions of equal valence with the demand of indissolubility, but because I wish to exclude from the issue internal forum solutions to the problem. Why? For two reasons. First, such pastoral solutions include the condition *secluso scandalo* and therefore when properly implemented should not, or at least need not, raise the indissolubility issue. Second, and more importantly, the usual instance of an internal forum solution is one where a conclusion of nullity of the first marriage is drawn on prudent and probable, but legally non-demonstrable or unacceptable grounds. If this is the case, the issue is not truly indissolubility itself as commonly understood, but the sufficiency of the legal structures whereby it is supported and adjudicated.

Within the confines of the above clarifications, the issue is the following: are those in a second canonically irregular marriage (and one that cannot be regularized and is not patent of an internal forum solution) necessarily to be excluded by policy from the reception of the Eucharist, the necessity being the demand of indissolubility? Or put differently, would the doctrine of indissolubility be intolerably undermined if the Church adopted a policy that allows some divorced-remarried to receive the Eucharist? Or again, can the Church maintain the doctrine of indissolubility and still administer the Eucharist to those whose life-status represents a violation of this teaching? Is not the indissolubility of marriage so fundamental to the Gospel and the Church's proclamation of it that violation of indissolubility implies rejection of a substantial element of the Gospel (and the faith) and therefore excludes one from celebration of the sacrament that is preeminently the celebration of unity in faith? The question can be worded in many ways, some more tendentious than others. My pleonasms here are simply an attempt to formulate the problem as it might be formulated by a variety of publics.

We are aware that the answer given to this question *at the level of practice* varies. While this is to be regretted, it must not be our prime focus of concern here. For what is theologically enlightening is not one's ultimate posture or conclusion, important as it may be, but how one got there. It is just as theologically (and canonically) irresponsible to be warm-hearted but wrong-headed as it is humanly irresponsible to be cold-hearted and right-headed. A healthy pastoral policy can exist only if a warm heart is guided by a right head, in this case one that does not betray the Lord's teaching.

2. *The Negative response* (sc. the position that holds that reception of the Eucharist and indissolubility are a single issue in the sense that the Church cannot allow the Eucharist to the divorced-remarried without fatally undermining her commitment to indissolubility). To the best of my knowledge this position is not widely defined in recent theological writing but is found chiefly in the manualist tradition and episcopal statements. It is therefore what is properly known as "the official doctrine and policy."

First I shall state what I believe is the position itself, then the strongest arguments possible for it. A marriage that is *ratum et consummatum* is indissoluble by any human authority, be it the partners themselves (internal indissolubility) or any other authority (external indissolubility). In such a marriage, a bond comes into being that is dissolved only with the death of one of the partners. If the marriage factually breaks up and a partner to it remarries, his marriage is in violation of this existing bond. Such a partner, should he desire to remain in Eucharistic communion with the Church, has but two options. Either he must abandon the second marriage, or if he cannot (because of obligations that have arisen within it), he must live as brother-sister. That is a brief but, I believe, accurate summary of the official understanding of indissolubility and its pastoral concomitants.

There are three major arguments used to support this official position on the Eucharist for the divorced-remarried: the state of sin, imperfect symbolization, scandal. A word about each.

The State of Sin. It has been, and indeed still is, common teaching that one may not remain in the free proximate occasion of serious sin. If he does so he may not be absolved "for the will to remain in the proximate occasion of sin constitutes a new grave sin" (Genicot, *Theologia Moralis* II, n. 357). Obviously, if the person's very determination indisposes him for the sacrament of penance, it also indisposes him for the Eucharist. This indisposition is acknowledged both in the treatise on the recipient of the sacraments and that covering the duty to deny the sacraments to *indigni*. *Indigni* are described as those who are indisposed, "that is one who will receive a valid sacrament but not the grace of the sacrament" (Genicot, *loc. cit.,* n. 20).

Applied to the divorced-remarried, this means that unless they are determined to forego sexual relations, they are in a permanent state of grave sin (a free proximate occasion of the grave sin of adultery). Their sexual relations are adulterous as long as the first spouse is still alive. Therefore, their remaining together without the determination to live as brother-sister is persistence in the free proximate occasion of adultery.

Imperfect symbolization. This argument was used recently by the bishops of the Ivory Coast. They first reject the full impact of the state-of-sin argument as follows: "actually God alone fathoms depths and hearts and knows the real spiritual condition of men. It would be, for priests and members of the community, an error and a sin against fraternal charity to consider those to whom Church law forbids access to the sacraments as in a state of grave sin" (*Documentation Catholique* 69 [1972] 739).

Why, then, may the divorced-remarried not receive the sacraments? The bishops note that the sacraments have as one of their purposes "to build up the Body of Christ." Now in the Body of Christ, the divorced-remarried "cannot witness fully to the sanctity of the Church. It is because the sacraments are signs of the People of God for the world that those may not receive them who do not fulfill all the conditions required for being signs of the Church." Others might word the matter differently, but the substance of the argument is the witness or symbolization involved in sacramental participation.

This argument did not originate on the Ivory Coast. It is a concise statement of the rather traditional teaching on the obligation to administer the sacraments. Let me recall the highlights of that teaching. Moralists maintain that "one who has the care of souls *ex officio* is obligated in justice to administer the sacraments to those under his care who reasonably request them."(Genicot, n. 18. Canon 467 does not say *ex justitia;* it says only *debet.* But canon 892 #1 says it of penance. So it is an easy inference that the *debet* of c. 467 touches justice.) This means that the faithful have a right to the Eucharist, a right had by reason of the office undertaken by the minister. This right is conditioned by the phrase *rationabiliter petentibus.* When, then, do persons "reasonably request" the sacraments? Genicot answers somewhat broadly: "This is to be judged by the laws of the Church and local customs." I think it can be said that apart from the laws of the Church and local customs, the reasonableness of the request is determined by a combination of the need of the recipient and the inconvenience to the minister.

However, at this point we must, by extrapolation, include among those who do not "reasonably request" the sacraments the so-called *indigni* (those who would receive validly but not fruitfully). For if the minister ought to deny the sacraments to *indigni,* then clearly they do not request them reasonably. At this point Joseph Fuchs adds an extremely interesting sentence: "Equivalent to *indigni* are those who, though they are personally disposed for a fruitful sacramental reception, are however not to be admitted (to the sacraments) because of the common good of the Church and because of its concern for discipline and unity" (J. Fuchs, *De Sacramentis in Genere*, *De Baptismo*, De Confirmatione, 3 ed., 1963, p. 50).

In applying this to heretics and schismatics who are in good faith and personally well disposed, Fuchs notes: "The reason for the prohibition in this instance is different; it is that the sacraments are the greatest signs of ecclesial unity. Therefore, administration of the sacraments would easily promote indifferentism. And as a general rule *(per se)* unity in the sacraments supposes full unity in faith and discipline" (Fuchs, *loc. cit.*, p. 51).

If Fuchs' reasoning were applied to the divorced-remarried it would go as follows: since the sacraments are the greatest signs of ecclesial unity, their administration to the divorced-remarried would easily undermine that unity by undermining the permanence of marriage. For the permanence of marriage is indisputably a substantial element of the Gospel. He who rejects such a substantial rejects the Christ who demanded it. But since the Church must maintain unity in faith and discipline, she must not tolerate practices that undermine it. This is, in slightly different words, the argument used by the bishops of the Ivory Coast. And it is found widely in the manualist tradition.

It is forcefully stated by Karl Lehmann as follows: "As regards admission to the Eucharist anyone who publicly and permanently intends to persist in this state publicly contradicts the Lord's commandment by his adulterous life, while by taking part in the Lord's Supper he would simultaneously make a profession of faith in Jesus Christ. This intolerable discrepancy publicly displayed contradicts the meaning of faith, of the ecclesiastical community, and of the function of the sacraments as symbols effecting what they signify" (Karl Lehmann, "Indissolubility of Marriage and Pastoral Care of the Divorced Who Remarry," *Communio* 1[1974] (222-223). At this point Lehmann is stating the argument, not necessarily endorsing its every aspect or implication.

Scandal. This is but an explication of an argument already present in the second argument. But it is so important at the practical level that it deserves separate status. It would run as follows: if the divorced-remarried are allowed to receive the Eucharist, others will conclude that it is not wrong to remarry after divorce, that the Church is changing her teaching on indissolubility, that the Church is approving second marriages, etc. If this is the way the faithful would respond to a change in pastoral policy, then clearly we are dealing with a policy that would undermine the permanence of marriage by eroding the determination to permanence from the very beginning. Briefly, a policy that would constitute scandal in the theological sense.

The cumulative force of these three arguments is that indissolubility and reception of the Eucharist by the divorced and remarried are not separate or separable issues. A change in traditional pastoral policy will necessarily affect corrosively the teaching on indissolubility. For instance, if the second marriage (while the first spouse still lives) is *not* a "state of sin," then precisely what is wrong with entering this state? And if there is nothing wrong with entering this state, then what is left of the traditional notion of indissolubility? The same deductions could be drawn from the second and third arguments.

3. *The affirmative response.* Contemporary moral writing that adopts the position that the right to the Eucharist and indissolubility are separate issues usually proceeds in two steps. First, it shows the weakness of the arguments for the opposite position. Second, it attempts to show a variety of ways that it would be for the overall good of the Church's mission of reconciliation and mercy were she to adopt a policy that allowed some divorced-remarried access to the sacraments. A word should be said about each to fill out the theological *status questionis.*

The state of sin. Clearly there are some couples in a second marriage whose situation and personal awareness could be described as "the state of sin." But to say this of all second marriages that are canonically irregular labors under many telling, even fatal weaknesses. The following points are frequently made:

1. Some, even many couples are factually convinced that they are not living in sin, whatever may have been the sinfulness in the rupture of the first marriage and the entry into the second. The second union is stable, characterized by mutual respect and profound affection, and is often supported by deep Christian at-

titudes in all other spheres of life. To stigmatize this as a "state of sin" is to speak a language with little or no resonance in the couples' experience.

2. The state-of-sin argument identifies in the term *indigni* the external state of irregularity with a subjective and personal sinful will. Of this facile identification Karl Lehmann says: "This seems to be one of the really problematic presuppositions of the traditional argument" (*Ibid.* 223. Cf. also Ch. Robert, "Est-il encore opportun de priver des sacrements de la réconciliation et de l'eucharistie indistinctment tous les divorcés remariés? *Revue de droit canonique*[24] [1974] 152-176 at 158; H. B. Meyer, "Konnen wiederverheiratete Geschiedene zu den Sacrament en zugelassen werden?" in J. David and F. Schmalz (eds.) *Wie unaufloslich ist die Ehe?* [Aschaffenburg, 1969] 268-306 at 284 ff; Hans Heimerl, "Um Eine neue Wertung der nicht katholisch geschlosunen Ehen von Katholiken," in H. Heimerl (ed.) *Verheirate und doch nicht verheiratet* [Herder, 1970] 157-212 at 198).

3. In some instances the Church admits that it is humanly and Christianly better for the couple in the second marriage to remain together, deepen their Christian life, attend Mass, etc. This all supposes that they are living the life of grace and are not precisely in a state of sin ("Le problème pastoral des chrétiens divorcés et remariés," *Vie spirituelle: Supplement* 109 [1974] 125-154 at 146). As the French moral theologians state it: "From the moment that the Church recognizes that Christian divorced-remarrieds have the human and even Christian duty to live their second union, and not to ruin it or to attempt to revive the first marriage, she cannot impute sin to them or consider as a *state* of sin that which in other respects she considers their *state* of life and even as their obligatory *state*" (146).

4. The state-of-sin argument supposes the adequacy of the present tribunal system in determining the status of the first marriage and the freedom (or its absence) to enter the second marriage. It is canon lawyers themselves who have raised the most serious objections to this supposition. It further supposes a sufficiently well-developed theology of marriage to undergird any adjudicative system, a supposition denied widely within the theological community.

5. The official policy which sees the second marriage as a state of sin also sees this state of sin dissolved by a brother-sister relationship. But the notion of such a relationship has its own serious problems. First of all, there are the grave disorders that can arise for a couple and their children from an intimate life together without any sexual expression. *Gaudium et spes* recognized this when it stated: "But where the intimacy of married life is broken off, it is not rare for the faithfulness to be imperiled and its quality of fruitfulness ruined. For there the upbringing of the children and the courage to accept new ones are both endangered" (n. 51). Second, there is an attitudinal contradiction in the brother-sister relationship. On the one hand the Church views sexual intimacy as so essential to marriage that the marriage is not consummated without it (and is indeed dissoluble). On the other hand this intimacy is denied to the divorced-remarried at the very time the Church urges them (at times) to remain together and deepen conjugal affection (cf. Le problème pastoral . . ." *loc. cit.,* 136).

6. The state-of-sin argument seems to suppose that the morality of sex relations depends solely on the recognition of the legal validity of the union. This is not compatible with the Code's express admission (c. 1085) that even in invalid or irregular unions there can be a true marital intention. If such a marital intention were not present, the notion of *sanatio in radice* would be empty and erroneous (cf. Lehmann, *loc. cit.* 241, note 46).

7. To view all irregular second marriages as involving a state of sin is to make the rupture of the first marriage an unforgivable sin. The Church does this with no other failure even though the objective effects of the sins are irreparable (e.g., murder) (cf. "Le probleme pastoral . . ." *loc. cit.*). An analogy may help enlighten what is the true state of sin in this matter. It is not the thief who repents who is in a state of sin. It is the thief who intends to continue to thieve who is. His very mentality and outlook constitute a state of sin. Similarly, it is not the divorced-remarried person as such who is in a state of sin; it is the divorced-remarried person who is unrepentant and intends to continue to allow his union to go stale and to remarry. If we say anything else we have made divorce and remarriage an unforgivable sin.

8. Finally, and quite tellingly, it is argued ("Le problème pastoral . . .") that if indissolubility is denied by reintegration of the divorced-remarried, it is because one concludes that no matter what the state of the second union, *the first still exists*. And thus the state of sin. There are two weaknesses to this conclusion. First, this means that indissolubility assures the existence of a reality with no other content, no other properties. This is an unacceptably legal or juridical notion of indissolubility. Second, this notion of indissolubility contradicts official pastoral practice. For this practice often and rightly attempts to promote the Christian life of the couple in the second union. The Church demands of the divorced-remarried a life of faith, attendance at Mass, the fulfillment of all familial obligations. This she does not do with bigamists as the term is popularly used. In other words, the Church acts as if the first marriage no longer existed.

In summary, then, the present official pastoral policy which sees the second union in which sexual intimacy occurs as a state of sin is, it is argued, impaled on contradictory attitudes. It both recognizes the marriage, but does not recognize it. It both recognizes the necessity and desirability of a Christian life for these Christians, but does not recognize it completely (cf. "Le problème pastoral . . ." *loc. cit.* 139). The French moral theologians have summarized very trenchantly the difficulties in the state of sin approach. "The single thing apropos of which one can speak of a personal actual sin, according to presently admitted pastoral practice, would be the practice by the partners of sexual union. This is why it is demanded of them that they abstain from the sacraments. But we have repeatedly underlined the paradoxical character of this demand. On the one hand, what notion of marriage and sexuality underlies the position of the Church that demands of Christians that they honor all the dimensions of their union with the exception of the sexual? On the other hand, what conception of the sacraments and of sexuality leads us to the notion that the sacraments would be compatible with the exercise of all the other dimensions of the conjugal union but that they would not be compatible with that of sexuality?" ("Le problème pastoral . . ." *loc. cit.*, 145).

Imperfect symbolization and the Church's concern for unity in faith and discipline. The answer to this second argument is not the denial of the Church's concern for unity in faith and discipline. It is rather that the form this concern takes can and must vary depending especially on one's assessment of two factors: the nature and purpose of the Church (and of the sacraments as actions of the Church), the cultural and theological perspectives on lack of full integration with the Church. In other words, the argument supposes that the administration of the Eucharist to those who do not fulfill all the conditions for complete ecclesial integration will de facto undermine unity in faith and discipline, and thus undermine the common good of the Church. If that were true, the Church would have little choice in her pastoral response to the problems of the divorced-remarried. But whether it is true is highly questionable, so it is argued and the determination of this revolves especially around the two factors just mentioned.

First, the nature and purpose of the Church. In the mind and words of the Second Vatican Council, the Church has a double finality which it expresses in its sacramental life: the unity of the Church (the only Body of Christ), the indispensable means of grace and salvation (cf. Ch. Robert, *loc. cit.*, 169). Just as the Church is both the sacrament and the means of salvation, so her ministry has the twofold finality. As Robert has pointed out, neither of these finalities can be suppressed or forgotten. In concrete circumstances it is necessary to balance and compromise to do justice to both finalities. Concretely, the Church judges it appropriate at times to renounce the fullness of the conditions of integration which she imposes in principle in order to extend more widely the means of grace.

This she does, for example, when dealing with common worship. In the Decree on Ecumenism the Council stated: "Such worship (common) depends chiefly on two principles: it should signify the unity of the Church; it should provide a sharing in the means of grace. The fact that it should signify unity generally rules out common worship. Yet the gaining of a needed grace sometimes commends it." (n. 8).

This dialectical balance was applied explicitly to common

worship with the eastern churches. In the *Decree on Eastern Catholic Churches* we read: "Divine Law forbids any common worship (*communicatio in sacris*) which would damage the unity of the Church, or involve formal acceptance of falsehood or the danger of deviation in the faith, of scandal, or of indifferentism. At the same time pastoral experience clearly shows that with respect to our Eastern brethren there should and can be taken into consideration various circumstances affecting individuals, wherein the unity of the Church is not jeopardized nor are intolerable risks involved, but in which salvation itself and the spiritual profit of souls are urgently at issue.

Hence, in view of the special circumstances of time, place, and personage, the Catholic Church has often adopted and now adopts a milder policy, offering to all the means of salvation and an example of charity among Christians through participation in the sacraments and in other sacred functions and objects" (n. 26).

Therefore, once the Church's double finality is acknowledged, there is nothing *in principle* that prevents sacramental reception by those who are incompletely integrated into the Church. If that is true of our separated brethren, is it not at least as true of those who are not separated but have encountered marital tragedy or failure?

Whether there is *in fact* (in our present circumstances) something that would prevent reception of the sacraments by the divorced-remarried is closely associated with our cultural and theological attitudes toward those who do not fulfill all the conditions for full integration in the Church. For example, whether granting the sacraments to heretics (in good faith) and schismatics will foster indifferentism and undermine unity in the faith, depends heavily on the prevailing attitudes toward heretics and schismatics. If the age is unecumenical and the atmosphere is one of religious distance and warfare between Protestants and Catholics—the Protestant being viewed dominantly in terms of what he does *not* share with Catholics—and if the atmosphere is one of suspicion, fear, and rather low-grade apologetics, common sharing in the sacraments will more readily lead to practical indifferentism. If, however, our Protestant brethren are viewed as believing, good-faith separated *brethren* who share in most of our beliefs and with the Spirit's help and guidance are seen as struggling with us toward unity, then the atmosphere is such that common worship would not involve the same degree of danger of indifferentism. This the council itself clearly concluded.

Something similar can be said of divorced-remarried. What are the dominant notions or perspectives that lead to the conclusion that unity in faith and discipline would be threatened if some divorced-remarried could receive the sacraments? They are above all two: 1) the "state of sin" view of the second union; 2) the implication that the ability to receive the sacraments is tantamount to full legal good standing—sc., legal approbation of the second marriage with connotation of its validity before God—with the further connotation that marriage is dissoluble, a connotation at odds with the basic Catholic understanding of marriage.

However, if we have changed our perspectives on these two dominant notions, then the danger of undermining unity in faith and discipline by undermining marital permanence is profoundly lessened. Enough has been said about the "state of sin" to indicate that at least theologically the designation is, as a generalization, unsupportable.

The second notion needs attention here. The implication that the ability to receive the Eucharist is tantamount to full legal good standing or integration is an implication with roots in a widespread popular and highly legal mentality. That is, this is how many people think about the sacraments. They believe that going to communion is a sign to themselves and others that their marriage is accepted and approved by the Church. And obviously they *want* this to be the case since their own peace of mind is closely connected with such acceptance and approval. In this sense, it is a popular mentality that makes of indissolubility and reception of the Eucharist a single, non-separable issue.

However, with a fresh awareness in the post-conciliar Church that we are a pilgrim Church, in need of sacramental sustenance not because of our sanctity and wholeness but precisely because we are weak, are sinners, are only more or less possessed by the faith we profess, are only more or less led by the charity that defines our being, we are well positioned to distinguish between sacramental nourishment at the Eucharistic table and full legal integration into the Church. Thus, though it can be admitted that the integration of the divorced-remarried into the Church is incomplete (as whose is not in one way or other?), still this incompleteness is, in a pilgrim church, hardly reason for denial of the sacraments, sacraments of whose need and importance to the Christian life the Church herself has spoken so eloquently.

Briefly, a policy allowing some divorced-remarried to receive the sacraments would undermine unity in faith and discipline only if we (quite unrealistically and inconsistently) demand full integration into the Church as a condition of sacramental life, and if we (quite legalistically) allowed participation in the sacraments to be viewed as the equivalent of complete integration or legal good-standing. Since we need do neither—though some popular mind-changing might be called for—the argument for imperfect symbolization is no insuperable obstacle to a change in pastoral policy.

Scandal. The third argument uniting inseparable indissolubility with sacramental reception was scandal. That is, people would conclude that, if the second union is not a "state of sin" and the partners may receive the Eucharist, it is not wrong to remarry after divorce, that the Church is abandoning indissolubility, etc.

The answer given to this type of objection in the literature is simple, perhaps too simple. It is insisted that forgiving the reconciling need not and does not imply approval of what has gone before and even now come to be. Thus, the objection centers on the wrong thing. The precept of permanence is what the Church proclaims and what the couple must live. *That* is not affected by forgiving those who have failed, even sinfully, to live that command and find themselves in a position of irregularity as a result. Therefore, if the people are properly prepared for this change of approach by a careful explanation of its meaning, no scandal need occur.

Once the weakness of the arguments uniting inseparably indissolubility and reception of the sacraments has been shown, the theologians who espouse the position of separability of issues develop other arguments to show why the Church ought to adopt a cautious policy of readmission to the sacraments. Some of the arguments are the following: (1) The need of the partners for sacramental sustenance. (2) Readmission to the sacraments better manifests the reconciling role of the Church in a sinful world and her message that it is always possible to begin anew. (3) An open juridically practicable policy avoids the confusion, abuses, disarray associated with the clandestinity of internal forum approaches. (4) The right to marry is a very fundamental right. Given the many doubts about the extent and meaning of Christ's injunction against divorce and remarriage, and of its practical consequences in the contemporary world, the Church ought to honor the fundamental character of this right by leaving the validity and dissolubility of the first marriage to God and put more emphasis on "the present dispositions and good consciences of those second-marriage Catholics who meet the four conditions I have described" (Charles Whelan, "Divorced Catholics: A Proposal" *America* 131 [1974] 363-365 at 365).

In short, I suppose that the cumulative force of these arguments reduces to the general principle that of the two options discussed (continue present policy, change to readmit some divorced-remarrieds to the sacraments), the second represents the lesser evil, or viewed positively, the greater good.

This is the way the discussion has proceeded. It is fair to say that most recent writing (at least of my acquaintance) favors a policy of *cautious* readmission of *some* divorced-remarried to the sacraments. I say "cautious" because the literature lists in detail the conditions that ought to be observed. I say "some" because I know of no serious literature that proposes a kind of conditionless and indiscriminate "amnesty" for all divorced-remarried persons. In this sense, then, it is true to say that contemporary theological writing moves in the direction of answering the question posed by the title of my report as follows: indissolubility and the reception of the Eucharist are separate issues, at least in some cases. The reasons for this conclusion are, I believe, substantially the ones I have reported here.

4. *Personal reflections.* This study began with the threat that it would conclude with some personal reflections. Let me now make good that threat. I believe that indissolubility and reception of the sacraments by the divorced-remarried are separable issues.

That is, a practicable public policy of admission of some divorced-remarried persons to the sacraments need not constitute a challenge to the teaching on indissolubility of marriage, and thereby weaken the Church's unity in faith and discipline.

I use the word "separable" designedly. For at present at the popular level and in the public mind, so to speak, they are possibly not separate issues. What does this mean? It means that for many decades, even centuries, the Church has interpreted the indissolubility of marriage in a particular way and drawn certain consequences from it with regard to pastoral policy. This has had the effect of inculcating a mentality in the faithful, a mentality that views indissolubility as capable of but one pastoral policy where the divorced-remarried are concerned. Change the pastoral policy and you have changed or revoked the teaching. I may be wrong in this assessment of public attitudes, but if this is actually the popular understanding of things, then obviously a change in policy will indeed harm the common good of the Church by seeming to deny or weaken one of its substantial teachings. Therefore, some readjustment of perspectives is called for, first theologically, then at more popular levels, before indissolubility and reception of the sacraments by the divorced-remarried can become actually *separate* issues at the practical level.

What is this adjustment? In other words, what is the basic theological justification for saying that indissolubility and reception of the sacraments by divorced-remarried are separable issues? There are, I believe, two possibilities: (1) an adjusted understanding of the meaning of indissolubility; (2) the principle of the lesser evil. I am torn as to which one ought to function as the basis for a modified pastoral practice in the Church, torn because I have not received sufficient theological response to the proposals I made in fear and trembling in *Theological Studies* (36[1975] 113-114) on an adjusted understanding of the meaning of indissolubility.

Let me briefly review that analysis first. For many centuries this was understood in a highly juridical sense, not least of all because marriage, as a basic human institution, needs legal supports and controls. When a marriage was sacramental and consummated, a *vinculum* was said to come into existence which no human power, neither the pope (extrinsic indissolubility) nor the marriage partners themselves (intrinsic indissolubility), could untie. Thus, one form of pastoral accommodation for marital distress was "dissolution of the bond." Once indissolubility is conceived in this way, it seems to dictate inexorably certain practical conclusions—the state of sin being one of them.

But should indissolubility be conceived in this way? Or better, is this the only way indissolubility can be conceived if we are to be true to the Lord's command? (Here I refer back to my suggestion that we talk of indissolubility *in se*.) Perhaps not. I would like to suggest, very probably for your enlightened disagreement, that indissolubility ought to be thought of above all and primarily as an absolute moral percept, a *moral ought* inherent in the marriage union. Because marriage represents the most intimate union of man and woman and is inseparably tied to the procreation and education of children it ought to be one and permanent. That is, from the very beginning there is a most serious obligation upon the couple to support and strengthen this marriage. They are absolutely obliged not to let the marriage fall apart and die. This is particularly binding on those who have made their marriage a sacrament to the world because they have undertaken a true ministry to the world: to mirror Christ's love for and fidelity to his church. The moral ought of which I speak, in its imposing urgency, is rooted in faith in the redemption. With Christ's redeeming grace we know we can do what might appear to be impossible to sinful men.

Indissolubility as a moral ought implies two things: (1) the couple must strengthen and support their union and not allow it to die; (2) when the relationship has fallen apart and separation occurs, they must resuscitate it. A too quick conclusion that the marriage is dead is itself a violation of this ought, much as a premature pronouncement of death in a heart donor is a violation of his life.

If indissolubility is thought of in this way, then when a marriage irretrievably breaks down it can be said that at least one of the partners (whether through weakness or sinfulness can be left, indeed must be left, to God's merciful understanding) has failed to live up to the precept of indissolubility. What ought not be has come to be, a serious disvalue, both personal and social, has occurred.

But when a marriage is truly dead, then it seems meaningless to speak of the moral ought of not letting the marriage die. If indissolubility is conceived in highly juridical fashion, the unbreakable *vinculum* continues, and subsequent remarriage is in violation of this *vinculum*, is an objective state of sin, etc.

What I am suggesting, therefore, is that it may be quite possible to conceive of the permanence of marriage in a way compatible with Christ's command without viewing it in terms of a continuing moral and legal *vinculum*. And if this *vinculum* is not present, then the basic reason preventing reception of the sacraments disappears. Another way of wording this would be the following: the indissolubility of sacramental and consummated marriage prevents the institutional possibility of another *sacramental* marriage, but not of another non-sacramental marriage. This seems to be the direction of the Church's pastoral practice when she advises some couples to stay together rather than break up the second union. But her recognition of this second union is incomplete and inconsistent as noted. To circumvent this inconsistency the Church would have to abandon her teaching that every true marriage between the baptized is thereby a sacrament. If this notion of indissolubility is viable, then it seems quite clear that indissolubility and reception of the sacraments by the divorced-remarried are separable issues. Is it a viable notion? Here I must await the responses of the biblical, systematic and canonical communities.

If such a modification of the meaning of indissolubility is not possible, and if we must continue to speak of a *vinculum* surviving the death of the first marriage (whether the language used to convey this bond be legal or more biblical, e.g., a kinship bond), then there remains the possibility of the use of the principle of the lesser evil. (I cannot accept other suggested solutions, e.g., the notion of indissolubility as an ideal, nor can many exegetes.) The principle could be applied in either of two ways, one general, the other individual. First, it might be argued it is factually a lesser evil if all divorced-remarried Catholics are admitted to the sacraments. The difficulty in proceeding in this way is that it is extremely difficult to show how and why this constitutes the lesser evil in our times. Second, it could be argued that *in some individual cases* (the conditions being carefully spelled out) it is, all things considered, the lesser evil. The constituents of this judgment would be the following: the basic character of the right to marry, the doubtful character of the theology and jurisprudence presently limiting that right, the importance of the sacraments for spiritual growth and salvation, the overall good dispositions of the couple, the fact (if it is such) that people would not be scandalized or misled by such a policy, the reconciling mission of the Church, the fact that the Church's commitment to indissolubility (in the traditional sense) is sufficiently manifested and protected if she refuses to bless second marriages and so on.

If the calculus in individual instances is that readmission to the sacraments is indeed, all things considered, the lesser evil, then I think it is clear that the two issues we are discussing are separable issues. For if indissolubility were intolerably compromised by such a judgment, we could never draw such a conclusion. If it is not so compromised, it seems a separable issue. This formulation of the matter is at some point probably circular. So, it assumes what is to be proved.

One final remark to this admittedly tentative probe. If indissolubility and reception of the sacraments are not only *separable* issues, but are to be practically *separate*, then it is clear that the validity of the slightly dejuridicized notion of indissolubility I have proposed or the soundness of the factual judgment about the lesser evil in individual cases must not only be established in the academic community. It must be prepared for, understood, and accepted at the popular level. Otherwise, at the level where scandal and division ought not to be, it will continue to be and grow. As Charles Whelan noted: a modified pastoral practice "would require careful explanation to the membership of the Church of the reasons for the change in discipline. It must be abundantly clear that the purpose of the change is to show compassion and to do justice, not to introduce another form of divorce into the Church, (*Loc. cit.* 365).

"Abundantly clear." For if this is not the case, the Church will be seen, in adopting a more lenient policy on reception of the sacraments for divorced-remarrieds, to be adjusting not her partial and historically-conditioned grasp of the consequences of indissolubility, but she will be seen as revoking the very notion of indissoluble marriage. That I think she cannot do, nor can she tolerate the conclusion by the faithful that this is what she is doing.

"It must be abundantly clear. Can this be achieved? Yes, I think so. For I suggest that the issues are separable issues—one way or another."

The Right of Catholics
in Second Marriages to the Eucharist

Anthony J. McDevitt

The saying has it that if you are not part of the solution, you are part of the problem. While it is unlikely that cannon law and pastoral policy have had much influence upon the alarming increase in marital breakdown, this scarcely means that the Church bears no responsibility. At the very least we might say that in those situations where alienation and estrangement prevail the Church's mission of uniting all things in Christ has somehow been obstructed and frustrated. Divorce is society's way of acknowledging that a marriage has failed: the Church's perceived response to that acknowledgement has, by and large, been quite negative.

The topic given me directs my remarks to the area of Church law, and more especially to penal law. At least, that is my understanding of the title of this address: Excommunications and the Right of Catholics in Second Marriages to the Eucharist.

By its very nature law has but a limited role to play in social interaction. It is a means by which acceptable standards of conduct are articulated and sanctions for non-compliance imposed. So understood, the law expresses the self-awareness of the society from which it emerges. Unless it gains wide acceptance law is ineffectual, for it will not be observed and cannot be enforced. Thus it projects the values which the social grouping in a particular set of historical and cultural circumstances considers to be paramount. These limitations become glaringly apparent in the aftermath of historical developments and cultural shifts which magnify the provisional quality of the legislator's perspective. This dynamic is also operative in canon law. The fact that a revision of the Code is underway gives practical recognition to these limitations. Hopefully, future legislation will take into account factors which the membership of the North American Conference of Separated and Divorced Catholics are most keenly aware.

Future solutions, however, don't solve present problems. It is my thesis that widespread misapplication of criminal sanctions has served to aggravate, rather than to contain, and much less to alleviate a massive problem within the Church. I wish to emphasize that word, misapplication. The framers and promulgators of legislation now in force, with all its limitations and deficiencies, ought not to be held accountable for the misuse to which their laws have been put, albeit unwittingly. It is understandable, of course, that institutional inertia would prize total and uncritical compliance with all laws, thus eliminating dissent. It's understandable, too, that the institution should penalize those who fail to conform to its expectations. Any discernible deviation from the norm provokes a strong negative reaction. Church history contains numerous examples of those who challenged the inequities of the system, and were ostracized for their efforts, and were vindicated and rehabilitated only after the merits of the reforms they proposed had gained popular acceptance. For many of them, unfortunately, recognition came posthumously!

Behavior which does not conform to prevailing expectations inevitably creates tension. The way in which the social grouping deals with that tension is the measure of its ability to respond to challenge, to flourish, is the measure of its soundness and maturity. If adjustment to cultural factors is inadequate, and adaptation to other environmental pressures unsatisfactory, conflict remains unresolved and the wounds begin to fester. Without the capacity to tolerate considerable deviation from the ideal a society becomes rigidly doctrinnaire and tragically oppressive. As regrettable as such a development may be in civil society, it is totally repugnant to the image of the Church as a people brought together under the sign of God's forgiving love, a community of universal reconciliation.

Since ostracism means that conciliation has failed, and excommunication is the ecclesiastical term for ostracism, the effectiveness of Church ministry to those in canonically irregular situations might well be measured by the frequency of its usage. Just as excommunication represents the nadir of the ecclesial process, so does Eucharistic sharing represent its zenith, "the summit toward which the activity of the Church is directed". (*Sarcrosanctum Concilium*, #10). To pronounce excommunication is to acknowledge failure; to effect reconciliation is to announce the power of God's unfailing mercy toward his sinful creatures. Just as the restoration of unity among the family of Christian Churches was one of the chief concerns of the II Vatican Council (*Unitatis Redintegratio*, # 1), so within the Roman Catholic family our forebearance of one another's mistakes and failures becomes the sign of unity in the Spirit of the Risen Christ. In both ventures, ecumenical and domestic as well, union can be achieved and celebrated only at the banquet table of the Lord!

In acknowledging that the law has contributed to the Church's ambivalence, if not schizophrenia, toward the casualties of marital breakdown, I do not infer that a reformulation of law will reverse or even retard the trend toward more divorce. (It doesn't appear that we have yet reached agreement on how best to tackle that multifaceted problem!) As the letters of Paul to the Romans and Corinthians and Galatians repeatedly remind us, the function of law among God's people is quite modest. Yet, unless regulations are precisely formulated, clearly presented, and equitably applied, even that subordinate role is seriously compromised and subverted. By way of atonement for the mistreatment which victims of broken marriages have received from malpractitioners of the law, I will review with you the norms that have been invoked. From a brief analysis of the provisions of the general law, contained in the Code of Canon Law, and of particular legislation for the American Church in the III Plenary Council of Baltimore, and of policy that has evolved from these enactments I will draw conclusions that suggest a significant change in pastoral practice, but one that is fully consistent with the actual provisions of law, and which does violence neither to public order nor to the rights of individuals. These are the conclusions reached by a special committee of the CLSA on Alternatives to the Tribunal, of which I was privileged to serve as chairman.

A Fundamental Right.

Let's start at the beginning! The fundamental right of every Catholic to receive the Eucharist is guaranteed in law. Canon 853 states: "Every baptized person who is not restrained by law can and should be admitted to Holy Communion."

Supporting that and other similar provisions of law are the affirmations of the II Vatican Council such as this: "The laity have the right, as do all Christians, to receive in abundance from their sacred pastors the spiritual goods of the Church, especially the assistance of the Word of God and the Sacraments" (*Lumen Gentium*, #37). Moreover, since the exercise of this right to the sacraments is not optional, but mandatory for us all, it imposes some obligations upon pastors. Because we have the duty of full, conscious and active participation in the liturgy (cf. *Sacrosanctum Concilium*, #13) there is a corresponding obligation to provide us an ample opportunity for such sharing.

Underlying this right conferred by membership in the Church is the very dignity of the human person. The Pastoral Constitution on the Church in the Modern World makes a declaration which could well serve as the preamble to a Christian Bill of Rights. "(T)here is a growing awareness of the exalted dignity proper to the human person. . . . The ferment of the Gospel . . . has aroused and continues to arouse in man's heart the irresistible requirements of his dignity" (*Gaudium et Spes*, #2). So universal and inalienable are his rights and responsibilities that the Declaration on Religious Liberty (*Dignitatis Humanae*, #2) insists that within the limits imposed by public order the individual is not "to be restrained from acting in accordance with his own beliefs, whether privately or publicly." Speaking to this very point in publishing guidelines on "Due Process" of law within the Church (page 5), our American Bishops acknowledge that "the principles of fundamental fairness and the universally applicable presumption of freedom require that no member of the Church arbitrarily be deprived of the exercise of any right or office." The inference is compelling: in the event consideration is given to the restriction of any right of Christian membership the burden of proof should rest with those who charge that it is forfeit. Canon 87, the very first in the section of the Code dealing with the rights of persons, sets forth that basic guarantee. "By baptism a person becomes a member of the Church of Christ with all the rights and duties of a Christian unless there is some obstacle impeding the bond of ecclesiastical communion or a censure inflicted by the Church."

The trend in law after Vatican II has been to discard penalties that are incurred automatically, and to curtail all criminal sanctions. The Pontifical Commission for the Revision of the Code of Canon Law, which, to my knowledge, has never been accused of excessive liberality, confirms that tendency. Prefacing its draft legislation on penalties is this statement: "Of greatest import are the norms of the draft which have the purpose of reducing the use of penalties in the Church and rather of employing other pastoral, and even juridical, means before resorting to penalties" (*Schema de Poenis et Delictis,* p. 6). The influence of the Vatican Council's Declaration on Religious Freedom is undeniable. "It is completely in accord with the nature of faith," that document proclaims, "that in matters religious every manner of coercion on the part of man should be excluded."

Pending the revision of law, however, there are provisions in force which do impose sanctions upon those involved in irregular conjugal situations. First let's look at the legislation in the Code of Canon Law.

The Code.

Two canons are of major interest. Canon 2356 establishes an automatic penalty for bigamy. "Bigamists, that is those who in spite of the conjugal bond, attempt another marriage, even a so-called civil marriage, are *ipso facto* infamous; and if, in spite of warning by the Ordinary, they continue in the illicit relationship so begun they are to be punished by excommunication or personal interdict according to the gravity of the case." Be it noted here that only the judgment of infamy is automatic; the other penalties require some kind of procedure. The next canon, #2357, assigns a comparable sanction for the crimes of adultery and public concubinage. "They shall be excluded from legitimate ecclesiastical acts until they have given signs of true repentance." While partners to a canonically irregular union have in certain quarters been characterized as living in adultery or in concubinage the definitions of such offenses in penal law are quite circumscribed. Another canon gives the legal definition of a crime: "In ecclesiastical law a crime is to be understood as an external and morally imputable violation of the law to which a canonical penalty has been attached." Moreover, in order for the crime to qualify as public, the violation of a criminal statute as well as the fact of an irregular union must be of common knowledge, or committed under such circumstances that it can be safely concluded that it will easily gain notoriety (canon 2197, n. 1). Thus, in the matter of adultery, even if the fact of an earlier marriage of either party is known, there is no public crime as long as grave moral culpability remains occult (canon 2197, n.4.). The matter of determining what constitutes public concubinage is even more problematic. Despite wide usage among canonists and casuists concubinage does not lend itself to easy definition. The usual connotation is that of a casual, rather unstable affair in which the couple recognize no serious reciprocal obligations. Such an arrangement offends Christian sensibilities and is condemned by the Church because it violates all the basic values of the conjugal relationship.

Now even if all the conditions for the commission of one of these crimes are shown to exist it still does not follow that the delinquent is thereby excluded from participation in the Church's sacramental life. The penalty of exclusion from legitimate acts, imposed for adultery and concubinage, does not prohibit access to the Eucharist (canon 2256, n. 2). Neither does infamy of law. These are punishments which forbid the exercise of certain rather esoteric rights, already largely reserved to clerics (canon 2294, n. 1). In specifying the type of infamy which does exclude from reception of the Eucharist the Code requires that there be notoriety. "They are to be excluded from the Eucharist," states canon 855, #1, "who are publicly unworthy, as those who are excommunicated, interdicted, and those who are manifestly infamous, unless their repentance and amendment is publicly known and they have already repaired the scandal that has been caused.'' Punishment is confined to those who show open and willful disregard for the institution of Christian marriage and this is emphasized in the proposed reformulation of the pertinent canon. It reads: ''Those who have committed a serious delict and who persevere in evident contumacy are not to be admitted to celebrate the Eucharist or to receive Communion'' (*Schema de poenis et delictis*, canon n. 75).

From this examination of the general law of the Church it is readily apparent that no member is to be denied the Eucharist unless there is grave moral culpability in the transgression of a law to which that penalty is expressly attached. Since the criteria for the commission of a delict are quite strict and demanding, criminal guilt cannot be lightly or casually assessed.

The law itself calls for extreme caution in the curtailment of any ecclesial right (canon 2214, #2). It also guarantees that in the absence of certitude regarding the commission of a crime, the penalty attached to it may not be enforced without due process of law (canon 1933, #4). At the very least, equity demands that the accused be afforded the opportunity to oppose allegations brought against him, and that practical avenues of recourse from an adverse judgment be provided. To put the shoe on the other foot, if such safeguards are not made available the one whose rights have been unduly abridged may claim damages for defamation of character! (canon 1938, #1; 2355).

Moralists quite generally are coming to recognize what most of you can attest to from personal experience. Here is the testimony of one, Franz Bockle: ''The reasons for the failure of a marriage are manifold and complex; very often one cannot even talk about a marriage which has been broken through the guilt of one of the parties, or where one must regard the contracting of a new marriage as a grave moral wrong. We are generally faced with the facts that cannot be changed either by repentance, or the desire to make good the wrong that has been done; the moral obligation toward the new partner and the children will make it essential that the second marriage should remain in being.'' How then can one presume to impose sanctions that interfere with the fundamental right to Eucharistic sharing without a balanced inquiry into actual notoriety, into the circumstances which may have diminished imputability, and into the myriad other considerations which may undermine a judgment of manifest contempt for Church order or lack of repentance?

The Plenary Council of Baltimore.

At the request of the National Conference of Catholic Bishops the Holy See recently removed the automatic excommunication which the III Plenary Council of Baltimore had imposed upon those who "after obtaining a divorce dare to attempt civil marriage" (n. 124). In taking this action the Holy Father repealed a piece of legislation that affected only the American Church. Already in 1966 the general law imposing automatic excommunication for those who entered marriage before a non-Catholic minister had been abrogated (canon 2319). The common opinion among canonists (cf. "Committee Report on Legislation of the Councils of Baltimore," *CLSA Proceedings, XXXI*, pp. 140-141), even before the announcement, was that it no longer obliged, so radically had the situation changed since the enactment of the penalty in 1884. At worst, the excommunication was incurred only in those exceptional circumstances when, without any diminution of culpability, the party audaciously flaunted Church discipline. The psychological value of this development goes far beyond its legal import (cf. "What did the Bishops Decide about Divorce and Remarriage?", *Origins*, Vol. 7, (1977), p. 56). The elimination of that single statute is a heartening expression of our growing sensitivity toward those caught up in a highly complex problem. At the same time it affords an opportunity for the reexamination of the other aspects of Church discipline bearing on this issue.

Custom with the Force of Law.

Although the law itself does not warrant a blanket condemnation of the divorced and remarried, it cannot be denied that conventional pastoral practice sometimes leaves that impression. But even a widespread misunderstanding does not justify the practice on the grounds that it has gained legitimacy through long standing custom.

While custom is, indeed, the best interpreter of the law, it acquires legal force only if it is reasonable, and lawfully prescribed by continuous and uninterrupted usage. Since indiscriminate exclusion from the Eucharist violates those fundamental principles of canon law (canon 19) we've already considered, as well as the explicit requirement that penalties derive only from a strict reading of express statutory provisions, the practice is unreasonable and can never acquire the force of law no matter how long and frequent the abuse; even though numerous individuals over generations may erroneously have assumed that their own actions did in fact constitute grounds for automatic excommunication. As outrageous as this misinterpretation of canonical discipline is, we may at least be consoled by the fact that its discontinuance does not require any repeal or amendment of the law!

Worthiness.

The mere absence of excommunication or of other canonical penalties does not, of course, insure worthy reception of the Eucharist. Those involved in irregular marriages, no less than others, are subject to the same imperatives which bind all believers. Paul's admonition (I Cor. 11:27-28) to take care that we do not "eat the bread or drink the cup of the Lord unworthily" requires a kind of discernment that is the proper responsibility of each individual, and that no authority can rightfully preempt. Even in those instances when a canonical penalty has certainly been incurred pastors of souls may not demand its observance unless the fact is notorious in that particular congregation or unless a declaratory judgment has been rendered (canon 2232, #1).

It should also be emphasized that the Eucharist is not a reward for perfect adherence to moral and juridical standards. Were that the case none of us would qualify. Rather it is the central celebration of a pilgrim people who, in the words of Father Richard McCormack, "will always be characterized by the unachieved and imperfect.'' To bar any member of the Church from the Eucharist as a penance or as a punishment is intolerable, for it falsifies completely the meaning of the sacraments.

While the situation of the Catholic who is remarried may be juridically ambiguous it does not follow that he is either unworthy or improperly disposed. If the Ecumenical Directory issued by the Secretariat for the Promotion of Christian Unity (May 14, 1967, #55) permits the ministration of the sacraments to the non-Catholic, who does not subscribe fully to the teaching or discipline of the Roman Church regarding marriage or divorce, and who may in fact actually be divorced and remarried "so long as he declares a faith in these sacraments in harmony with that of the Church and is rightly disposed,'' how can the needs of Roman Catholics be considered less urgent or less deserving?

Conclusion.

The major conclusion I draw from these considerations is that the admission or divorced and remarried Catholics to the Eucharist does not involve a shift in Church doctrine. It is not a matter of denying the indissolubility of a ratified and consummated marriage. Neither does it excuse bigamy, adultery, or concubinage, or claim for these offenses immunity from punishment. No compromise of sound moral and canonical principles is insinuated. The issue, put quite simply, is whether within the framework of current canonical discipline, the spiritual needs of the individual and the common good of all God's people might not be more effectively accommodated. The answer can be no other than an emphatic, "Yes." If the Church is to present herself as a community of reconciliation it can no longer tolerate practices that obscure the very purpose of the sacraments. Pope Paul's address, inaugurating the recent Holy Year, seems to contain the appropriate charge to action. "Let all in unison commit themselves to creating a climate in which reconciliation can become effective." That seems to be another way of stating Our Lord's admonition: "Let the man among you who is without sin be the first to cast a stone . . . " (Jn. 8:7).

Part III
Pastoral Ministry to the Divorced

Indissolubility of Marriage and Pastoral Care of the Divorced Who Remarry

Karl Lehmann

Translated by W. J. O'Hara

Every priest in his parish work and many Catholics are familiar with the thorny problem that pastoral care for divorced persons who have remarried very soon ends up in a practically hopeless blind alley. Even when such persons show the greatest readiness that can be expected in view of the circumstances to live a Christian life, such contact as is officially possible for the priest is extremely limited. It is true that the divorced who remarry are not ipso facto excommunicate (cf. CIC, can. 2356), as is often assumed, but to all intents and purposes they are excluded from the Church community;[1] this is most obvious in the refusal to admit them to the sacraments of penance and the Eucharist. In Canon Law they count as bigamists and automatically incur loss of normal rights (*infamia iuris*).

The question of sacramental practice is, of course, certainly not the only problem presented by second marriages of this kind. Even if the divorce is felt to be a liberation, it involves harsh consequences. Loneliness, the experience of estrangement, the sense of failure, the struggle for their rights, the children's future, questions of housing and financial and economic burdens are only a few items. Precisely in this situation exclusion from the sacraments means alienation from the Christian community, which often treats hardheartedly those who have married after divorce, showing no understanding at all and making them feel cut off and socially isolated. The Church community surely ought to create an atmosphere in which people who have been hurt like this may find serenity and support?

Pastoral workers have always tried to find ways and means to give help in this distress, sometimes desperate expedients such as renunciation of conjugal relations in the second marriage, and consequent possibility at least of deathbed reconciliation, administration of the Eucharist without the knowledge of the congregation, etc. There is an ever-increasing tendency to admit persons divorced and remarried to the sacraments on certain conditions.[2] Previously the individual pastor in an individual case of conscience took such a favorable decision, or else the episcopal chancelleries adopted exceptional solutions in individual cases (e.g., on the occasion of the children's first communion). What is in fact being done at the present time is leading in the long run to a scarcely tolerable situation when pastoral solutions are being applied which are contrary to Canon Law; this practice is detrimental to the parties concerned, to priests and to Church order, and is causing many bishops serious concern. There therefore seems to be an urgent need, not only to deal seriously with the disciplinary question, the "wild growth," but above all to come honestly and openly to grips with the problem itself. In view of this situation, we may also expect the various synods to take up this urgent but unsolved problem.[3] Some even want to make it a test-case for the Synod. Various reasons therefore make it indispensable for the Church authorities to reflect on the situation and the problem at issue. Any short-circuit reaction would be fatal.

In what follows only a few remarks can be offered on the problem. This is not without its dangers, because many standpoints adopted on this controverted matter ultimately prove untenable because they treat the problem in too isolated a way, without wider comprehensive anthropological and theological context. The practical problem in many cases is dealt with in a narrow perspective of casuistic moral theology or Canon Law, or commonplace pastoral exhortations. Some people dismiss the whole problem by mere reference to the dogma of the indissolubility of marriage. If we can succeed in placing this problem in its correct perspective and propounding the real questions that have to be answered, the purpose of this contribution will be more than achieved.[4]

The main arguments for the Church's present attitude

In the first place we must examine the reasons given for the teaching and practice of the Church as at present still in force.[5] In the Church's judgment, remarried divorced persons are living in a sexual association which is not a valid marriage, which is contrary to the will of God and therefore sinful. As long as they do not alter this state, and are not willing to give up their sinful will, they are lacking in the necessary dispositions for sacramental forgiveness of sins and consequently for admission to the Eucharist. If for grave reasons they cannot give up the new partnership they have entered into, and at the same time are prepared to renounce sexual relations and to live like brother and sister and to avoid proximate occasions of sin, they can be publicly admitted to the sacraments. This indeed is only possible in places where their true situation is not publicly known and no scandal is to be feared. Consequently, admission to the sacraments usually takes place solely in a parish where they are not known.

The essential basis of this attitude can be made even plainer theologically. Remarried divorced persons, according to the Catholic principle of the indissolubility of marriage, are living in an invalid marriage; since their marital relations are in contradiction to the clear percept of Christ, they are remaining in a sinful condition (as in the case of all extra-marital sexual relationships). On the ground of their objectively invalid marriage, we can and must conclude—so it is mostly assumed as a matter of course—that personally and subjectively their own will is a sinful one.[6] As regards admission to the Eucharist anyone who publicly and permanently intends to persist in this state publicly contradicts the Lord's commandment by his adulterous life, while by taking part in the Lord's Supper he would simultaneously make a profession of faith in Jesus Christ. This intolerable discrepancy publicly displayed contradicts the meaning of faith, of the ecclesiastical community, and of the function of the sacraments as symbols effecting what they signify. It is therefore better that such people should admit with dignity and respect that they are transgressing Jesus Christ's commandment, and take responsibility for the consequences.[7] Otherwise there is danger of deceitful maneuvers which may mean total living contradiction.

Objections raised against the basis of present practice

The strength of this argument is its plain meaning and coherence. Those who contest the continuing validity of previous doctrine and practice have a difficult task, by the very nature of the case. They are often really discussing other different problems—e.g., whether the general grounds of nullity should not be extended, whether instead of the sexual, "physical" consummation of the marriage, the dynamic personal and "existential" maturing and complete realization of the will to marry should not be taken more seriously into account, whether even a valid sacramental and consummated marriage might not be dissolved by the Church, whether a second conjugal association of divorced persons might not also be sacramentally contracted, etc.[8] Since, however, a solution of these questions will demand an incalculable length of time the opponents of what until now has been standard doctrine and practice limit themselves in the first place to a critical scrutiny of the traditional arguments deployed against admission to the sacraments. It is less a question of the formal validity of the arguments than of a critical discussion of the presuppositions on which they depend and which are often simply taken for granted.

In the first place, reference is made to God's limitless readiness to forgive: this, it is said, will not halt even at the serious guilt incurred by divorce and remarriage, especially if the failure involved is acknowledged and any share of guilt is made good as far as possible. When a Christian resolutely and contritely admits his guilt, it is said, he may also hope firmly and confidently in God's forgiveness and mercy. Total "reparation" is often impossible to achieve—e.g., in a marriage that has irreparably broken down on both sides.[9] This applies above all when one or other partner has entered into a new union which cannot be terminated for external and internal reasons, or would not be morally justified—e.g., on account of the children of this union. Admission of guilt, repentance, and penitential disposition do not therefore in every case and absolutely entail abandoning the new union and a return to the first partner. Besides, in many cases those concerned are not conscious of guilt. A lack of any sense of guilt in this connection can be due to various causes and must be judged very cautiously, [10] so that in concrete individual circumstances it is not admissible to speak automatically of a state of grievous sin.

Two particular considerations are of special weight in this argument: (1) There can be cases in which it may be morally permissible for remarried divorced persons to continue in their invalid marriage and even their sexual relations if, for instance, a concrete estimate of the balance of values involved shows that the situation and range of their present obligations are not *in themselves* bad, although the law of unicity and indissolubility of marriage is transgressed. [11]

(2) The second argument concerns the judgement passed on sexual relations within the new conjugal association. The reason for the sinfulness of cohabitation is almost exclusively considered to be the illicit character of the sexual relations. They are equated with pre-marital sexual relations (a point which we cannot further discuss here). Now doubt is raised whether the evaluation of human sexuality implied by such a judgement can still be objectively and convincingly defended today: the sexual relations in the second marriage, which of course are often the expression of a newly matured, irreversible, and serious interpersonal reality, cannot without further ado and from the start be condemned as bad *in themselves*. And the individual elements and decisive factors needed for a full estimate of the position of remarried divorced persons, can hardly be adequately judged solely in terms of pre-established moral categories. Consequently the self-critically aware and conscientious conviction of the partners themselves must be consulted and respected to a very much greater extent. Such regard for conscientious conviction means neither Church recognition of divorce as such nor any kind of equating of civil marriage with sacramental marriage.

The search for an escape from the dilemma:
is there a third alternative?

Such in brief outline are the arguments of supporters or opponents of previous teaching and practice as it has been until
now. There is no doubt that the grounds on both sides could each
be considerably deepened theologically. It also seems to me
indisputable—quite apart from whatever position one adopts
oneself—that the justification of present practice in the form in
which it has usually been presented hitherto, is inadequate, and in
that form cannot claim incontestable certainty and therefore absolute validity in every case. Mere reaffirmation of the previous
attitude and doctrine without explicit discussion of the objections
raised to it, can claim neither truth nor pastoral consistency. In
any case the two positions mostly stand irreconcilably opposed.
Is there any escape?

The most striking thing is that in average arguments on the
matter, the reasoning really only appeals to "secondary"
grounds.[12] Fundamental dogmatic considerations, for example,
are hardly employed. It is more or less clearly presupposed that
on the basis of the indissolubility of Christian marriage, viewed
globally as a truth to be maintained by the magisterium, no
modification of existing teaching and practice is to be expected
anyhow.[13] That is why scarcely any statements of views on the
question have been made by dogmatic theologians.[14] However, it
must now be examined whether, from the central Christian view
of marriage, there are nevertheless ways of solving this distressing pastoral problem.

Unequivocally definite and bi-polar statements
in the New Testament

The question of divorce is dealt with in five passages in the
New Testament (Matt. 5:32/Luke 16:18; Mark 10:2-12/Matt.
19:3-9; ICor. 7:10-16),[15] and in them we note a striking and peculiar difference in the attitude adopted. According to Matthew
10:2ff., and Luke 16:18, the prohibition of divorce is absolute.
The Matthean "fornication clauses" (Matt. 5:32; 19:9) and the

Pauline "privilege" (I Cor. 7:10f.; 7:15) testify to the limited possibility of a separation of the partners. This applies quite apart from the question, still not completely solved, whether the Matthean fornication clauses[16] allow actual divorce in the case of one partner's grave sexual fault (this is probably the fundamental sense of the word used, *porneia*, "fornication" or "adultery"). In Paul, the apparently almost contradictory facts of the case become even clearer: Jesus' statement on divorce, unrestrictedly formulated as an absolute requirement, stands next to the "restriction" introduced by Paul's authoritative interpretation — there can be a situation in which the Christian must not oppose divorce, namely if the pagan partner in a mixed marriage demands and effects the divorce. On this basis the conclusions to be drawn for our purpose are:

(1) I Corinthians 7:10-16 in particular shows that Paul's directive is linked with Jesus' prohibition of divorce which was understood to be absolute. Jesus' pronouncement is not felt to be weakened or relaxed in any way by Paul's attitude.

(2) In all these cases Jesus' original directive is given concrete form and embodiment. The "concessions" indirectly prove that Jesus' pronouncement was understood to be a binding precept capable of realization in this world.[17]

(3) The apostle Paul and the "Matthean" church regarded themselves as authorized in certain circumstances, notwithstanding the absolute obligation of Jesus' command, to concede the possibility of divorce.

(4) Separation is in no case imposed (as it was later in the post-New Testament period, e.g., in Hermas). Nor is remarriage anywhere recommended. Consequently it is historically and, as regards the New Testament, doctrinally meaningless to speak of a "right" to divorce and remarriage in Scripture.

Tensions and struggle in the history of the Church

It is difficult for us today to discover anything but a contradiction in the interconnection and juxtaposition of Jesus' absolute precept, which is maintained in principle, with "concessions" in individual cases.[18] Either the toleration of remarriage is regarded as abandoning the principle of indissolubility, or one is left with an unrelated and featureless juxtaposition of two statements which have little reciprocal significance.[19] We must once again clearly realize the fact that in certain situations the real possibility of divorce and remarriage is conceded, without this being regarded as weakening or relaxing Jesus' absolute command.

This duality of view is also attested in the post-New Testament period. Nowhere is this extreme tension clearer than in a passage of Origen's Commentary on Matthew:

> Already some of the leaders of the Church contrary to what is written have allowed a wife to marry in her husband's lifetime. In this they are, it is true, acting contrary to the words of Scripture where it is said, "A wife is bound to her husband as long as he lives" (I Cor. 7:39), and "Accordingly, she will be called an adulteress if she lives with another man while her husband is alive" (Rom. 7:3). And yet their action was not entirely without foundation, for it may be supposed that they permitted it to avoid worse, though certainly in contradiction to the law established in the beginning and to the words of Scripture.[20]

Testimonies of this kind could easily be multiplied.[21] The constantly repeated dramas involved in the realities of human marriage demanded an answer: a man's adultery with his wife's sister, the infidelity of a wife who had become a prostitute, the future lot of one partner suddenly, secretly (and permanently?) abandoned by the other, enforced separation from wives and families by war, imprisonment, the caprice of those in power, deportation, etc. In a long tradition, the Church found ways of escape for such distressing cases in the sense of a less rigorous practice. Some decisions were even enacted by qualified papal decrees (e.g., of Leo the Great, Gregory II, etc.).[22] At the same time they were always aware of the contradiction to Scripture, and saw in this action the possibility of avoiding even greater evil (in other words, they applied the principle of the lesser evil). Before a second marriage was tolerated therefore, a canonical penance was imposed.[23]

Theological elucidation of the data of tradition

The usual view taken in the history of dogma of the sacrament of matrimony and its indissolubility has not devoted sufficient attention to this other, second line of ecclesiastical action, which always has to be seen in conjunction with the absolute precept of unconditional fidelity in marriage. Such cases have been considered more as archaic traces of retrograde tendencies which from the dogmatic point of view had not yet been regularized, and as the expression of questionable pastoral indulgence. No real theological relevance was attributed to these testimonies as long as a particular mode of thought prevailed. That is in fact correct to the extent that the significance of that practice in detail should not be theologically overestimated without further examination, for behind it there also lay, for example, theologically unexamined ideas, questionable pastoral practices, accidental factors, etc. From the beginning of the 13th century onwards, the principle of the indissolubility of marriage quite definitively prevailed in the decisions of the popes and in canon law (even in regard to non-consummated Christian marriages, except in the case of religious profession). A systematic marriage-law, which aimed at grasping a priori and arranging logically the conditions for contracting matrimony and possible grounds of nullity drawn from experience,[24] had as its purpose the avoidance of subsequent breakdown of recklessly contracted marriages, or, as the case might be, to establish their invalidity more readily. It is hardly possible to overestimate the human and religious importance of this victory of the principle of unconditional fidelity in marriage as something that has to be carried out in real life. Nevertheless the struggle of tradition with actual difficulties and distress in individual cases, notwithstanding its unbroken certainty and abiding conviction of the indissolubility of marriage, constitutes a striking testimony which cannot be equated with, or explained away solely by, theological backwardness, laxity, or an as yet insufficiently enlightened moral consciousness. The courageous endurance of the tension between Jesus' fundamental precept which is never doubted for a moment *and* pastoral concern for the failures in certain particular emergencies—leaving aside the admittedly problematic aspects in individual cases—presents a valuable example and significance as a guide to the Church at the present day.

Later restriction to the juridicial method, to an exclusively legal and procedural mode of envisaging the question and the predominance of formal viewpoints (e.g., defects of form, etc.), despite its indispensable advantages of juridical classification, did involve, as compared with the Church's earlier practice, a certain narrowness which in this sole and exclusive form is not permanently justified either by Scripture itself or by the full breadth of the attested tradition of the Church. It is evident here how even in theology and the Church every progress in some matter—often after a long period of incubation and even after incontestably important and successful reforms—has its drawbacks. The mental distress of some of those responsible for the Church's matrimonial jurisdiction has become evident,[25] the questions have been squarely raised,[26] and, furthermore, even under the surface, changes cannot be denied to have occurred in matrimonial law and tribunals.[27] The question therefore arises whether legal methods and proceedings must remain the only way by which "justice" in a radical sense can be made to prevail.

The meaning of the Tridentine dogma

All attempts at giving current practice a new direction appear, however, to break down over the crystal-clear words of the Council of Trent:

Anyone who says that the Church errs in having taught and in teaching that according to the teaching of the Gospel and the apostles . . . the bond of matrimony cannot be dissolved because of the adultery of one of the spouses and that neither, not even the innocent party who has given to occasion for adultery, can contract any other marriage during the lifetime of the other partner; and that the husband commits adultery if he marries again after divorcing his adulterous wife and similarly the wife if she marries after divorcing her adulterous husband,—let him be excluded.[28]

The researches of P. Fransen on this text have shown that even this Council was still aware of the tension attested in Church tradition, even if this is not immediately evident in the text itself. Thus it is demonstrated that the Tridentine decision does not concern and condemn the practice of the Eastern Churches, which in the sense of Origen and St. Basil takes a milder form. (There is no valid sacramental marriage in the lifetime of the first partner in the East either; the second marriage is tolerated, it is true, but is not recognized by the Church in a way comparable to the first at all. Reception of the sacraments is accorded by way of the "economy"). The Eastern Churches certainly maintain quite unambiguously the indissolubility of marriage.[29] Only the practice of tolerating a second marriage has a different significance.[30] The Council of Trent *consciously* did not condemn this pastoral practice of the East, but rather let it stand as an integral part of the form of life (rite) of a particular Church.

The Council Fathers of Trent wanted above all to reject the calling in question of the authority of the Church officially to teach the doctrine and morals of Christian marriage, since Luther in particular had accused the theory and practice of the Roman Catholic Church of being contary to Scripture. As opposed to this, the Council declared that the teaching and practice of the Western Church are in fact "in accordance with (*iuxta*) the teaching of the Gospel." P. Fransen[31] has worked out the exact shade of meaning of this precise formulation: the Western practice, as it has more and more definitely prevailed, is *not* simply *the* teaching of the Gospel; it is therefore to a certain extent left open whether there are other modes of action in conformity with the Scriptures which can also appeal to Scripture; but its own teaching and practice is preserved and defended to the extent that it is *positively* declared to be "in *accordance* with the teaching of the Gospel." The theory and practice of the Catholic Church are therefore, regardless of other possible interpretations, inspired by revelation, are in line with the Gospel and give concrete expression to the Gospel. In any case (and the importance of this must not be minimized) the text was formulated so carefully not only with an eye to the Eastern Churches, but also out of regard for other differing Catholic doctrinal views on the interpretation of the fornication-clauses (Cajetan) and on the toleration of a second marriage (Ambrose, in reality Ambrosiaster).

*Consequences for a dogmatically soundly-based
pastoral care in cases of marriage after divorce*

The Council of Trent did not therefore condemn in certain difficult situations the indubitably existing line of milder practice attested by Western tradition in the early Church and the Middle Ages. This means that even from the official doctrinal standpoint on certain conditions (of which more later) genuine scope opens out for truly responsible pastoral care in cases where marriage break down—which is an extremely urgent matter today. This does not mean that the Western Church must adopt the practice of the Eastern Churches. On the contrary, it will very carefully have to avoid making their mistakes. But anyone who does not acknowledge the real possibility of a new orientation in actual practice is not admitting established facts in the history of dogma and is defending the really binding doctrine of the Church in a way that is in fact lacking in precision.[32] In the question of the admission of divorce and remarried persons to the sacraments a trustworthy dogmatic foundation is thus available, and on this basis the pastoral task can be cautiously elucidated. The controverted problem therefore need no longer be dealt with in a dogmatic no-man's-land, with pseudo-dogmatic claims, or only on the ultimately "secondary" plane of particular determinations of casuistic moral theology and Canon Law, but finds in this context a firm and dependable basis. The problem itself is not indeed made any easier, as will at once be shown.

A new pastoral order—in what sense?

Until now we have seen the two lines of an unbroken certainty of the validity of Jesus' absolute requirement and of a practice of toleration only in the tension of their juxtaposition. *Each* line involves a doctrine about practice and an element of actual practice that requires elucidation by dogmatic reflection.

On closer examination it is at all events clear that the two strands of tradition do not simply run parallel, equally justified, for the principle of the indissolubility of marriage claims an inherently higher normative force of a different quality from the concession of a milder practice in this or that particular case. The tension in tradition is of course an expression of the almost contradictory opposition between the fact that while the Lord's words "in themselves" represent what alone is correct and right, behavior that deviates from them in some particular situation is "not entirely without foundation." The "concessions" therefore in a certain respect have precisely the function of drawing attention to the obligatory character of Jesus' directive and of ensuring as far as possible its maintenance in principle and practice.

The concession of milder practice must not turn into an independent system, relatively or at least in fact indifferent to the principle of indissolubility. For it is outside the limits of what in faith indubitably ought to be the case, and consequently there is no place for it *purely and simply in itself*. There is, therefore, fundamentally no intrinsic "right" to divorce, remarriage, and eventual subsequent readmission to the sacraments. To be sure the Church can and must create a responsible and to a certain extent juridically practicable order for the pastoral regulation of such emergencies. But from the central doctrine of unconditional fidelity in marriage there can be no juridical *claim* in the sense mentioned.

Jesus' example: no justificatory "permission"

Any idea of that kind is excluded by Mark 10:2ff., in controversy with the Pharisees. The Pharisees were asking about a "permission," a legal provision which concedes a certain range of freedom of action ultimately to a man's own advantage. Jesus, however, does not go into the question of a "permission" at all, but by his counter-question, "What did Moses *command* you?" he emphasizes God's original will. The opponents are aiming at exceptional situations which are to be legitimized by general legal dispensations. "Jesus asks about God's will, the others about what is their due. But by this way of raising the question—by asking how within the range of the permissible one can contrive to get as much as possible for oneself—marriage is already destroyed before it has been contracted."[33] Precisely because the original will of God is manifest once more with unmistakable clarity through Jesus, the possibility is excluded of thinking oneself justified before God by appeal to a questionable "right." "Jesus thereby, as in the antithesis of the Sermon on the Mount, pierces through the juridical sphere which his opponents equate with the will of God, turning it into an ultimate authority, in order to hide the injustice of their lives behind formal legality. By opposing the will of God to law, Jesus uncovers the life of disorder behind the then current order."[34] Jesus' claim, therefore, is greater and more than a law understood as something purely external, and this of course increases the binding character of what he demands.

On the theological and practical logic of an exceptional situation

Jesus' attitude warns us not to see some supposed "right" in a pastoral regulation for broken marriages. But if in Scripture and tradition divorce is conceded in certain particular and limited situations, this makes it unmistakably clear that a certain room for maneuver is available which in itself ought not to exist and which nevertheless in view of man's sinful reality cannot be excluded as "totally unfounded."[35] Consequently what is "legally regulated" in this domain—here our very language comes dangerously near to being double-tongued and perverted—is fundamentally only possible relative to human "hardness of heart" and is shown in Scripture itself to be a "measure of necessity of the old aeon."[36] The mystery of evil lies in a regulation in which what ought not to be can become a normative factor. The Church cannot admit here *in the same way* a "right" to separation, divorce, and remarriage, as it is bound to determine its teaching and practice by our Lord's words. After all, the Church is not arbitrarily holding fast to this indubitable commandment of Jesus, and it is a profound question of theological judgement and discernment to decide to what degree it can transform the conceded possibilities of tolerating a second marriage into an (always questionable) "regulation" of its practice. In the Eastern churches, of course, as can easily be shown,[37] it was not in the strict sense pastoral grounds alone which encouraged the practice. The abuses are obvious even today. What can be envisaged in the sense of an extreme marginal possibility as a "concession," must in no case become so much the rule that it soon becomes the preponderant everyday practice and hides the original sense and requirement of Jesus' pronouncement. Otherwise, even the principle of the indissolubility of marriage though maintained in theory will become unconvincing and in fact radically violated.[38]

Against this background we can form some idea why the Western Church at Trent, for its own sake and for the truth of Christian faith, insisted with utter firmness that it was acting in fidelity to the teaching of the Gospel in its admittedly stern and hard practice. Consequently J. Ratzinger[39] is quite right in not wanting to speak at all of a "two-sided state of affairs"—i.e., indissolubility of marriage and practice of divorce—but only of *one* reality, clear in itself but at the same time exhibiting as it were marginal breaks and blurred edges. "The Church cannot do both. *Per se* there is only one thing it can do: live and teach 'in accordance with the teaching of the Gospel and the apostle.' But it cannot completely exclude marginal cases where in order to avoid worse things, it has to remain below what it *really* ought to be."[40]

Greater insistence on unconditional fidelity
and the form of an exceptional regulation

Pastoral methods in the Church intended to help divorced and remarried, cannot—if they are to maintain their indispensable theological context—by the nature of the case constitute a self-contained system or a separate set of guide-lines. Otherwise all too easily a new "legality" would arise such as Paul so drastically described. Consequently the doctrine of the indissolubility of marriage cannot simply be presupposed by a few stereotype traditional formulas and then detailed new regulations for the pastoral care of broken marriages put forward. Anyone who does not at the same time with even greater insistence and vehemence awaken a deep realization of unconditional fidelity in marriage, theologically forfeits the right seriously and responsibly to devise pastoral assistance in these second marriages after divorce. Consequently our question is not sufficiently elucidated by considerations of moral theology aimed at a finely-shaded judgment of individual difficult cases—that would involve the danger of a new and no better casuistry.

In view of all this, the question arises whether the Church can lay down a *general norm* at all here? Rather than a systematic regulation, which would always remain a problematic one, and which would always be impaled on the dilemma of making generally possible something that after all is "in itself" impossible, it will be a matter of the education, spiritual capacity, discretion, and prudence of those Christians and especially of pastors, who in frank discussion with remarried divorced persons are able to estimate the particular situation and so give responsible assistance. This point of view seems to me to have been largely overlooked in the discussion.

Concrete conditions of a new orientation in pastoral care

Changes in the Church's marriage laws are obviously mainly effective when a transitional missionary situation calls for answers to new questions. This can be observed in New Testament times with Paul in particular (I Cor. 7:10ff.),[41] during the transition from Christianity in the ancient to the Germanic world,[42] and in the 16th century when new questions arose in the missionary countries.[43] These are limiting cases on the collective scale, and the question is whether and how far such decisions react on the traditional legal structure.

1. Our present situation is different from but not unrelated to this experience of the Church. Many particular considerations in pastoral theology inescapably pose the question to what extent the Church today must consider acting differently towards those who have remarried after divorce. At all events in situations of obvious distress and difficulty the Church can in principle admit clearly delimited exceptions to avoid worse evils. In adopting any such position, of course, it has to be borne in mind that it involves the inevitable danger that the concession of such exceptions will be abused in the sense of extending the original will of God and therefore favoring a lax view of marriage and divorce. Anyone

who can cast even a brief but sobering glance from a distance into the offices of our divorce lawyers and divorce court practice, will realize at once that in face of so much "hardness of heart," much unthinking talk of the duty of mercy merely sounds naive. In present-day discussions about the renewal of pastoral care of divorced and remarried persons, the great yet delicately sensitive sayings about forgiveness, indulgence, and peace are quite often used in a vapid and jejune way. Certainly many a well-meant statement based on real experience of difficulty and distress can be explained as understandable protest against many a case of narrowness, obscurity,[44] and harshness in present marriage law and tribunals. Nevertheless the talk of mercy and forgiveness sometimes has a ring about it that recalls to mind Martin Luther's phrase about "grace that costs nothing," as though real indulgence and a serious new start were possible without conversion and decisive change of heart. Those who postulate mercy without judgement and love without justice (and vice versa), or think to escape from this humanly insoluble tension by a one-sided slogan, must ask themselves just how valid their idea of God really is.

2. While the Fathers of the Church and the Middle Ages imposed grave canonical penances in connection with the toleration of a second marriage, we today on different presuppositions are bound to formulate with very great caution the conditions for such an admission of remarried divorced persons to full Church life. To elucidate the situation three sets of questions have to be examined: responsibility for the first marriage, nature of the second marriage, and request for participation in the sacramental life of the congregation. As far as I can see, most authors are agreed on the following criteria for such action (here they are expanded by a few points of view of my own):

(a) Toleration of a second marriage, and admission to the sacraments linked to it, must in no way call in question the obligatory basic form of indissoluble marriage. Appropriate pastoral care must awaken and strengthen in the parties concerned and in the Christian community an awareness that the situation is exceptional and that help is being given in clearly circumscribed emergencies.

(b) When the breakdown of the first marriage involved grave

fault, the responsibility incurred and the sin committed must be acknowledged and repented. Possible wrong and damage inflicted must be made good as far as possible, which in certain circumstances will not exclude a return to the first partner.

(c) If return to the first partner is impossible, it must be convincingly shown that with the best will in the world the first marriage cannot be remade. Here particular attention must be paid to whether the first marriage has irreparably broken down for *both* partners.[45]

(d) A subsequently contracted second marriage must have stood the test for some considerable space of time as a determined will[46] to live together permanently in matrimony, and proved itself as a moral reality.[47] It must also be examined whether the maintenance of this union has become a new moral obligation in relation to the partner and children of the second marriage. Both partners would have to demonstrate that they are trying to live by the Christian faith and are asking to share in the sacramental life of the Church for religious reasons and after serious examination of conscience.

(e) Both partners and the responsible pastor must see to it that no justified scandal is caused in the congregation and that the impression is not created that the Church no longer takes the indissolubility of matrimony seriously.

On such presuppositions and conditions, in my opinion, divorced persons who have remarried could be allowed access to the sacrament of penance, and receive communion with the congregation. The decisive presupposition remains: Only on the basis of Jesus' original precept can something that ought not to be, be "regulated." "If the extreme case becomes the normal case, the essence of Christian and Church will have gone."[48]

3. With the doctrinal creation of a certain room for maneuver, the pastoral situation is of course far from being mastered. The present article aimed at discussing only the fundamental theological principles. It is obvious that there are objections to establishing a catalogue of conditions and criteria drawn from moral theology. All one can say is that it must not be affirmed out of hand that a new orientation of pastoral practice is completely impossible and not to be expected. The anxieties of a bishop and a

priest about their responsibility in this respect are very under-standable.[49] But are our congregations so incapable of under-standing exceptional situations of the kind we have been describ-ing, and of accepting them as such? Is there not a no less horrible hardness of heart behind many a refusal to try to see things in a new way for once? Much time and work will be needed for Chris-tians to become capable of understanding the distress of their brothers and sisters, of respecting the conscientious decision, and to enter into truly fraternal relations with them. The whole con-gregation must forestall marital difficulties even before divorce and remarriage, by thorough preparation for marriage and in mar-riage.[50] Sins of omission in this domain make the indissolubility of marriage even more vulnerable in the world of the present day. What is done on the congregational plane in this respect?

Genuine pastoral care for broken marriages concerns the whole congregation, and demands a change of heart on the part of all. We must not be under any illusions about where Jesus sees "adultery" already accomplished: "Everyone who looks at a woman lustfully has already committed adultery with her in his heart" (Matt. 5:28). As long as we do not take such a saying in deadly earnest, the finger of scorn pointed at remarried divorced people easily becomes a pharisaic lie. A special, separate pastoral care for broken marriages may readily turn out to be the contrary of its good intentions.

What is needed in a new orientation in pastoral care for bro-ken marriages is, when clearly examined, not so very different from what Christians generally are endeavoring to achieve and what the responsible pastors of the Church are concerned with. Only in a larger context is there any guarantee that a newly oriented pastoral care would not favor divorce and the readiness to divorce, but would promote the renunciation of divorce, which is what Jesus commanded. Only then is that unity of mercy and justice promised us what we ourselves cannot create and which we nevertheless are constantly seeking. Only in the forbearance and the tranquility of the jealous, just, and loving God can that attitude be obtained as a gift, which is the basis of all true pastoral care: "Not to go too far in severity, not to shock by weak in-dulgence.[51]

Notes

1. Cf. on this J. G. Gerhartz, "Exkommuniziert—ein Leben lang?" in *Signum* 41 (1969), pp. 44-50; H. Heimerl, "Ungeordnete Ehen vor dem Kirchenrecht," in *Der Seelsorger* 35 (1965), pp. 116-123.

2. In addition to the bibliographical survey referred to in note 5 below, cf. the French collective work, *Divorce et indissolubilité du mariage*. Congres de l'Association de théologiens pour l'étude de la morale (Chevilly-la-Rue, 18-20 September 1970), (Paris: 1971), pp. 127-152 (F. du Plessis, A. Petitcolas, P. de Locht).

3. The General Synod of the Dioceses of the German Federal Republic prepared in the face of numerically small but "strong opposition" (F. Böckle, Chairman of the relevant subject Commission IV) "Guidelines for pastoral assistance for divorced persons who have remarried and wish to share in the sacramental life of the Church." The draft-text (5 pages) was duly completed by the Commission itself. On grounds of form and content the Synod Central Commission proposed to the Plenary Session to insert this theme in the wider context of fundamental statements about Christian married life; this need not mean minimizing the gravity of this distressing pastoral problem, as if it were just one more marginal problem among many. In giving its approval to the subjects for discussion (which need not necessarily be identical with the draft-texts submitted), the Bishops' Conference qualified its agreement by the stipulation "that the question of the guidelines for pastoral assistance to divorced people be dealt with in the whole context of *one* draft-text, "Christian Married Life." The explanation was that "the Bishops' Conference is fully aware that from the pastoral point of view it is an important and urgent task to open out to divorced persons who have remarried, ways of living their religion within the Church. It is nevertheless of the opinion that in our time it is an even more comprehensive and pastorally no less urgent task of the Synod to help the faithful to a better understanding of Christian marriage, fidelity, and the sacramental nature of marriage. The bishops are accordingly of the opinion that without attentive awareness of the indissolubility and sacramentality of marriage, no practicable ways can be indicated by which remarried divorced persons can be helped to lead a religious life." The Plenary Session for its part approved the proposal of the Central Commission on 14 May 1972. On the subject, cf. also in interview with Prof. Böckle in *Herder-Korrespondenz* 26 (1972), pp. 69-73. In the meantime the Commission "Marriage and Family in a Changing Society" of the 1972 Swiss Synod has presented for discussion under the title "Marriage in Development and Crisis" (Sec. 24/25) a first draft dealing with the topics that concern us here (cf. *Schweizerische Kirchenzeitung* No. 15/1972). Its statements are largely the same as the suggestion of R. Gall, *Fragwürdige Unauflöslichkeit der Ehe?* (Zürich, 1970), pp. 198ff., 200ff.

4. Many fundamental problems of a theology of marriage must be

omitted in the present article, e.g., that of the "marriage bond," etc. Cf. on this a few indications in K. Lehmann, "Zur Sakramentalität der Ehe," in F. Henrich/V. Eid (Ed.), *Ehe und Ehescheidung* (Munich, 1972), pp. 57-72, esp. p. 61f. For general bearings, cf. the copious bibliography in H. Stirnimann (Ed.), *Christliche Ehen und getrennte Kirchen.* Ökumenische Beihefte 1 (Freiburg, 1968), pp. 95-124, and E. Christen, "Ehe als Sakrament—neue Gesichtspunkte aus Exegese und Dogmatik," in J. Pfamatter/F. Furger (Ed.), *Theologische Berichte* I (Zürich, 1971), pp. 11-68.

5. The following outline can be brief because I can refer the reader to a detailed and up-to-date bibliographical survey by W. Löser, S.J., "Die Kirche zwischen Gesetz und Widerspruch. Für und wider eine Zlassung widerverheirateter Geschiedener zu den Sakramenten," *Herder-Korrespondenz* 26 (1972), pp. 243-248. I should like particularly to draw attention to the materials assembled there.

6. This seems to be one of the really problematic presuppositions of the traditional argument. Cf. in particular H. B. Meyer, "Können wiederverherheiratete Geschiedene zu den Sakramenten zugelassen werden?" in J. David/F. Schmalz (Ed.), *Wie unauflöslich ist die Ehe?* (Aschaffenburg, 1969), pp. 268-306, esp. p. 284ff.; in addition to the bibliography there, cf. A. Roper, *Objektive und subjektive moral—Ein Gespräch mit Karl Rahner* (Freiburg, 1971).

7. These and other considerations have been vigorously urged by I. F. Görres, *Was Ehe auf immer bindet.* Ehe in Geschichte und Gegenwart 1 (Berlin, 1971); cf. esp. pp. 74-89. Nevertheless the more disturbing calls for reform contained in this book should not be overlooked either, e.g., pp. 69-74.

8. Cf. on these questions the circumspect and learned observations of the Zürich judge in matrimonial cases R. Gall, *op. cit.* (n. 3 above).

9. It is astonishing how frivolously the concept of "irreparable breakdown" is taken over from the civil divorce law into theological discussions; cf. my essay referred to in n. 4 above, esp. pp. 67f., 70f.

10. Cf. W. Löser, *op. cit.,* pp. 246ff.

11. Cf. more precisely on this point, H. Heimerle, "Sakramentenempfang für Wiederverheiratete" in *Theologische Quartalschrift* 151 (1971), pp. 61-65.

12. "Secondary" because the fundamental theological questions are scarcely dealt with or only superficially. Of course these "secondary arguments" have their own place and importance.

13. To the extent that these problems are gone into in some publications, it is often in what—from the point of view of dogmatic theology—is a dilettante way, so that contradiction is quite in order.

14. One exception is now represented by J. Ratzinger, "Zur Frage nach der Unauflöslichkeit der Ehe" in F. Henrich/V. Eid (Ed.), *op. cit.,* pp. 35-56, esp. pp. 54ff.

15. The recent literature on the matter is immense. We therefore

only mention the latest contributions (further bibliographies will be found in them): R. Schnackenburg. "Die Ehe nach der Weisung Jesu und dem Verständnis der Urkirche," in F. Henrich/V. Eid (Ed.), *op. cit.*, pp. 11-34; G. Schneider, "Jesu Wort über die Ehescheidung in der Überlieferung des Neuen Testaments," in *Trierer Theologischer Zeitschrift* 80 (1971), pp. 85-87; R. Pesch, *Freie Treue. Die Christen und die Ehescheidung* (Freiburg, 1971); B. Schaller, "Die Sprüche über Ehescheidung und Wiederheirt in der synoptischen Überlieferung," in E. Lohse (ed.), *Der Ruf Jesu und die Antwort der Gemeinde* (Festschrift für J. Jeremias) (Göttingen, 1970), pp. 226-246.

16. As well as the works just mentioned, cf. A Sand, "Die Unzuchtsklausel in Matthew 5:31-32 und 19: 3-9," in *Münchener Theologische Zeitschrift* 20 (1969), pp. 118-129.

17. Consequently, as many exegetes agree, it is not possible to interpret it in the sense of a goal to be aimed at, or an ideal to be preached. Surprisingly, the Swiss Synod draft-text (cf. n. 3 above) includes such an interpretation under No. 24.2. On this, cf. also n. 18 below.

18. The reflections which follow are a first attempt to express doctrinally in a single concept this duality of aspects. But this would not itself fulfill the more comprehensive function of a fundamental hermeneutical reflection, which must concentrate also on the problem of the relation between general and particular, on the meaning of a precept (of Jesus), etc. Similarly, a critical examination of the linguistic usage of "absolute" in this connection needs to be undertaken. An acute study has been devoted to the word "radical" by B. Schüller, "Zur Rede von der radikalen sittlichen Forderung," in *Theologie und Philosophie* (1971), pp. 321-341. But in our context this question cannot be dealt with adequately without more extensive exegetical work.

19. This also applies to some exegetical attempts at explanation which, by working our various strata in the history of tradition (for instance in regard to Matt. 5 and 19) or by hypothesis of another kind (necessary alteration of Jesus' precept on account of the delay in the Parousia), no longer inquire into the meaning of the relationship between the statements in the texts as they now stand—whereas this is a task which systematic dogmatic theology cannot escape.

20. In Matt. 14:23 equals PG 13, 1245.

21. For the ancient period, cf. B. Kotting in *RAC* III, Cols. 1016-1024; J. Moingt, "Ehescheidung 'aufgrund von Unzuche' (Matt. 5:32/19:9)" in J. David/F. Schmalz (Ed.), *op. cit.* (n. 6 above), pp. 178-222; P. Stockmeier, "Scheidung und Wiederverheiratung in der alten Kirche," in *Theologische Quartalschrift* 151 (1971), pp. 39-51; and now, decisive by its abundant materials: H. Crouzel, *L'Eglise primitive face au divorce*, Thèologie historique 13 (Paris, 1971). The controversy between J. Moingt/H. Crouzel still requires examination by other specialists.

22. Cf. on this B. Primetshofer, "Zerbrochene Ehe und Ehesecheidung," in *Theologische parktishe Quartalschrift* 119 (1971), pp. 117-130; P. Manns, "Die Unauflösbarkeit der Ehe im Verständnis der frühmittelalterlichen Bussbücher," in N. Wetzel (Ed.), *Die öffentlichen Sünder oder Soll die Kirche Ehen scheiden?* (Mainz, 1970), pp. 42-75, 275-302; E. Schillebeeckx, *Le mariage I.* Cogitatio fidei 20 (Paris, 1966); the contributions of J. Gaudemet and G. Fransen in R. Metz/J. Schlick (Ed.). *Le lien matrimonial.* Hommes et Eglise I (Strassburg, 1970), pp. 81-105, 106-126; R. Weigand. "Das Scheidungsproblem in der mittelalterlichen Kanonistik," in *Theologische Quartalschrift* 151 (1971), pp. 52-60 (with bibliography).

23. Examples in H. Crouzel, *op. cit.,* pp. 148ff. (St. Basil speaks of canonical penances lasting for years); on the early Middle Ages, cf. P. Manns, *op. cit.,* pp. 60ff.

24. This structure has been little studied as far as I know, but cf. J. Danviller, *Le mariage dans le droit classique de L'Eglise* (Paris, 1933); G. H. Joyce, *Christian Marriage* (1934); H. Portmann, *Wesen und Unauflöslichkeit der Ehe in der Kirchlichen Wissenschaft und Gesetzgebung des 11 und 12 Jahrhunderts* (Emsdetten, 1938).

25. Cf. on this R. Gall, *op. cit.,* pp. 197ff. (with bibliography).

26. Cf. for example R. Schnackenburg, *op. cit.* (n. 15), pp. 24ff., 27ff., 32ff.

27. Examples in P. Huizing, "Das kanonische Ehescheidungsrecht seit dem Konzil von Trient," in N. Wetzel (Ed.), *op. cit.* (n. 22), pp. 76-93.

28. DS 1807-NR 65 (Canon 7 of Council of Trent on matrimony). Cf. the summary of his own researches by P. Fransen, "Das Thema 'Ehescheidung nach Ehebruch' auf dem Konzil von Trient (1563)," in *Concilium* 6 (1970), pp. 343-348 (with bibliography); H. Jedin, "Die Unauflöslichkeit der Ehe nach dem Konzil von Trient," in K. Reinhardt/H. Jedin, *Ehe —Sakrament in der Kirche des Herrn.* Ehe in Geschichte und Gegenwart 2 (Berlin 1971), pp. 61-135 (with bibliography).

29. Cf. J. Meyendorff, *Marriage: An Orthodox Perspective* (St. Valdimir's Seminary Press, 1970), pp. 11ff., 32ff., 35ff., 42ff.; E. Melia, "Le lien matrimonial a la lumière de la théologie sacramentaire et de la théologie morale de l'Eglise orthodoxe," in R. Metz/J. Schlick (Ed.), *op. cit.* (n. 22 above), pp. 108-197.

30. On this cf. also J. Kotsonis, *Problèmes de l'économie ecclésiastique.* Recherches et syntheses, dogme II (Gembloux, 1971), pp. 187ff.

31. P. Fransen, *op. cit.* (n. 28), pp. 345f., 347, and J. Ratzinger, *op. cit.* (n. 14), p. 49f.

32. Recognition of such research work in the history of dogma is, of course, the presupposition on which the above reflections are based. Anyone who debars from the dogmatic method the fruitful use of the findings of critical historical research can no longer pursue theology

today on the specialist level. The non-specialist's suspicion that dogma here is being tampered with and manipulated is understandable enough, but quite unfounded.

33. E. Schweitzer, *Das Evangelium nach Markus*. NTD 1 (Gottingen, 1967), p. 115

34. G. Bornkamm, "Ehescheidung und Wiederverheiratung in Neuen Testament," in *Glaube und Geschichte*. Gesammelte Aufsatze III (Munich, 1968), pp. 56-59; the quotation is on p. 57f.

35. Fundamentally this already applies to the "separation from bed and board" which in Canon Law is relatively easy to obtain (cf. CIC, can. 1128, 1129, 1131).

36. G. Bornkamm, *op. cit.*, p. 58.

37. Cf. N. van der Wal, "Aspekte der geschictlichen Entwicklung in Recht und Lehre. Einfluss des profanen Rechts auf die kirchliche Eheauffassung im Osten" in *Concilium* 6 (1970) pp. 337 to 339; P. von Chersones, "Ehescheidung in der Theologie und im Kirchenrecht der Orthodoxen Kirche," in J. David/F. Schmalz (Ed.), *op. cit.* (n. 6), pp. 337-351, esp. 343ff., 349ff., and the works listed in n. 29.

38. Cf. J. Ratzinger, *op. cit.* (n. 14), pp. 49-51.

39. Cf. also similary J. Ratzinger, "Zur Theologie der Ehe," in H. Greeven and others, *Theologie der Ehe* (Regensburg, 1969), pp. 81-115, esp. 111-113; H. U. v. Balthasar, "Christ auf Zeit," in *Klarstellungen* (Freiburg, 1971), p. 178f.

40. J. Ratzinger, "Zur Frage . . . ," p. 51.

41. Cf. on this H. Greeven, "Ehe nach dem Neuen Testament," in H. Greeven, *op. cit.* (n. 39). 73-77; R. Schnackenburg, *ibid.* pp. 21ff.

42. CF. the works listed in n. 22.

43. On this cf. P. Huizing *op. cit.*, (n. 27), pp. 81-87; but the minimalist interpretation of the Council of Trent expressed there must be disputed.

44. To give only one example: Church recognition and blessing of a second marriage after a first purely civil marriage (and one, for example, which is abandoned after a considerable length of time and on frivolous grounds). Cf. also on these problems J. Neumann, "Unauflösliches Eheband?" in *Theologische Quartalschrift* 151 (1971), pp. 1-22 (with bibliography).

45. Cf. on this R. Gall, *op. cit.* pp. 200ff.

46. The morality of sexual relations in a marriage does not depend solely on legal recognition of its validity. As Canon Law expressly acknowledges (cf. CIC, can. 1085), even in an invalid marriage there can be a genuine marital intention; otherwise there could be no such thing as *sanatio in radice*. In the question of admission to the eucharistic community, this consideration is of extreme importance.

47. Some authors ask further whether in the individual case a life together as brother and sister (without sexual relations) could not after all be demanded as meaningful and not impossible of fulfillment.

48. H. U. v. Balthasar, *Klarstellungen* (Freiburg, 1971), p. 179.

49. Whether the establishment of a "Pastoral Marriage Commission" (as in the Swiss Synod document, n. 24 above; cf. R. Gall, *op. cit.,* pp. 198f.) sufficiently objectifies and facilitates decisions, still needs to be shown. At all events optimism in this respect is not justified.

50. Cf. on this the voluminous work of G. Struck/L. Loffler (Ed.), *Einführung in die Eheberatung* (Mainz, 1971), and also F. Henrich/V. Eid (Ed.), *op. cit.* (n. 4), pp. 84-108, 109-118 (Contributions of K.H. Mandel and G. Struck).

51. Gregory of Nazianzen, quoted by J. Kotsonis, *op. cit.* (n. 30), who premises this sentence as epigraph to his book. On the reality in question, cf. also F. Bockle, "Die gescheiterate Ehe, Thesen und Vorschlage aus moraltheologischer Sicht," in F. Henrich/V. Eid (Ed.), *op. cit.,* pp. 131-132; H. Heimerl, *Verheiratet und doch nicht verheiratet* (Vienna, 1970), esp. the contributions of P. Alonso, Ch. Munier, B. Häring and the editor's concluding article.

Spiritual Direction for the Divorced and Remarried Catholic

John T. Finnegan

For many years the canonists have said fine things in regard to the pastoral care of the invalidly married. Beginning with *The Bond of Marriage* Symposium at Notre Dame in October 1967,[1] and right up to this present convention, the Canon Law Society of America has worked on two fronts to renew and reform the pastoral care of marriage. First, the revitalization of the external forum, the Marriage Tribunal, and to insure that law incorporates all the modern advances of the behavioral sciences, theology and the renewed interest in history.[2] All this is done to insure that the Church "as a society . . . as a visible assembly and spiritual community . . . forming one interlocked reality . . . comprising divine and human elements" (*Lumen Gentium,* art. 8) will be a sign of human dignity, conjugal fidelity and permanence of commitment freely made in Christian marriage. A second approach of the Canon Law Society, and canonists during the past decade, has been to look at the pastoral care of the invalidly married, and the possibility of ecclesial reconciliation when the external forum procedures are unavailable, or to no avail, and when personal conscience permits.[3] This is the delicate area of the "internal forum solution," and a point on which the Canon Law Society made an extensive study in 1969,[4] and concerns a point that has received widespread concern by the magisterium, and the religious press during the past year. At the present time, the entire Church seems to be involved in this issue; the magisterium,[5] the Catholic Theological Society of America,[6] renowned moral theologians,[7] and canon lawyers[8] who continue, as the agenda of this convention suggests, to research this issue. The national press has also shown great interest here, as well as television. It is quite legitimate to expect that research will continue in both of these areas for some time to come. But what about the poor parish priest in the service of his people? Should there be a new genre of literature directed to him, and his pastoral and spiritual formation, so that he addresses himself to his people as a "specialist of the life within," and not a mere functionary of an external discipline?

After a decade of dealing with Catholic divorce and remarriage on the level of the Marriage Tribunal and the obtaining of official Church annulments, and of offering pastoral counsel to scores of people who were unable to obtain such annulments, I would offer four preliminary remarks:

1. The professional societies for all the good they do on the theoretical level by their scholarly studies may well do pastoral harm on the practical level if their studies do not include some reflection on the pastoral skills necessary to cope with and implement their reflections. The gap between the canonical-theological studies and pastoral expertise at the local level is nothing short of mammoth.

2. There is an insufficient understanding and attention among Catholics in general, and priests in particular, concerning the specific features and genius of the Catholic tradition and commitment. Advice that fails to take this into consideration can deaden faith and weaken the coherence and plausability of life in Christ as a Catholic Christian.

3. Certainly conscience and personal identification with Christ are operative principles in our tradition for Christian behavior, but they run counter to a communitarian emphasis built on an ecclesiology of the Body of Christ that has a remarkable grip on the faith commitment of our people. It does little good in some cases to counsel conscience, and personal identification with Christ if in the process the framework supporting this commitment collapses.[9] As a matter of empirical fact few Catholics over thirty are able to act against the community's evaluation of

their marital status. We are reluctant nonconformists, and at this point magisterial pronouncements and the Catholic conscience resonate as one.[10]

4. The local priest is still the pivotal person in the care and upbuilding of the community. His role demands an increased sensitivity to conscience problems; the understanding of marital hurt and pain, and an appreciation of the peculiar personal and psychological problems of the Catholic divorced. The priest must see himself as a spiritual director; one who discerns and tests the spirits; one who insures that every act of his people is Christian and Catholic and represents growth in Christ . . . even if that act does not conform to community, canonical, and magisterial expectations. If a priest does not have the necessary skill to deal with the "imperfect response,"[11] he should not do so. Certainly, priests who are themselves experiencing confusion and pain in ministry should not counsel at this level. It has been my experience that the "ex opere operato" mentality[12] is still in possession concerning our pastoral approach to the divorced Catholic. Leaving aside the theological issues, the practice of *telling people* to return to the sacraments (in the case of the invalidly remarried Catholic) without a great investment of time and energy and pastoral expertise is counterproductive, and may lead to a deadening of faith.[13] The priest must remember that what the canonical judgment decision is in the external forum, discernment is in the internal forum. In an age of interiorism this is of great pastoral importance. Our Canon Law conventions generally offer us food for thought. How is this thought working out in practice?

The Peculiar Problem of the Catholic Divorced

In his review of Garry Wills', *Bare Ruined Choirs*, the distinguished American churchman, John Tracy Ellis, criticizes the author for his failure to manifest "the instinct of Catholic faith."[14] The instinctual response of Catholic faith apparently has something to do with elements of the tradition; certain ways in which the community experiences itself as being together in Christ; certain ways of ecclesial relationships that lead a person to affirm, "I love the Church." This can only mean a person loves the relationships, experiences, symbolizations, and institutions that mediate to him the life and vitality of Christ. The Catholic experience of the faith does bring to its people a special combination of intellectual and emotional inputs that can possibly not only change its adherents' world view, but also profoundly touch the soul of man. What I am speaking of here is best summed up in a remark to me by an elderly Episcopal priest:

> What is there about you Catholics? After 45 years of parish work; and after involving many divorced and remarried ex-Catholics in the work of my parish . . . I have never once been able to convince them to join the Episcopal Church. Why is it they would rather die a bad Catholic than a good Episcopalian?

That this remark draws chiefly from past Catholic experience is indicated by the recent decision of John Cogley.[15] However, at the level of feeling most of us understand what this gentleman was saying. The "instinct of Catholic faith" needs some reflection as a preliminary to our work with the Catholic divorced and remarried.

This instinct of faith can cause great harm and pain to the Catholic divorced, and especially the innocent party. There is a feeling of rejection; loss of self-esteem, and a great sense of failure and unworthiness. In the era of the "physically battered-child" we have its counterpart in the "spiritually battered adult" . . . the invalidly married Catholic. While much of this alienation is closely associated with the human problem of divorce, the Catholic commitment can intensify it as the weight of religion is brought to this pain. As a community we Catholics cope with failure of this nature poorly, and we have few coping mechanisms and pastoral aids to offer. So, our people drift away by the scores, never receiving the consolation of the Church . . . its sacraments, or its forgiveness. And we, the Church, are less for their absence. What a tragedy it is to have so little to offer people in these situations. If the Matrimonial Tribunal cannot meet the needs of the Church, if it cannot render justice in a reasonable time . . . then our people have no where to go. The unexplored regions of conscience and the "internal forum solution" is small consolation to one who has obeyed the Church, at least in these matters, faithfully. Our people ask for the bread of mercy and forgiveness, and we give them stony silence. As priests our problem is acute also. We wish to be faithful ministers of the Church; the pain of any form of disobedience is burdensome for us; we adhere fully to the values of marital fidelity and generosity, and proclaim in season and out of season the prayer of the Eucharistic Liturgy . . . "Keep me faithful to your teachings Lord, and never let me be separated from you." Why is it that mercy and consolation frequently can only be given in the hushed silence of the rectory parlor? It is an odd experience to have tender consciences enjoying in the Lord your every word, but totally unable to act upon them.

Steps in Conscience Formation

Is it possible to use the resurgence of interest in prayer, the spiritual life, and the directed retreat, as a means of helping members of our community who have failed in marriage? Do these offer some skills and tools in conscience formation that might be pastorally beneficial, and offer religious communities some hard, real life situations to test their principles? Perhaps the privatized atmosphere of religious living is not the best locale to test these principles in the first place. We might even be made whole again if spiritual direction focused on failure rather then perfection.[16]

What follows is tentative program of pastoral care for the divorced Catholic. It is based on the conviction that the Church does have the motivation and zeal to care and serve in this manner where conflicting principles vie for our allegiance. Furthermore, it is based on the conviction that no member of the Church should ever feel outside the pale of our pastoral efforts. It is also based on the conviction that questions concerning readmittance to the Eucharist, civil remarriage in good faith, or even the respected petition for a marriage annulment, should not be resolved until the parties are deeply involved in a spiritual renewal program. It is understood that it is the obligation of the priest to seek out such people, to gain the support of the parish community, and to insure that such parish interest enhances the concern for family life while at the same time nutures the values of mercy, healing and reconciliation so mysteriously restorative to Christian idealism.

The first step in the spiritual renewal of the divorced Catholic is what the charismatic movement calls, "the healing of memories."[17] The divorced person has been through a harrowing, possibly dehumanizing experience. The memory is cluttered with fears and anxieties, and there is little spiritual freedom. Growth in spirituality is growth in memory; it is an increased awareness of where we come from . . . of all God's actions in our past . . . and our personal salvation history. Great pastoral skill is needed to comfort and create a new thirst for God. Remembering what God has done for us, and how he has been present in the past can be a source of personal renewal. The memory tends to protect itself from its wounds; the "black-and-blue" marks of the psyche are especially damaging. The use of Scripture and private prayer can be very effective here. It means, of course, that the priest is able to move comfortably in this direction. In this stage the priest tries to rehabilitate, establish personal worth, and the turning of vulnerability into wholeness. A good prudential and pastoral rule here is: no mention is to be made or discussed in this phase of doing anything canonically that is not permitted. The next step in the process is the realization of God's forgiveness. "Our God is the God of the nevertheless, and not the God of the therefore" says Karl Barth.[18] Our God does not tally up our failings and misadventures, and cry out, "*therefore*, I hate you!" Rather, the Lord utters after such a tally, if indeed he would make one, "*nevertheless*, I love you." A prayerful reading of the parable of the Prodigal Son is helpful here. The divorced Catholic frequently confronts co-religionists, members of their families, friends, and even their Church, who have a "therefore" mentality. The bruised reed is nearly broken and bent out of shape; the smoking flax is nearly extinguished, and the temptation of the divorced is to return hatred for hatred. After experiencing God's love and mercy in the kindness of the priest, the divorced person is brought slowly to the maturity of the "nevertheless." In spite of the hurt that brought the marriage to its breakup; in spite of misunderstandings at home and in the Church, they gradually can be led to pray, "*nevertheless,* I love you." The meaning of the Lord's Prayer may now be understood for the first time. If we are dealing here with a couple who are in a canonically invalid marriage with no possibility of annulment, or of terminating the relationship, the work at this point focuses on the quality of their relationship, and the integrity of Christian witness they offer the community . . . the Catholic portion of which does not recognize their marital status. Even at this point it is still premature to speak of reception of the Eucharist if that is their hope. While some may be able to attempt the "brother-sister" relationship,[19] and are capable of great heroism, pastoral experience proves that in these times of personalism and need for intimacy such a lifestyle cannot be borne by most. The priest should not feel constrained to mention it if he judges it unwise and impossible of fulfillment. For those not so able they should be willing at this point to abide by the principle that the sacraments are too communitarian and public by nature to be received by those whose state in life is not recognized by the Church. The emphasis remains on the healing power of God's forgiveness, and the quality of life in Christ which bespeaks his presence to the community and challenges the community's assessment of their life in Christ. For some, perhaps even most, this is as far as pastoral care will permit.

If at this juncture the priest feels that the research and the statements of responsible theologians and canonists are so suasive that he will continue his pastoral care, then he must do so responsibly. He should respect the parties' rights in the external forum, and always seek an annulment there first if that is possible. The more one deals with our people the more one realizes how important is the Matrimonial Tribunal. To neglect the adequate staffing and financing of the Tribunal is to be pastorally irresponsible.[20] If a priest or bishop defends vigorously the external forum, as one should, and fails to see that the Tribunal is rendering wise decisions based on the new law, and advances in the theological and behavioral sciences, then they will not be taken seriously.[21] There is too much rhetoric in support of the external forum. The priests and the laity will not take magisterial pronouncements seriously if they are not supported by action that will engender confidence that is here where justice and mercy meet. Inefficient, and laboriously canonical Tribunals do much to undermine the value that the external forum represents, and the fact that the Catholic magisterium should be seen as a gift to the community. The "good faith" or "good conscience" solutions so much in the news during the past year is another indication of how important an external judgment is to the practicing Catholic. [22]

There are some guidelines for the priest if he counsels people in the direction of "internal forum decisions." He should be familiar with the current writings of moralists concerning the "imperfect response," and the "theology of compromise." He should inculcate a reverence for the teaching authority of the Church, and be certain that personal decisions of conscience respect the Christian value of permanence in marriage. The priest can never ask his people to make a moral decision that they are unable to make; and one in which he does not support or fully believe. The priest never counsels his people in disobedience. He presides over a process . . . he tests it, directs it, seasons it with Gospel values, and insures that what is taking place is growth in maturity and love of Christ and his Church. This is a legitimate priestly endeavor, and our people have a right to expect it from us. They should not suffer because of our pastoral unpreparedness.

A third step in the spiritual renewal of the divorced Catholic is community affirmation and support that come from their peers in pain. The communities of "divorced Catholics" that have received notoriety are a significant and worthy development. [23] The priest has a role of presence in this setting, and he should bring to these communities resource personnel and encouragement. This is the atmosphere in which the priest can help people to confront failure and interpret it in the light of the theology of the cross. The mutual interaction of failure with failure presided over by the priestly witness is restorative for all and especially for the priest. Many Catholic divorced will become reconciled to their new celibate state if they are canonically unable to remarry. The amazing feature here is that they will do so with great love for the Church, and if there are children, they become the spiritual beneficiaries. Admittedly, some grow and heal to a point of seeking remarriage, even if not canonically recognized. The priest is always diminished when the idealism of the Gospel is impossible of fulfillment, and he anguishes and suffers as he supports the rights of the community, the magisterium, and personal conscience. Religious congregations can have special effectiveness here by creating situations where such communities of divorced may gather and where healing, growth in Christ, and responsible Catholic maturity of conscience may develop. Even within the prescribed limits of canon law and liturgical discipline there are many forms of worship that may be celebrated. These communities of divorced should not become known as a new avantgarde, or a reverse elitism, or people removed from the larger community so that the latter will be antiseptic enough to be called God's People. Each diocese should support a center of this nature as symbolic of its collective concern for those who have failed. The fear of the official Church of supporting an apostolate of this nature is understandable. Such fear may be based on the sound insight that our people would misinterpret such support. The Catholic community must be catechized regarding our tradition and the values of conjugal fidelity, indissolubility and marital holiness, and at the same time they must be brought to an awareness that this tradition is not compromised by gentle overtures and compassion to those who have failed, but rather blessed and enriched.

Ideally, and at the present time it is rarely the case; this is the situation where people are best able to handle tensions in conscience arising from disobedience of Church law. Such a situation is much more strict than some contemporary pastoral practices that welcome people in canonically invalid marriages back to the sacraments without a year to three years of pastoral contact. In a situation such as described, the priest can insure that the communitarian nature of the sacraments are fully appreciated; he can watch over the development of responsible Christian maturity; failure will be seen as an opportunity for growth in Christ, and not a disgrace; forgiveness and acceptance will be placed in a Christian perspective; the role of magisterium respected and understood so that the "instinct of Catholic faith" is nourished. It is my contention that it is never the role of the priest to encourage people to disobey the discipline and teaching of the Church. Traditionally this dictum has shut us off from the fragile, the frail and the wounded lest they embarrass and tempt us. The role of the priest in Christian marriage is more directly associated with the public, the external forum features of marriage and its witness to the larger community. However, he has the pastoral obligation to create situations whereby people can grow in responsible conscience formation. We should not fear involvement at this level. The priest is always tempted to be dogmatic or anti-nomain; to be a "good guy" at the expense of discernment, spiritual leadership and personal investment of time and energy. The priest finds himself burdened with family care in a child-centered Church; he finds himself living in the two worlds of theory and reality; he is unprepared to handle the moral problems and spiritual direction that his people place before him and expect of him. At this point the pain of ministry begins to comprehend the pain of his people. Divorced from his roots and training, and frequently misunderstood in his ministry, the priest begins to hear with his heart the agony of marital disruption. In meeting this need bravely and spiritually, and in finding a home in the Church for all the sinful and repentent the priest finds himself as pastor and "good shepherd."

The Role of Discernment in Conscience Formation

The priest who engages in the work of seeking out and counseling the divorced and remarried Catholic will be greatly assisted if he acquaints himself with recognized and approved techniques of spiritual direction. The priest is being forced by the pressures of contemporary living to consider himself as a spiritual director. Indeed, the sacrament of Penance will only be approached by some today if accompanied by such direction. Our people are gently nudging us toward expectations of genuine holiness, personal integrity and competence in the discernment of spirits.[24]

Of all the systems of spirituality in our Catholic tradition that are being revitalized today, the *Spiritual Exercises* take first place.[25] Not all are suited temperamentally or spiritually to give or receive spiritual direction in the Ignatian method. However, the *Exercises,* and the current literature surrounding their renascence, offer us a sound model to grapple with the conflicts of the individual conscience and the community consensus as formed by the superior. The *Exercises* place great emphasis on "senter cum ecclesia" with docile, filial obedience to God's leaders who direct a community of faith. At the same time, and counterpointed to this, the *Exercises* in their modern interpretation stress the individual, his/her needs, talents, and personal wishes. Models of dialogue, prayer and discernment emerge as the individual under the guidance of a director grapples with these polarities.[26] "Spiritual discernment" is the term that characterizes this process.[27] One of the most important conditions for the discernment process is consistent and dynamic contact with the total mystery of Christ; his life, death and resurrection. The divorced with their emotional depletion are frequently excited candidates for spiritual growth as the Paschal Mystery is such a distinctive feature of their lives.[28] The divorced person whose heart is not bitter is often on the verge of great sanctity. My most treasured correspondence is of the kind that states: "Father, you have made me proud to be a Catholic again." In most of these instances all that is done is common prayer, an outreach of understanding, and an offering of a systematized approach to growth in Christ.

A most important element here is prayer. Even if I am certain that parties are going to move in a direction contrary to canonical discipline, I insist that if our relationship is to continue it must be on the basis of prayer and testing of their decision-making process. If people cannot "disobey" the law in good faith then they should never do it. This is the most difficult juncture in direction of the divorced, and the about-to-be-invalidly-remarried Catholic. To assist a person to grow in spiritual freedom so that they can make a decision free of self-deception is in itself a pastoral skill gained only by personal prayer and priestly fidelity. The Holy Spirit always leads us back to community and so personal decisions are never made at the expense of our sense of churchmanship.[29] Here is where sub-communities can be supportive. In discovering the Spirit we must be aware that he does not contradict himself. If we discern properly according to the Spirit's lead, then both the individual and the community will be enriched. The scandal of Christianity is that it is the home of forgiveness and repentence. We have taken the scandal out of it, and have refused to give failure its privileged status. Our ministry as canon lawyers has brought us as professional men of the Church into contact with the broken-hearted and with the remnants of the intolerable marriage. As we have endeavored to reform our institutions; and as we have investigated rights of conscience, and the reform of Canon Law, let us lead the way in developing a wholesome, refreshing pastoral program of spiritual care for the divorced Catholic.

APPENDIX

Unofficial Translation of Letter of Congregation of the Doctrine of the Faith, April 11, 1973*

Your Excellency:

This Sacred Congregation, whose duty it is to safeguard the teaching of faith and morals throughout the Catholic world, has taken careful note of the spread of new opinions which either deny or attempt to call into doubt the teaching of the Magisterium of the Church on the indissolubility of matrimony.

Opinions of this kind have not only been published in Catholic books and periodicals, but have also begun to appear in seminaries. Catholic schools and even in the ecclesiastical tribunals of some dioceses.

The opinions, moreoever, have been joined to other doctrinal or pastoral reasons to form an argument for justifying abuses against current discipline on the admission to the Sacraments of those who are living in irregular unions.

Consequently this Sacred Congregation in its plenary meeting of 1972 examined the matter and now has the mandate, approved by the Supreme Pontiff, to strongly urge upon Your Excellency diligent vigilance, so that all those assigned to teach religion in schools of any level or in various institutes, or who function as "officials" in ecclesiastical tribunals, will remain faithful to the teaching of the Church regarding the indissolubility of marriage and will reduce this to practical effect in the tribunals.

In regard to admission to the Sacraments, the Ordinaries are asked on the one hand to stress observance of current discipline and, on the other hand to take care that the pastors of souls exercise special care to seek out those who are living in an irregular union by applying to the solution of such cases, in addition to other right means, the Church's approved practice in the internal forum.

Franjo Cardinal Seper, Perfect

The Wanderer, August 23, 1973

A private interpretation of the Letter

1. Like all documents coming from authority centers in the Church it needs interpretation (canons 17-20). The NC news dispatch printed in diocesan weeklies on June 22, 1973 states that "a Vatican official who knows well the mind of the Congregation claims that Cardinal Seper was speaking exclusively of the brother-sister relationship as the only solution approved by the Church." This remark, besides being of no official canonical value, breeds distrust of the magisterium. If the statement saw fit to leave room for development in keeping with the canonical dicta "expressa nocent" and "omnia definitio periculum est" it should not be "clarified" in such a casual manner.

2. The statement is confusing, but this is not to be faulted, but rather expected. Justice Holmes' remark that the role of Law does not follow the path of logic, but rather the ambiguous path of human nature is applicable here.

3. The strong affirmation or indissolubility is to be expected. However, there seems to be a misunderstanding of current Catholic theological literature when they infer that some are denying, or calling into doubt the traditional teaching. This is a reminder for those seeking to develop pastoral methods of reconciliation of divorced and remarried Catholics, that this should not appear to question the principle of indissolubility, or of the officially recognized status of the first marriage in the eyes of the Church.

4. All that the third paragraph of this document can be made to infer is if persons in irregular unions receive the sacraments,

they cannot justify their actions by questioning the indissolubility of marriage, nor the prior and privileged status of the first marriage. In other words the justification for return to the sacraments cannot involve the denying of the magisterium and its teaching on the permanence of marriage. The return to the sacraments, then, must be found in our renewed understanding of God's mercy; his reconciling power which he has given to the Church; the current pastoral sensitivity of the Church in being God's agent of forgiveness; as well as some possible merit in the current teaching of moral theologians regarding the "theology of compromise" and "the imperfect response."

5. The last paragraph is most significant even though it is garbled in translation. It clearly states the priest should seek out those in *good faith* (this is a legitimate inference here) who are living in irregular unions, and apply the internal forum solution. The clause in the second line: "in addition to other right means" is perhaps a reference to the external forum and the pastoral necessity of seeking a solution there first. However, if that cannot be done, then follow "the Church's approved practice in the internal forum." This would include the approved "brother-sister" relationship and the broadening of the internal forum solution to the responsible limits set by moral theologians and canonists (cf. The Jurist, 1970:1).

6. If this interpretation is legitimate then we are witnessing the development of the Eastern practice of economy (oekonomia); an enlargement of equity (epikeia); a recognition that principles can be upheld (indissolubility), but not urged in every instance (the pastoral ministry of mercy and forgiveness); a scriptural hermeneutic that interprets the logia of Christ as the ideal to be sought after, but perhaps not realizable in every instance due to sin and selfishness; a recognition that the priest enters ministry today principally as a pastor, and he must have a message and apostolate for the brokenhearted and alienated.

Notes

1. *The Bond of Marriage,* edited by William W. Bassett (Notre Dame: University of Notre Dame Press, 1968).
2. *The Tribunal Reporter,* edited by Adam Maida (Hunt-

ington, Ind.: Our Sunday Visitor Press, 1970); *Matrimonial Jurisprudence: United States 1968-1972* (Hartford: Canon Law Society of America, 1973); *Documentation on Marriage Nullity Cases,* compiled by Germain Lesage and Francis G. Morrisey (Ottawa: St. Paul's University, 1973). This latter work, which at present has only limited circulation is an outstanding contribution to the renewal of the Canon Law of marriage; Annulments, Lawrence G. Wrenn (Hartford: Canon Law Society of America—2nd edition, 1972); John T. Noonan, *The Power to Dissolve: Lawyers and Marriages in the Courts of the Roman Rota* (Cambridge: Harvard University Press—The Belknap Press, 1972). For some reviews of this outstanding work, cf., *National Catholic Reporter,* Dec. 22, 1972 by John E. Lynch, C.S.P.; *The Jurist* (1972-1973) review by William W. Bassett, pp. 419-424; and *Theological Studies,* March 1973, review by John J. Reed, S.J., pp. 168-173.

3. *Divorce and Remarriage in the Catholic Church,* edited by Lawrence G. Wrenn (New York: Newman Press, 1973); Stephen J. Kelleher, *Divorce and Remarriage for Catholics?* (New York: Doubleday and Co., 1973) for popularizations cf., Morris L. West, *Scandal in the Assembly* (New York: William Morrow and Co., 1970); Oliver Stewart, *Divorce Vatican Style* (Denville, N.J.: Dimension Books, 1971).

4. Cf. *The Jurist,* vol. 30, no. 1 (1970-1971).

5. Cf., infra., Appendix I

6. *CTSA Proceedings of the Twenty-Seventh Annual Convention,* vol. 27 (Bronx, N.Y.: Manhattan College, 1973), "The Problem of Second Marriages," pp. 233-240. Also in *Origins*—NC News Documentary Service, vol. 2, no. 16, October 12, 1972. This report is weak and does not respond to the numerous theological issues raised by canonists, theologians, historians, and Scripture scholars during the past decade.

7. Richard A. McCormick, "Notes on Moral Theology," *Theological Studies,* March 1971, "Theology and Divorce," pp. 1-7-122; by the same author, and in the same journal, March 1972, "Divorce and Remarriage," pp. 91-100; Bernard Haring. "The Internal Forum Solution to the Intolerable Marriage Cases," *The*

Jurist (1970-1971); also by the same author, "The Normative Value of the Sermon on the Mount," *Catholic Biblical Quarterly,* July 1967; and again by Haring, "A Theological Appraisal of Marriage Tribunals" in *Divorce and Remarriage in the Catholic Church,* edited by Lawrence G. Wrenn, op. cit., pp. 16-28.

8. For bibliographies on this issue, cf., *Annulments,* Lawrence G. Wrenn, *op. cit.*: William W. Bassett, "Divorce and Remarriage: The Catholic Search for Pastoral Reconciliation," *American Ecclesiastical Review,* January 1970, pp. 20-36, and February 1970, pp. 92-105. In this latter article the author concludes on pp. 100-105 with a bibliography.

9. Cf. remarks by Peter Huizing in *The Jurist* (1970-1971), pp. 15-20. In a subsequent article the author makes a attempt to correlate personal conscience with community values; *The Jurist* (1972-1974), "The Sacramental Structure of Church Order and its Implications," pp. 479-493. For some insight on the peculiar problems of the Catholic divorced, cf., James J. Rue and Louise Shanahan. *The Divorced Catholic* (New York: Paulist Press, 1972).

10. The traditional teaching on conscience formation is interesting to check at this poing. Cf., M. Zalba, *Theologiae Moralis Compendium,* vol. 1, "De Conscientia," p. 354ff.; B. H. Merklebach, *Summa Theologiae Moralis,* vol 1, "De Conscientia in generali," p. 186ff; Henry Davis, Moral and Pastoral Theology, vol. 1, "Conscience," p. 64ff.; Bernard Haring, *The Lqw of Christ,* vol 1, p. 135ff; Louis Monden, *Sin, Liberty and Law* (New York: Sheed and Ward, 1965), pp. 102-144.

11. Cf. Henry Allard, "The Invalidly Married Catholic and the Admission to the Sacraments," *The Clergy Review,* January 1971. The "imperfect response" is close to the "theology of Compromise" suggested by Charles E. Curran, *Contemporary Problems in Moral Theology* (Notre Dame: Fides Publishers, Inc., 1970), pp. 102, 244ff.

12. *The Catholic Priest in the United States: Psychological Investigations* (Washington: USCC Publications Service, 1971), pp. 10-11; *Spiritual Renewal of the American Priesthood* (Washington: USCC Publications Service, 1973), p.12.

Canonical-Pastoral Reflections on Divorce and Remarriage

Thomas J. Green

This article surveys some of the more significant canonical-pastoral developments regarding divorce and remarriage in the Catholic Church today. It should be read in the broader context of the church's ministry to those who are about to be married; to married couples, especially those who are finding it hard to sustain the responsibilities of marriage and family life and to the divorced, whether or not they have remarried. The church has a catechetical and pastoral responsibility in preparing couples for marriage, supporting them in their commitment and helping those who have suffered through the breakdown of a marital union to rebuild their lives.

Much tension within some local church communities has resulted from the failure on the part of their members to be informed about and to appreciate changes in outlook and practice regarding divorce and remarriage.[1] The specialized ministry to the divorced has become a pressing pastoral concern in recent years. Probably 5 million American Catholics are divorced. It is estimated that nearly 3 million could initiate annulment proceedings, with about one third of that number obtaining decrees of nullity according to present jurisprudence.[2] Since only 9300 annulments were granted in 1974—the last year for which reliable statistics are available—the magnitude of the problem is apparent.[3]

Various factors are forcing a new look at church policy and practice regarding ministry to divorced Catholics. There are new biblical and theological insights into the nature of sacramental marriage. Historical studies have illumined ancient usage. Ecumenical contacts are revealing wide variations in pastoral practice. Opinion polls indicate a growing acceptance of divorce and a favoring of liberalized divorce laws even by Catholics. The behavioral sciences are clarifying the social and psychological demands of marriage as well as the capacity of individuals to assume marital responsibilities. The Canon Law Society of America has pointed up some of the inconsistencies in present marriage legislation and the inadequacies of marriage tribunals to cope with the large number of cases which come before them.

Although a comprehensive pastoral ministry must take cognizance of all these developments,[4] our scope in these pages is much more limited. Our primary focus here is on the ministry to the divorced. First, we review the canonical legislation governing annulments and the dissolution of the marriage bond in the external forum, that is, in the arena of one's relationship to the church as a society governed by laws. Next we consider the church's pastoral ministry to the Catholics who have divorced and remarried and for whom canon law offers no ready legal recourse. Finally, some particular attention is given to the question of their receiving the eucharist and internal forum solutions, that is, in the arena of one's personal relationship to the Lord.

Annulments and Dissolutions of the Bond

In dealing with the age-old practice of divorce, church courts have had to define the meaning of Christian marriage in legal terms. Two notable institutes have developed: annulment and dissolution of the bond. These, however, can be properly understood only within the broader context of church marriage law. A fundamental reality is the ecclesial dimension of the sacraments. They are faith experiences expressing the church's life to the world and offering men and women access to deeper union with the Lord. Every sacrament involves an interaction between the Lord and the believer within the community. Church law governing sacramental practice attempts to ensure the authenticity and integrity of that encounter. Marriage as a sacrament is a unique interpersonal relationship between consenting parties who accept certain rights and responsibilities. Hence, marriage law tries to safeguard the integrity of that relationship not only for the benefit of the parties themselves but also for the well-being of society as a whole. The church does this by establishing norms for preparation for marriage, determining certain impediments, specifying the way of expressing consent, adjudicating cases of marital invalidity, etc.[5]

Annulments. Canon law takes appearances at face value, presuming that all marriages are valid. An annulment, however, means that contrary to appearances a given relationship does not fulfill the legal requisites for community recognition. The contract governing the rights and responsibilities of the consenting parties is, in fact, invalid. This may result from a deficiency extrinsic to the couple, e.g., not marrying before a priest and two witnesses. There are also deficiencies intrinsic to the couple, e.g., an incapacity to sustain a lasting relationship or perhaps a defective attitude regarding the traditional values of permanence, fidelity and procreation.[6] Annulments have been granted for centuries. However, only within the past few generations have church tribunals adjudicated a large number of cases. Until recently divorce was not socially acceptable, and extended family units supported those experiencing marital difficulties. As a result, the validity of the marriage bond was not often challenged. Socio-cultural upheavals and changes in civil law have considerably altered the situation.

Jurisprudence does not operate in a vacuum. A complex interaction of law, theology, historical contingencies and sociocultural factors affects tribunals.[7] There has been a significant shift affecting marriage cases in the theological-legal context of jurisprudence since Vatican II. At the risk of oversimplification, one might say that from the Middle Ages to recent years church law and the practice of jurisprudence shaped the Catholic theology of marriage, but since Vatican II jurisprudence has been shaped by theology.

Before the recent council, marriage was viewed as a contract between two parties granting mutual and exclusive rights to the body of the partner for procreative acts. The primary end of marriage was defined in terms of the procreation and education of children. Its secondary ends were mutual help and the allaying of concupiscence (cf. can. 1013). Juridical emphasis was placed on the expression of marital consent freely, knowingly and according to proper form. The uniqueness of marriage consent was acknowledged. However, there was a tendency to operate legally within a rather narrow contractual framework. About the time of Vatican II, however, one could observe the beginnings of a shift in tribunal practice. The change was due partly to deeper theological insights into marriage as covenant and sacrament and partly to the influence of the behavioral sciences.

Contemporary theology discusses marriage as much more than a contractual consent to sexual intercourse. It is a commitment to a total life relationship in faith that ideally reflects God's unfailing love for his people.[8] The traditional qualities of permanence and exclusivity are related especially to marriage's being an institutionalized way of life responsive to personal and social exigencies. Vatican II transcends the code's dualistic expression of a hierarchy of purposes in marriage in favor of a more integral partnership-procreation relationship. The deepening of the couple's relationship is the milieu within which a genuinely human procreation and education of children takes place.[9]

What are the implications for annulments of this change in theological perspective? It has meant in practice that the conditions requisite for a valid marriage are more demanding, and conversely a considerable broadening of the grounds for annulments. Tribunals have become more interested in the couple's lived relationship than their momentary intentions at the time of consent. In effect, tribunals are afforded greater options in dealing with marital breakdown.[10]

It is not enough for a valid marriage that the consent of the parties be knowing, free and according to prescribed formalities. Marriage presupposes the physical, psychological and emotional maturity necessary to assume and fulfill the responsibilities of a lifelong heterosexual union. It is one thing to know about marriage intellectually and to desire such a commitment. It is another to be physically equipped to sustain conjugal and parental responsibilities.

The past decade has seen a growing awareness on the part of the church that certain individuals are incapable of marriage. This admission is a most significant jurisprudential development because it comes as a result of fruitful dialogue between canonists and behavioral science experts. At one time an individual had to be clinically insane for a marriage to be invalidated on psychological grounds. We now realize that numerous individuals not so disordered are nevertheless psychically incapable of marriage.[11] New church law proposes three general categories of marital incapacity. The first two relate to marital consent: 1) a mental disturbance impeding the use of reason; and 2) a serious lack of discretion regarding marital rights and obligations.

The third incapacity relates more to the lived experience of marriage. It is the inability of assuming the essential obligations of marriage because of a serious psycho-sexual anomaly.[12]

Dissolution of the Bond

Another legal remedy for the divorced, probably less well understood, is "the dissolution of the bond." A dissolution differs from an annulment in that it presupposes a valid marriage. Some marriages, however, lack a certain quality which can later become the grounds for dissolving the bond. Since even in these cases, the marriage bond is lawful and binding the union may not be dissolved by the spouses on their own volition but only by church authority. (Not all writers agree on the theoretical basis for this action by the church. Some ask whether the dissolution process really involves any positive action by church authority terminating the marriage bond or whether it is simply a declaratory recognition of a de facto broken union and consequent acknowledgment of the parties' freedom to enter a second marriage.)

The absolute indissolubility of a sacramental consummated marriage has been fundamental to canonical theory and practice since the 11th century. On the other hand, the church has also recognized grounds for dissolution of the bond in sacramental marriages which have not been consummated. ("Sacramental" means a marriage between two baptized individuals whereas "consummation" refers to the act of sexual intercourse.) In this legal framework, consent suffices for a valid marriage whereas consummation alone makes a marriage indissoluble. Although the rationale for the absolute indissolubility of sacramental consummated unions continues to be discussed[13] by canonists and theologians, there is general agreement that such marriages have a special quality because they symbolize the faithful union of Christ with the church.[14]

As mentioned before some marriages lack a certain quality which can later become the grounds for dissolving the bond. The so-called "Pauline Privilege" and its later extensions are the best known examples of dissolution of the bond. The origin of the practice is attributed to St. Paul (cf. I Cor. 7:12-15). It involved two non-baptized spouses, one of whom became converted to Christianity. If the non-baptized spouse was unwilling to be baptized or at least to permit the convert to practice the faith in peace, the church declared that the convert was not bound by that marriage. In the eyes of the Christian community the freedom of the Christian spouse to practice the faith took precedence over the prior marriage bond ("favor of the faith").

During the centuries the church developed certain legal formalities for dealing with such cases. However, the church had to respond creatively to new pastoral needs during the 16th century when there was a notable expansion of her missionary effort. There were a number of cases when the strict requirements for a "Pauline Privilege" could not be met. Accordingly, the church extended the meaning of the "Pauline Privilege" to apply to these situations since the same spiritual grounds for such a policy were present. The 20th century has witnessed a further expansion of the occasions when the church has dissolved non-sacramental unions, i.e., those involving at least one non-baptized party.

This has resulted more from pastoral exigencies rather than a well worked out theory. (One wonders to what extent the Lord's call to permanence affecting all marriages is compromised by an ever widening dissolution practice.)[15]

In brief, whenever a marriage involves at least one non-baptized person or at least the marriage has not been consummated after the baptism of the previously unbaptized party, that marriage can be dissolved "in favor of the faith" by the Holy See. This is true even if there is no conversion to the church by the one seeking the dissolution.[16]

The practice of dissolving non-consummated marriages began in the Middle Ages. The dissolution of the bond was first granted when one of the parties entered monastic life. The vows made at the time of solemn profession (which implies a lifelong commitment) took precedence over the marriage vows. Later, popes extended this kind of dispensation from the marriage vows to a wide range of cases where there was an adequate spiritual reason and no danger of scandal.

One might note a contemporary effort to refine the meaning of "sacramental" and "consummation." Given their significance for marital indissolubility, it is imperative that the need for canonical precision not preempt theological reflection in an issue transcending purely juridical categories.

The Code of Canon Law identifies the sacrament with the marriage contract between baptized persons (cf. can. 1012, 2).

Yet such "automatic sacramentality" is questioned because of a renewed sense of the sacraments as actions of a believing community. Unfortunately, numerous couples reflect minimal or immature faith at the time of marriage. Their awareness of the covenant relationship embodying God's love for his people seems tenuous. It has been suggested by some that we should distinguish between marriage as a natural human reality (recognized as valid) and as a sacrament to which such couples would be admitted only after a period of catechesis.[17]

There is a similar effort to come to an understanding of consummation which is more expressive of a genuinely human act, reflecting conjugal commitment and embodying the deepening of marital love over a period of time. If marital intercourse is to symbolize Christ's union with the church, it would seem that something more is called for than a single physical act prescinding from other considerations.[18]

Pastoral Ministry: Admission to the Sacraments

The church's official position on indissolubility and its pastoral implications might be summarized as follows:

A marriage that is *ratum et consummatum* (sacramental and consummated) is indissoluble by any human authority, be it the partners themselves (internal indissolubility) or by any other authority (external dissolubility). In such a marriage, a bond comes into being that is dissolved only with the death of one of the partners. If the marriage factually breaks up and a partner to it remarries, his [her] marriage is in violation of this existing bond. Such a partner, should he [she] desire to remain in eucharistic communion with the church, has but two options. Either he [she] must abandon the second marriage, or if he [she] cannot (because of obligations that have arisen within it) he [she] must live as brother-sister.[19]

The preceding section discussed annulments and dissolution of the bond freeing an individual to enter a second marriage recognized in the church. However, what about those whose first marriage has neither been annulled nor dissolved? Are they excluded from the eucharist? Recent developments shed light on this question and should be brought to the attention of the Catholic community to facilitate a more balanced approach to the issue.[20]

Issues involving a believer's marital status should be resolved through the church's regular legal channels if possible. Respect for human and Christian dignity grounds a basic right to a readily accessible church hearing for an annulment or dissolution within a reasonable period of time.[21]

The ecclesial implications of marriage preclude its being arbitrarily declared invalid or prematurely dismissed as "dead." Marriage is both a personal and a social reality; and marital stability is a fundamental human value. Accordingly, the community should be involved in a crucial human reality as divorce — whatever form that involvement may take. However, despite contemporary procedural and jurisprudential developments, it is painfully evident that the tribunal system is having increasingly serious difficulties in meeting the demands placed upon it.[22]

Furthermore, there is a renewed awareness of the law's limitations in clarifying marital status. Law is primarily concerned with the good ordering of society. It can never be so precise as to grasp all the particulars of a concrete situation. Hence, it always falls short of a full approximation of reality. Legal relations, however important, can never be primary realities in a community whose priority is union with the Lord. Canonical conformity and righteousness before the Lord are not identical. Frequently, the truth as known to God is not the truth as perceivable by the community. Tensions between the arena of conscience and the arena of church order may be minimized but not eliminated before the Lord's second coming. The conscientious decisions of couples should be respected even if contrary to church order. Yet, the community should assist them in forming a right conscience.

It is false to put in one category all divorced and remarried persons who have not received annulments or dissolutions. Statements that all such individuals are excommunicated and excluded from the sacraments are unfounded either in moral theology or canon law.[23] On the contrary we must *differentiate* the *varied situations* of such persons. Perhaps the following distinction may help:

a) Conflict situations between internal and external forum that arise from the fact that a marriage was invalid before God but cannot be proved as such before the community.
b) Hardship situations that arise from the fact that a marriage, valid before God and the community, has taken place and broken up; one of the parties remarried; how he [she] wishes to return to full ecclesiastical communion without abandoning the second marital union.[24]

Subsequent comments focus primarily on reception of the eucharist. Recognition of the second marriage is a more perplexing issue, especially in the hardship situations given the principle of indissolubility.[25] Likewise, we are entirely concerned with a couple's conscientious decision regarding reception of the sacraments (internal forum). We are not talking about official community authentication of their ecclesial status (external forum).

1. *Conflict situations*. (Probably invalid first union which cannot be established in the external forum.) At stake is a person's solidly based conviction that some element essential to the validity of his/her first union was lacking, but he or she cannot establish the grounds for the claim to the satisfaction of the tribunal. It may be that some key evidence is lacking. Perhaps the only tribunal to which one has ready access if unwilling to process a case on grounds generally acceptable in other tribunals.[26] Or it may be that a given tribunal for one reason or another simply does not function or is inadequately staffed so that an oppressive backlong of cases means a prolonged delay of several years. Despite procedural and jurisprudential developments, there are still serious problems for many in expediting their marriage cases.

Thus the issue in many cases is not the weight of evidence for an annulment but the insufficiency of the legal structures designed to verify such evidence.

As a consequence, pastors and confessors are more and more counselling individuals who have entered a second marriage to receive the eucharist. The well-being of the community and prudence dictate that certain conditions be met:

> If a couple decided after consultation, reflection and prayer that they are worthy to receive the sacraments, their judgment should be respected. If the consultation and judgment that takes shape around it are to be responsible, they must center on the quality of the present union, its fidelity and stability, the state of conscience of the couple, the quality of their Catholic lives in other respects, their acceptance by the community, etc.[27]

In these circumstances the second marriage may be regarded as valid and perhaps sacramental in the *forum of conscience* even given its non-recognition officially because of the above-mentioned difficulties. Given its redemptive importance for the majority of people, the supporters of this practice argue that the fundamental human right to marry prevails over ecclesiastical law requiring a church declaration of nullity or dissolution for official recognition of one's freedom to remarry.[28]

2. *Hardship situation*. McCormick poses the issue sharply:
. . . are those in a second canonically irregular marriage (and one that cannot be regularized and is not patient of an internal forum solution) necessarily to be excluded by policy from the reception of the eucharist, the necessity being the demand of indissolubility?[29]

This situation is the focus of recent moral-pastoral discussions. A scholarly consensus is emerging endorsing the admission of *some* such persons to the eucharist *under certain conditions*. The indissolubility of marriage and the reception of the eucharist are thus coming to be viewed as separate issues even though they have in the past been seen as inseparable.

The arguments for excluding individuals in the situation described by McCormick from the eucharist, always and everywhere are not entirely convincing. There seem to be sound reasons for a change in practice, though it is recognized that to admit everyone indiscriminately to the eucharist is irresponsible. The arguments customarily advanced to justify the exclusion from the eucharist of persons in a second marriage fall under three headings: 1) the state of sin argument; 2) the "imperfect symbol argument"; and 3) scandal.[30]

The first, the state of sin argument, takes the position that when one or both partners have been married, they are living in adultery unless they forego sexual relations while the first spouse is alive (so-called "brother-sister solution"). Otherwise, their state of serious sin makes them unworthy of the eucharist.

This position, however, frequently runs contrary to the profound convictions of couples whose second union is stable, characterized by mutual respect and affection and supported by Christian attitudes in other areas of life. Canonical irregularity does not necessarily mean subjective sinfulness. In fact, prudent pastoral practice encourages such couples to remain together and deepen their conjugal and familial life. It is confusing and even contradictory to say that these couples are living in a state of sin. Furthermore, the "brother-sister solution" erroneously isolates sexual intercourse from the totality of the marital relationship and fails to perceive the grave disorders for conjugal and parental relationships occasioned by such a practice. Furthermore, to view such situations categorically as a state of sin, in effect, makes divorce and remarriage unforgivable and restricts the church's power to pardon and reconcile. No such limits are placed on the church's power to bind and loose regarding other sins even though their effects are irreparable (e.g., murder).

The second, the imperfect symbol argument, says that reception of the eucharist by such individuals implies a contradiction. The syllogism is constructed as follows: Taking part in the eucharist is a profession of faith in Christ and a sign of full union with the church. Yet, such twice married individuals violate the Lord's call to indissolubility and, therefore, have compromised the ideals held up in the church's teaching on marriage. Hence, the symbolic meaning of the eucharist is seriously compromised by their receiving it.

Above and beyond the questionable assumption of a serious state of sin, this view wrongly implies that reception of the eucharist by one lacking full integration within the church always undermines her faith and discipline. It ignores the teaching that the eucharist is not only a sign of unity in Christ, but is at the same time a means to that unity. Present ecumenical policy which allows under certain circumstances, Christians not in communion with Rome, to participate in the eucharist, presupposes this twofold finality of the sacraments. Although full unity in Christ should precede common worship and sacramental sharing, the need for spiritual sustenance and the support of the Christian community sometimes commends it.[31] Post-conciliar ecumenical policy has attempted to realize these two basic values in a variety of situations.[32] As ecumenical relationships have deepened, the degree of unity between the various communions has become more evident and the dangers of such sharing less threatening. By the same token, the incomplete integration of such divorcees in a pilgrim church does not seem like an adequate reason to exclude them from the eucharist. The eucharist is not a reward for full conformity with a perfect and unalterable church order, but a means to union with Christ in the Christian community.

The third argument offered to exclude twice married persons from communion derives from the scandal that might ensue and the weakening of church discipline. It is said that a change in pastoral practice will lead people to conclude that the church no longer takes indissolubility seriously, that it is not wrong to marry after divorce, etc.

This objection is to be taken seriously. However, with proper education of Catholic communities on the complexities of the issue, the danger of scandal can be minimized. There is some evidence that attitudes seem to be changing;[33] that Catholics, without compromising the ideal of permanent marriage also recognize that the church has a pastoral responsibility toward the divorced. Religious educators, in particular, are called upon in their treatment of the sacraments of marriage, penance and eucharist to inform Catholics about the changes in pastoral practice and the reasons for it. And who is to judge what is the greater cause of scandal: individuals seeking the forgiveness and support of eucharistic communion; or the overly judgmental attitudes of the Catholic community towards divorcees, and the difficulty of getting a prompt hearing before diocesan marriage tribunals.

Reasons for a change in practice. There is an increasing consciousness of the eucharist's importance, strengthening us in our weakness and deepening our faith commitment to the Lord and to one another. Certainly, the eucharist is not the only way of deepening one's spiritual life. Perhaps we underestimate our other spiritual resources. Yet there is a particularly strong post-conciliar emphasis on eucharistic reception as an integral part of our liturgical life.[34]

Cautious admission of some divorcees to the eucharist would show the Lord's mercy towards those repenting their failure to live up to their gospel commitment. God does not demand the impossible of individuals striving to realize the fullness of Christ's self-giving, however imperfectly.

There is a conflict of values. On the one hand a couple should maintain their present union in view of conjugal and familial responsibilities. On the other hand one cannot simply prescind from the prior union even though now existentially defunct. However, it seems the greater good to offer access to the eucharist. This indicates the possibility of beginning again in the Lord and more authentically embodying Christian values.

Conditions for admission to the eucharist. Indiscriminate access to the eucharist for all such divorcees is irresponsible. The following conditions reflect a consensus on the prerequisites for such access:

a) The previous marriage is irretrievably broken down and reconciliation is absolutely impossible.

b) There is repentance for one's sinfulness in the breakdown of the first marriage and a willingness to discharge obligations to one's former spouse and children.

c) Obligations arising from the second union are being responsibly discharged and there is evidence of love, fidelity, openness to children, and a commitment to live together permanently in a Christian fashion.

d) There is a willingness to live the faith within the Christian community; and every effort is made to minimize scandal.

It is assumed that marital indissolubility is not to be called into question, and that the church is not asked to sanction divorce. The couple must make a conscientious decision and not expect official approval of the church authorities. Any community involvement, be it by clergy, marriage counsellors, or religious educators, can only be of the nature of private acceptance and support in arriving at a well-formed, responsible decision. There will always be tension within the church on this issue. Though the bishops may alleviate it by issuing precise guidelines for pastoral practice, the difficulty of reconciling the ideals of Christian marriage with the reality of divorce, cannot be readily overcome.[35] The strain within the family caused by the breakdown of marriage is felt in the community at large. I have spoken of "scholarly consensus" in this article to indicate an evolution of perspectives within the academic community. However, significant numbers of clergy and laity undoubtedly are acting according to the views expressed though perhaps not always as responsibly as desirable. Without official pastoral guidelines it will be difficult to educate the faithful widely on the complexities of the question, e.g., the ideal of marital indissolubility, the non-fulfillment of this ideal in a sinful world, the rights of innocent persons harmed by divorce, the sensitivities of believers who have striven to live up to their understanding of church teaching by not remarrying after divorce even at great personal cost, etc.[36] Only such education will minimize justified scandal and create a climate for a more supportive healing presence by the community to its divorced members.

So-called "internal forum solutions" are unique realities addressed to the particularities of a given pastoral situation. Each couple brings to the counselling situation their own distinct horizons and faith experience. It would be pastorally detrimental simply to state general guidelines for eucharistic reception with minimal awareness that they must be adapted to each situation. The community through its clergy and religious education personnel needs to invest time, energy and pastoral concern in enabling the divorced to experience God's healing mercy and gradually enhance their new relationship. Hopefully, they can be guided to deeper maturity in Christ and enabled to make conscientious decisions free from rationalization and self-deception.

Furthermore, there must be a serious effort to improve the efficiency of external forum procedures in view of providing an indispensable service to those seeking annulment or a dissolution of the bond. This should be a concern not simply of a few canonists but of the Catholic community at large. Perhaps the community's pastoral care for divorced couples can be better exemplified through another vehicle than the present tribunal system. The informed and prayerful collaboration of all members of the community is indispensable if the sacredness of marriage in Christ and the legitimate aspirations of divorced couples are to be realized in practice.

Notes

1. On tensions within the church because of divergent practice regarding divorced and remarried Catholics and the need of more enlightened pastoral care, See A. Coyle and D. Bonner, "What's Hap-

pening to Marriage for Life? in *The Church Under Tension*, New York: Catholic Book Publishing, Co., 1972, pp. 76-96; esp. 76-77; 91-96.

2. See. J. Bernardin, "Pastoral Planning: Focus on Marriage," *Origins* 3 (Oct. 25, 1973), 277.

3. See "Tribunal Statistics: January 1, 1974-December 31, 1974," in *Proceedings of the 37th Annual Convention of the Canon Law Society of America* (1975), 154-159.

4. See. W. Bassett, "Divorce and Remarriage," 20-36; 92-105.

5. On the presuppositions of church marriage law see W. Bassett, "Valid Contract or Valid Sacrament," in *The Bond of Marriage*. Notre Dame: University of Notre Dame Press, 1968, pp. 117-179; esp. 121-122. By jurisprudence in this article is meant the ongoing art of applying relevant law to specific conflict situations.

6. A particularly useful work for priests, religious and laity engaged in advising individuals on grounds for annulment is E. Hudson, *Handbook for Nullity Cases*, Ottawa: St. Paul University, 1976 (2nd edition). There are some particularly helpful tables on the grounds for nullity on pp. 44-56.

7. For a magisterial study of the evolution of jurisprudence through a detailed examination of selected cases see J. Noonan, *The Power to Dissolve: Lawyers and Marriage in the Courts of the Roman Curia*. Cambridge: Belknap Press, 1972.

8. See the *Pastoral Constitution on the Church in the Modern World*, Nos. 47-52. The following works are helpful for their insights on significant theological-canonical factors affecting post-conciliar jurisprudence. B. Haring, "Fostering the Nobility of Marriage and the Family," in *Commentary on the Documents of Vatican II*, H. Vorgrimler (ed.). E. Hudson, *Handbook for Nullity Cases*, pp. 1-28. W. LaDue, "Conjugal Love and the Juridical Structure of Christian Marriage," *The Jurist* 34 (1974), 36-67. G. Lesage, "The Consortium Vitae Coniugalis: Nature and Applications," *Studia Canonica* 6 (1972), 99-113. F. Morrisey, "Preparing Ourselves for the New Marriage Legislation," *The Jurist* 33 (1973), 343-357. P. Palmer, "Christian Marriage: Contract or Covenant?" *Theological Studies* 33 (1972), 627-665.

9. For a nuanced presentation of the more integral conciliar view of marriage see C. van der Poel, *God's Love in Human Language*. Pittsburgh: Duquesne University Press, 1969.

10. Developments in jurisprudence are not confined to psychic incapacity for marriage. For example, tribunals are taking more seriously the influence of cultural change and especially the acceptability of divorce on attitudes to *permanence* as a basic value. See D. Fellhauer, "The Exclusion of Indissolubility: Old Principles and New Jurisprudence," *Studia Canonica* 9 (1975), 105-134. B. Griffin, "Future Challenges in the Area of Marriage Legislation," in *Proceedings of the 35th Annual Convention of the Canon Law Society of America* (1973), 22-32; esp. 23-26; 28-29. Hudson, *Handbook for Nullity Cases*, pp. 93-94; L.

Wrenn, "A New Condition Limiting Marriage," *The Jurist* 34 (1974), 292-315.

11. Some representative articles on the evolution of jurisprudence especially in so-called psychic incapacity cases are the following: R. Brown, "The Canonical Problem of Mental Incompetency in Marriage," *Heythrop Journal* 18 (1969), 146-161. J. Dolciamore, "Annulments: Marriage Psychology," *Origins* 3 (Oct. 25, 1973), 278-279; 283-288. J. Finnegan, "Current Jurisprudence Concerning the Psychopathic Personality," *The Jurist* 27 (1967), 440-453" 440-453; "The Capacity to Marry," *The Jurist* 22 (1962), 391-411. J. Keating, "Sociopathic Personality," *The Jurist* 27 (1967), 429-438; "The Legal Test of Marital Insanity," *Studia Canonica* I (1967), 21-36. W. LaDue, "The Expanding Limits of Lack of Due Discretion Cases," *Concilium* 87 (1973), 61-71, F. Morrisey, "The Incapacity of Entering Into Marriage," *Studia Canonica* 8 (1974), 5-21. L. Wrenn, *Annulments*, pp. 21-26.

12. See F. Morrisey, *"Defective Consent—Matrimony—Towards New Church Law," Origins* 4 (Nov. 14, 1974), 321; 323-328; esp. 325-326. Some commentators on the proposed new law judge the restriction of the last type of incapacity to psycho-sexual anomalies as unduly narrow and favor reworking the norm to be more open to other possibilities, e.g., annulment of marriage of sociopaths. See "Report of a Special Committee of the Task Force of the Canon Law Society of America on the Marriage Canons of the Proposed *Schema Documenti Pontificii quo Disciplina Canonica de Sacramentis Recognoscitur,"* in *Proceedings of the 37th Annual Convention of the Canon Law Society of America* (1975), 205-217; esp. 212-213 commenting on proposed norm 297.

13. See J. Gerhartz, "Can the Church Dissolve Sacramental Marriage?" *Theology Digest* 21 (1973), 28-32.

14. See Bassett, "Divorce and Remarriage," pp. 22-29; esp. 25-26.

15. See Task Force Report, p. 211.

16. It should be noted that the use of the so-called "Pauline Privilege" is authorized by the local bishop. This involves the dissolution of a marriage of *two* non-baptized persons, one of whom becomes a convert. See canons 1120-1124; 1126-1127 of the Code.

17. See W. LaDue, "The Sacrament of Marriage," in *Proceedings of the 36th Annual Convention of the Canon Law Society of America* (1974), 25-35. Also Task Force Report, p. 209.

18. See J. Bernhard, "A propos de l'indissolubilite du mariage chretien," *Revue des sciences religieuses* 44 (1970), 49-62 and "A propos de l'hypothese concernant la notion de consummation existentielle du mariage," *Revue de Droit Canonique* 20 (1970), 184-192. These reflections are commented on by R. McCormick, "Notes on Moral Theology," *Theological Studies* 32 (1971), 110-112. See also J. Bernhard, "Reinterpretation (existentielle et dans la foi) de la legislation canonique concernant l'indissolubilite du mariage chretien," *Revue de Droit*

Canonique 21 (1971), 243-277. These reflections are commented on by R. McCormick, "Notes on Moral Theology," *Theological Studies* 33 (1972), 93-94.

19. R. McCormick, *Proceedings,* p. 27.

20. On the divorce-remarriage issue from a moral-pastoral standpoint, cf. references at the end of this article.

21. The Canon Law Society has fostered legal reform to implement more adequately the procedural rights of believers. See T. Green, "The American Procedural Norms—An Assessment," *Studia Canonica* 8 (1974), 317-347; esp. 318 giving the text of two resolutions on this point passed at the 1965 Canon Law Society Convention. See also J. Coriden (ed.), "Toward a Declaration of Christian Rights: A Position Paper," in *The Case for Freedom,* Washington: Corpus Publications, 1969, pp. 5-14; esp. 10-11.

22. For some pertinent literature on the effectiveness of tribunals see the following: G. Arella, "Case for the Marriage Courts," *America* 123 (1972), 316-320. W. Bassett, "Divorce and Remarriage," pp. 97-100. C. Curran, pp. 227-239. D. Burns, "Do the Marriage Courts Creak?" *Origins* 3 (1973), 293-296; 303-304. T. Green, pp. 338-341. S. Kelleher, "The Problem of the Intolerable Marriage," *America* 119 (1968), 178-182; *Divorce and Remarriage for Catholics?* Garden City: Doubleday, 1973. L. Orsy, "The Function of Ecclesial Decision: A Theological Evaluation of Marriage Tribunals," *Concilium* 87 (1973), 34-46. M. Reinhardt, "Updating the Marriage Tribunal," *America* 119 (1968) 429-432. L. Wrenn (ed.), *Divorce and Remarriage in the Catholic Church.* New York: Newman Press, 1973. This last work is a particularly valuable exploration of the pertinent issues.

23. See part one of Alternatives Report cited in references for a balanced appraisal of the relevant legal issues involved in the Christian's right to the eucharist and the possible denial of access to the sacraments.

24. L. Orsy, "Intolerable Marriage Situations: Conflict Between External and Internal Forum," *The Jurist* 30 (1970), 10. This is part of the special issue of *The Jurist,* cited in references at end of article.

25. For somewhat differing approaches to this issue see Curran arguing for a change in church teaching on indissolubility and McCormick, cited in references at end of article arguing for a rethinking of an overly juridical understanding of indissolubility but not calling for a change in church teaching.

26. The special procedures called the "American norms" offer greater options to petitioners in finding a tribunal competent to handle their case. Norm 7 reads as follows:

> The first competent Tribunal to which a party presents a petition has an obligation to accept or reject the petition. The competence of a Tribunal of first instance shall be determined by the residency of either party to the marriage, the place of the marriage or the

decree of the judge to whom the petition is presented that his Tribunal is better able to judge the case than any other Tribunal. In this last instance, however, the judge may not issue such a decree without first obtaining the consent of his own Ordinary and the consent of the petitioner's Ordinary and chief judge.

27. CTSA Report, p. 260.

28. See *Pastoral Constitution on the Church in the Modern World,* No. 26 and canon 1035 of the code on the basic right to marry. See canon 1069, 2 of the code on conditions for official recognition of freedom to remarry. Given the official role of the priest as a minister of the church, caution is called for regarding his involvement in celebrating the couple's exchange of marital consent (second union) particularly but not exclusively in view of potential civil law complications. See McCormick, 1972 *Theological Studies,* 97-98 commenting on some pertinent observations by Catoir.

29. McCormick, *Proceedings,* p. 27. By "internal forum solution" he means the conflict situation previously mentioned.

30. *Ibid.* For another fairly comprehensive treatment of this issue see Ryan, pp. 523-539. It should be emphasized that permissible reception of the eucharist does not mean that all is right with the second union and one can prescind entirely from the reality of the first marriage.

31. See *Decree on Ecumenism,* No. 8. Also *Decree on the Eastern Catholic Churches,* No. 26.

32. See J. Hotchkin, "Principles and Policies for Eucharistic Sharing Since Vatican II," *The Jurist* 30 (1970), 271-289.

33. It is reported that the percentage of people approving remarriage after divorce has risen from 52% to 73% in the past decade. See A. Greeley, *Catholic Schools in a Declining Church.* Kansas City: Sheed and Ward, 1976, p. 35.

34. See canons 682 and 853 of the code. Also the *Dogmatic Constitution on the Church,* No. 37 and the *Constitution on the Sacred Liturgy,* No. 14.

35. Apparently a special subcommittee of the NCCB Committee on Pastoral Research and Practice is working on some pertinent guidelines. However, little is known about the progress of this endeavor. For a brief discussion of events of a few years ago when there was some controversy over divorce-marriage procedures in Baton Rouge, Louisiana, cf. Curran, pp. 249-251. Also, "Divorce, Remarriage and the Catholic," *Origens* 2 (1972), 130; 135-136. Also "Krol on Good Conscience Procedures," *ibid.,* pp. 176-177.

36. See Coyle-Bonner, pp. 91-96.

The Religious Educator and the Children of Divorce

James J. Young, C.S.P.

I thought I had it all worked out, but tears started coming to my eyes when I heard the pastor speak on Holy Family Sunday about those divorced people who had sinned and were unfaithful to their vows. My two teenagers were sitting beside me. What did they think? I wanted to run out of the church.

In my parish I was told I couldn't serve as a lector any more, now that I'm divorced, because we're a family-oriented parish.

On Easter Sunday, Mass went longer than usual, and the young woman who was minding the pre-schoolers told them not to worry—their parents would be along in a few minutes to pick them up. My five-year-old cried all the way home, because she thought her daddy would be coming with me to pick her up. We haven't seen my husband since we separated six months ago.

These painful words were shared with me in recent months by divorced Catholics in several parts of the United States. They tell me that although we are now recognizing that divorce is an enormous pastoral problem in the American Catholic community, we need to develop much greater pastoral sensitivity on the parish

157

level. The religious educator can be a key person in bringing the special needs of separated and divorced parishioners to the attention of the local community, and can be of great assistance to parents and children working through this difficult adjustment. I have seen priests, sisters and lay religious educators devise some practical, compassionate responses to parents and children experiencing marital breakdown. I would like to share some of these creative approaches with you and offer some personal observations drawn from some five years of pastoral work with separated and divorced Catholics.

The Scope of the Problem

There has been no precise measurement of the number of separated and divorced Catholics in the U.S. In order to get an estimate we have to extrapolate from U.S. Census Bureau statistics. As best we can estimate, there are at least six million divorced Catholics in the country of whom at least half have remarried. Last year in the U.S., there were one million marriages that ended in divorce. We can safely estimate that at least a quarter of them were Catholic marriages, and that at least 400,000 Catholic children began to live in single-parent homes. Of all Americans divorcing, it is estimated that 80% will remarry; there is no evidence that Catholics any longer choose not to remarry because of the church's prohibition of second marriages, unless a first marriage has been annulled. Canon lawyers estimate that between 15,000 to 20,000 Catholic marriages were annulled in the country last year, and even though this may be an impressive figure compared to the number granted ten years ago, it means that about 2% of all American divorced Catholics have been helped by tribunals. The implications of all this for the average American parish is that obviously every year there are more and more divorced Catholics in the pews, and more and more of their children in parish religious education programs. I heard one pastor estimate recently that in the surrounding parishes of a large urban area, as many as a quarter to a third of the children came from single-parent families or were living with remarried parents. It is my belief that every American Catholic family has experienced divorce among its immediate members.

What Message Does the Parish Send Out to Divorced Catholics?

Most divorced Catholics tell me that the basic message they receive from their parish is that they don't exist. Some can detail horror stories of pastors who told them to reconcile or they might lose their souls, or stories of being removed from the parish council after a divorce. One man was told that his parish was not for divorced people, and that he should go to a parish in another part of the city where they were interested in the divorced. These stories may not be typical, but there are many similar messages that go out to divorced Catholics from many of our parishes which are equally injurious. A parish staff and parish council might ask itself: Is there ever a mention from the pulpit of the church's concern for the separated and divorced? Does "family" when used in parish announcements always mean two parents and children? Is there notice in the bulletin of any special groups or services for the separated and divorced? Has any attempt been made to educate the parish about the special concerns of the separated and divorced?

Several years ago I was invited by the parish staff at Our Lady, Star of the Sea Parish in Marblehead, Massachusetts to meet with them to discuss the special needs of their divorced parishioners. The priests and the two sisters and laypersons on the staff had already met many divorced people in their ordinary pastoral rounds; they were sure that there were many more whom they had not met in this suburban Boston community. The whole parish team discussed at length their own pastoral approaches to the divorced, and found themselves in general agreement about the need to foster reconciliation for these men and women who felt alienated from the church. A Sunday was chosen when the priests preached at all the masses a simple homily about the parish's concern for those of its members who might be experiencing marital breakdown; they wanted them to feel most welcome at Star of the Sea. The general response of the people was enthusiastic; many remarked that they had never heard the word "divorce" mentioned in church before, and they were pleased to know that their parish was really concerned. It was announced that I would be speaking at the parish center the following Thursday night, and that my talk would provide an opportunity for parishioners to learn more about the current discussion in the church about divorce and remarriage. About 70 people came out to the talk that following Thursday, and after my talk, when the layman who was responsible for adult education, asked how many present would be interested in forming a support group, over two dozen volunteered. The first meeting of the support group was held two weeks later, and has been meeting ever since. Now the parish bulletin of Star of the Sea lists the Divorced Catholics Group as one of its regular parish organizations. I have seen this process repeated in another dozen parishes.

Separated and divorced Catholics say they find it most helpful knowing that their parish not only knows that they exist, but that it takes them into serious account. Parish staffs, including especially secretarial staff who often talk to people on the phone, should be included in a consciousness-raising process so that any inadvertent preaching or practice which might alienate the divorced can be checked. I would further suggest that this consultation should at some point include some divorced parishioners to give their evaluation of the parish's present posture. I am convinced that this evaluation of the basic parish structure and the messages it sends forth must precede any attempt by a religious educator to build in more sensitivity to the children of divorce. If the parish in its life is exerting a negative influence on the lives of the divorced and their children, the religious educator's role will be enormously complicated.

When a homily on divorce is given at the Sunday liturgy, I think it should not be a theoretical talk on contemporary marriage breakdown or a presentation of changing annulment procedures. Rather the priests or deacons might suggest that those going through divorce remain parishioners in good standing, and they should call upon fellow parishioners to surround them with love and support during this difficult time. Some practical suggestions might be offered parishioners about dropping by or baby-sitting or helping with meals for the new single parent. So often the newly separated experience discomfort or avoidance from neighbors and friends at this difficult time.

Such concern need in no way imply that the parish leaders are backing off the church's traditional preaching of the Lord's call to permanence and fidelity in Christian marriage. This message can and must be presented in season and out, without in any way implying fault or blame on those who have not realized it in their marriages. We need here the kind of balance that we find in John's Gospel, where the Lord himself, who preached such a powerful ideal of lasting marriage, was able to reveal himself so warmly to the five-times married woman at Jacob's well. In revealing compassion and concern for those of its parishioners who suffer marital breakdown, the parish can do a great service to those whose marriages are intact, bringing them into real contact with the contemporary struggle to make real the call of the Lord. If we believe that the hunger for permanent and lasting marriage has been planted in every human heart by God himself in the act of creation, we Christians have nothing to fear by reaching out to the divorced. In the past five years I have never met a divorced Catholic who did not accept the gospel ideal, and who did not wish that he or she had been able to achieve it in his or her own marriage.

Sensitizing the Parish Religious Education Faculty

The parish director of religious education should take time to sensitize the faculty to the special needs of the children of divorce. Such a meeting might well include some divorced parents to share their special concerns about the parish program. The coordinator should devise some way during registration to find out the family status of children in the program; teachers should be apprised in advance if children in the class come from a family in which there has been a recent parental separation or if the child lives with a single parent.

Teachers with small children should be careful that when family examples are used in class, the model is not always that of an intact family. Examples of thoughtful children who generously help their single parent or who assume new responsibility for other siblings because of parental divorce might be used as well. Sometimes first communion programs which have a family receive together should be evaluated to see if single parents are comfortable with the way it is done. Those teachers who treat marriage, especially on the secondary school level should be especially sensitive to the way marital breakdown is presented. Is divorce presented as a sin? Is the implication that a child's parents are sinners? I recall a child who said to her mother, "Mommy, did you and daddy commit a sin in getting divorced? Our teacher said that Elizabeth Taylor did."

Teachers might well in their presentations honor those widows, widowers and divorced people, who with considerable Christian dedication, keep their broken families together. When home projects are assigned to children, the teacher should be especially careful that they do not explicitly call for both parents to participate. Suggested family prayer services should not call for the father of the family to preside, but might suggest that roles be divided up among all participating.

Some Special Issues Facing the Children of Divorce

Dr. J. Louise Despert, child psychiatrist and author of the highly-respected *Children of Divorce,* found that among all the troubled children she had treated or was consulted about, there were proportionately far fewer children of divorce than are found in the general population. "It is not divorce, but the emotional situation in the home, with or without divorce, that is the determining factor in the child's adjustment. A child is very disturbed when the relationship between his parents is very disturbed. Divorce in these circumstances is not automatically a destructive experience. It may also be a cleansing and healing one, for the child as well as the parents. Divorce is not the costliest experience for a child. Unhappy marriage without divorce. . .can be far more destructive."

Dr. Robert Weiss, author of *Marital Separation,* and an expert on the effect of divorce on children, says that although most children regain their balance rapidly despite the initial upset of parental separation, some do have continuing trouble. Among younger children one sign that things are not going well is regression to earlier behavior such as temper tantrums in the classroom. The teacher should deal directly with bad behavior by telling the child *privately* that even though he or she may be unhappy, disturbing the class or fighting will be of no help. The peer group of the classroom may be an important support for the child, and it is crucial that he or she feels welcome at this time. Some children's books about divorce or examples of children from divorced families might be used in the class presentation and could be especially helpful to this child.

Mel Krantzler, author of *Creative Divorce*, observes that school is one of the most common areas in which a young child will express his/her anxiety and fears. It is not unusual for good students to get failing grades under the initial impact of their parents' divorce. Such deterioration in schoolwork may reflect the child's anxiety over his/her disturbed family relationship, or his/her desire to punish him/herself for "causing" the divorce. It may also result from an unrecognized urge to "get even" with the parents for having separated by refusing to "perform" in endeavors that he/she knows are important to them such as Sunday school. Sometimes a child thinks, unconsciously, that by making things hot for his/her parents he/she can bring about their reconciliation.

Adolescents may pose some special problems for the religious educator. Weiss insists that it is normal for a teenager to test limits and get into some scrapes, so one should not be unduly alarmed by what may be typical teenage behavior on the part of the adolescent child of recently divorced parents. Teachers again should react directly and plainly to unacceptable behavior here. It is important not to be too permissive out of a false sense of compassion, because the teenager needs to belong to the group and be accepted.

Wallterstein and Kelly in their study of the effects of parental divorce observed in the teenagers they studied precipitous de-idealization of parents, anxiety about future marriage, and loyalty conflicts. "The family disruption by virtue of the peculiar interplay between the divorcing adults and the interplay between each of the parents and the adolescent poses a very specific hazard to the normal process of progressive detachment of the primary love objects. As such it carries the potential for severely overburdening the adolescent ego in it maturational, time-appointed tasks." The ideal parent, now divorced, becomes all too quickly the fallen idol. The parents now appear to be inadequate and ineffective role models. The teenager is presented with a close-up picture of adult failure and betrayal. The fearful prospect for the teenager is—If I cannot identify with this model, who am I? On top of this the fundamental continuity of family life is ruptured and the ground is quite literally sometimes removed from beneath the child's feet.

The parents' failure may make the teenager feel betrayed and he/she may respond with overt rage and hostility, which are only defensive masks to cover a deep sadness over loss. Yet some adolescents seem to react very cooly at this time and ask parents why they waited so long to end their unhappy marriage. If the child becomes a pawn, caught in warfare between the parents, this may induce severe conflict. The anger at being forced into this plight and the guilt at siding with one parent at the expense of the other, or neither to avoid taking sides, may plunge the adolescent into profound depression. The inner conflict provoked by this situation may cause a rupture in the process of self-definition and leave the young person in the grip of severe doubt about his/her ability to achieve meaningful relationships. Such a teenager may state baldly in class, "I'm never going to marry." For this child marriage may never have been seen as a warm, loving, caring reality; rather it has been full of conflict, alienation and ultimate breakdown. This highlights the importance of the teacher presenting a balanced outlook on marriage. The newer approaches which see marriage as an ongoing process of growth, developing commitment and rewarding struggle may be most helpful to this young person. The adolescent needs to be reminded that one's future is not completely determined by one's past, and most people have the capacity to develop those skills necessary to form a lasting, marital relationship.

Nonetheless, there is evidence that divorce patterns seem to repeat themselves in some families, and when the children of divorce think of marriage, they present a special responsibility for the church to provide more careful and effective marriage preparation.

The child of recently separated parents may voice guilt over the parents' divorce. A priest friend of mine, who has worked extensively with adolescents, Basil DePinto, O.S.B., says that the guilt a child feels allows him/her to feel in some way responsible, and therefore in control of the events he/she is undergoing. Without this guilt feeling he/she may be victimized by the terror of having no influence whatever on the course of events swirling about him/her. The guilt may be the most effective and healthy way for him/her to survive. These adaptive and defensive maneuvers must be respected during the period when they protect the child in the throes of severe adjustment from feelings of overwhelming fear.

Including Divorce in the Class Content

In secondary level classes about marriage, divorce should certainly be treated. It is important to deal realistically with the times in which we live, and the teenagers are well aware of the fact of broken marriages all around them. Too often we have analyzed the failure of marriage, almost entirely in terms of moral failure on the part of the husband and wife. We speak of "falling out of love," "not working hard enough at marriage," and "being unfaithful to their vows." The Orthodox have looked at divorce as a sign of the forces of evil at work in the world wounding the kingdom sign which is the marriage covenant. They see in marital breakdown an interaction of societal forces and personal weakness of one or both partners. This perspective helps us attend more seriously to the contemporary climate which makes lasting marriage difficult. We must take into consideration such damaging socio-economic forces as poverty, unemployment, poor housing, poor education, poor physical and emotional health, as well as such cultural factors as early marriage, rootlessness, consumerism and the worship of material success. The contemporary attempt to separate human sexuality from loving commitment and widespread doubt about the possibility of permanent relationships have a sad effect. These insights can help students see the partners of a broken marriage as victims of rapidly changing social conditions.

Furthermore, we should not be content with painting a bleak portrait of contemporary marriage, but should attend to the many positive features of the satisfying marriages we see around us. We see an enhanced role for women in the partnership of marriage, a more tender and human role for men, more wholesome views of sexuality in marriage, a deepening contemporary marriage spirituality, and greater social awareness of the responsibility of each family to other families in the society, especially those in need. The contemporary phenomenon of divorce can be seen as part of a larger phenomenon of "rising expectations in marriage:" never before have so many men and women looked for so much from their marital relationships, and never before have so many men and women invested so much in making their marriages work. The church can be a great resource in helping young people confront the "why's" of contemporary divorce, while helping them get realistically into touch with the demands of contemporary marriage.

We need to prepare them for marriage by having them appreciate the need for their own personal development as well as a realistic appraisal of the social pressures they will confront when they marry. They need to appreciate the power of our traditional Christian values of permanence and fidelity and the role of Christian faith and commitment in helping men and women achieve the lasting love they seek. If such education encourages young people to delay marriage or consider remaining single it may well have succeeded.

A Special Opportunity for the Teacher

Many times children in distress over separation and divorce may seek out a trusted adult to share their problems, and this person might well turn out to be a religious education teacher. The child may need a responsible third party he or she can talk to and share things with, even things he or she would be afraid to share with parents. Parents who are divorcing are involved necessarily in their own emotional upset, and they usually have little energy left to spare during the divorce crisis to devote to the needs of their children. If parenting patterns have not been strong prior to the breakup, this period may be all the tougher for the children.

It is important for the teacher to see him/herself as a caring adult, but not as a therapist. The child most likely will not be looking for interpretation and analysis, but more for acceptance and affirmation. The teacher should not underestimate the value of friendship and sensitive listening at this time. Raymond and Robin Yerkes, a child psychiatrist and his counsellor wife, write that many adolescents search out a trusted adult, other than a parent, to fulfill many parental roles. This helps the teenager develop a capacity to relate to others older than him/herself, but without the strong feelings associated with parents. From this adult the adolescent can accept advice that might not be accepted from parents, and the adult may offer a variety of alternatives for the modeling of roles and the development of positive ideals — suggestions that might not be available in the parental home.

If the teacher feels inadequate to relate to a child in this transition and is puzzled by particular behavior, it would be wise for the teacher to check things out with an experienced child counselor.

A therapist friend once remarked that the slender sapling, because it is so young and flexible, can often successfully withstand the raging storm around it. Generally, we need not be pessimistic about the potential for the children of divorce to cope with the pressures they face. Many observers find that these children can learn to mature more satisfactorily and more deeply than would be the case if they had not gone through this particular trauma. Robert Weiss remarks that "most children seem to recover quickly from their initial upset. Within three or four months they are once again giving their energies to their own concerns. Indeed, some parents have said that their children recovered more rapidly than they did themselves."

In conclusion, the religious educator can help the children of divorce by being attentive to the special stress the child is working through, while continuing to treat the child outwardly with the same even-handed attention the other children get. Most of all, these children need space, a sense of belonging in the peer group, and ordinary approval, so that he or she can have room to handle his or her own life pressures privately. If as often happens, a child seeks out a trusted teacher to share pain or seek advice, the teacher can serve the child well by listening, encouraging him or her to rely on his or her own strengths, and reminding him or her that this shock will pass. It is important that such conversations always be kept confidential; a teacher should never consult a parent without the child's permission.

The young person, especially the adolescent, can be helped to deal with such common issues as guilt, de-idealization of parents, and fear of future marriage by realistic education and open peer discussion. The religious education class may be a fine Place to present counter messages that affirm individual capacities to shape one's future and to suggest the kind of personal development necessary for happy marriage.

The religious educator will be helped enormously if the parish or the diocese has some local support group to help parents move successfully through the separation transition. The more competently the parent-at-home handles this adjustment, the easier it will be on the children. If the parish can find ways in its visible life, to show loving concern for the separated and divorced, the whole family will be helped.

Pastoral Work among the Divorced and Invalidly Married

Bernard Häring

Translated by Mark Hellebone

Pastoral work in this connection should not be thought of in the narrow sense of restoring the affected parties to the sacraments. Primary is the practice of the life of faith and the anchoring of trust in God, and Christian love. It is not only a question of regularizing a marriage but also of helping the couple concerned to love one another in a way that brings them nearer to God. They can themselves become examples of a right attitude to marriage by humbly confessing their faults to their friends, and by urging others not to resort to divorce, or at least not to remarry should they do so. By bringing up their children well, they can be a good example to others. They can play their part in the apostolate. By resolutely refusing to discriminate, those engaged in pastoral work will encourage others in the Church community to behave similarly towards the couples concerned.

I make these initial comments in order to make it clear from the outset that nothing in this article should be taken as an attempt to restrict the scope of this type of pastoral work to mere sacramentalism. Naturally enough, believing that the Church is the sacrament of reconciliation whose centre is the Eucharist, the question of readmitting the partners of such marriages to the sacraments will not be ignored. One often hears it said that even when divorced couples who have remarried outside the Church are for ever excluded from the sacraments, they can for their comfort be reminded of these words of the Lord: "he who comes to me I will not cast out." (John 6. 37). But is that really good enough? Isn't it an unacceptable restriction of the Church's sacramentality? Through the Church, Christ wants to make his redemptive love sacramentally visible, in the spirit of Leo the Great's comment: *"Quod redemptoris nostri conspicuum fuit in sacramenta transivit"*.[1] The Church, surely, should be at least as visibly welcoming as Christ to sinners who do penance and sincerely seek God's will? And could such a welcome exclude the "visible signs of grace"?

I

PASTORAL QUESTIONS IN A NEW CONTEXT

Pastoral attitudes should respond to the needs of the time and to man's own awareness of himself. A standard that proved fruitful in one culture could be damaging in another. Consider, for example, the legal and pastoral discrimination against unmarried mothers and illegitimate children. Although this was never a typically Christian attitude, it could feature as one of the defences against pre-marital and extra-marital sex. But the same sort of attitude today would simply strengthen the massive trend towards the systematic use of contraceptives and abortion.

The situation is similar with regard to the permanent exclusion of invalidly married people from the sacraments. This is a measure that needs to be seen against the prevailing social background and its particular circumstances, for it was this social milieu, its economic and social structure, that guaranteed marital stability, and in which the separated partners were received back into their own families. In addition, there was a substantial group of unmarried people, peasants and unskilled workers, for whom marriage was made impossible by hopeless economic circumstances. All this was considered normal. Those who nevertheless married outside the Church knew themselves to be public sinners and so considered it proper that they should be excluded from the sacraments.

But nowadays the victims of broken marriages are in a much more painful position. They are legion and rootless. And as industrialization has made marriage possible for everyone, it is seen as one of the most important basic human rights. Alone and isolated, separated couples not only feel discriminated against, but frequently, and in spite of the best of intentions, fall victim to the grave temptations that arise from the worlds of work and leisure, and the widespread depersonalization of sex. Most of those whose marriages break up find it existentially impossible to grasp that for the sake of the Kingdom of Heaven they are expected to accept in courage and patience a future without marriage. They think it would be better to marry again than to endanger the marriages and moral lives of others.

In consequence of all this, and of contemporary ecumenism, the theology of marriage is also undergoing unrest. As the matter is hardly academic, the debate has to take place in public. The inadequacies of canon law's statements on marriage are widely discussed. And in addition there is the widespread growth of a critical attitude towards all structures that appear to confine or restrict life and happiness. It is in this atmosphere that people's consciences form and in which they subsequently make their conscientious decisions.

Often, even the most pious of pastoral workers is convinced that the partners to a marriage contracted outside the Church could not separate without doing themselves and their children real harm. When he sees the female partner of a broken marriage living in harmony with another man, and notes also that a firm relationship is developing between them, he is bound to heave a sigh of relief at this choice of a "lesser evil" when he recalls that this same woman had previously been driven to the verge of prostitution and promiscuity.

II

TOWARDS PASTORAL SOLUTIONS

I have no illusions with regard to our unequivocal doctrinal solutions to these tricky problems. Our theological discussions of these questions must start from the standpoint of current Catholic teaching, though we must try to set in motion a reform of ecclesiastical legal thinking. Pastoral solutions should make every possible use of the possibilities that already exist.

In my opinion, well-intentioned Christians who are truly

sorry for their sins and who have to the best of their ability maintained order in their lives, should not only be released from the bans of excommunication but should also be readmitted to the sacraments.[2] The readmission should be a demonstration of the truth that "God does not ask the impossible but through his commandments admonishes us to do what we are able to do, and for the rest, to pray".[3] This Augustinian principle, made more explicit by the Council of Trent, should be interpreted in context. Augustine is speaking of the man who welcomed the merciful Samaritan to his inn, and who, though already saved, still has much to learn.

The question of readmitting someone to communion poses more troublesome pastoral problems than readmission to the sacraments. In this connection ecclesiastical pluralism is necessary. There will be Eastern Christians brought up in an awareness of God's mercy who will simply not understand why people who are now living to the best of their ability and who have showed sorrow for past sins should be excluded from full participation in the Eucharist. Whereas in local communities of a more traditional stamp or of a more inbred cultural outlook such public forgiveness could give rise to scandal. In the case of public admission to communion, we are concerned with a process devolving upon episcopal authority, the facts of the case are known, and a fresh start is being made. But the situation is quite different when the partners of invalid marriages receive communion at times and places when and where their marital situation is unknown or where at least it is assumed that all is well. Those concerned should use their discretion. When there is public talk in the parish this can be a good opportunity for the parish priest to set the record straight in public.

But whatever the pastoral solution, we must be clear that both the theological discussion concerning the practice in the Eastern and Reformed Churches, and the search for merciful solutions in special cases, are doomed to failure unless the Church as a whole educates for fidelity through intelligent education for marriage, marriage guidance and constant reminders of the importance of forgiveness.

III
THE DIFFERENT PERSONAL SITUATIONS

The admission to the sacraments of divorced people who have not remarried presents no particular problems. But such people do need a lot of help if they are to make the best of their new position, and above all to find it in them to forgive and, if possible and desirable, achieve a reconciliation with a view to the resumption of married life.

Fro the invalidly married who continue to live together, readmission to the sacraments should not be made quite so straightforward. First, we should differentiate between the various possible situations:

1. In cases where it is canonically possible to regulate a union (for example, invalidly contracted mixed marriages, or remarriage after a first marriage that from the point of view of canon law was very probably invalid) there must be a desire to regulate matters in accordance with canon law. The tendency to minimize this aspect should not be encouraged. But if the legal process is made unreasonably difficult, or is unreasonably prolonged, then in my view it is not necessary to delay absolution until every legal hurdle has been overcome. The couple will often become convinced that in spite of outstanding legal complications they are, before God, properly married. Some couples, on the other hand, will feel themselves bound in conscience not to live as man and wife until the juridical aspects are settled once and for all. In every case there should be respect fo conscience and a scrupulous avoidance of crude attempts to encourage an attitude or recommend a way of life that to this or that couple simply doesn't make sense.

2. In the many cases that cannot be resolved *in forum externum*, further important distinctions should be observed:

(*a*) It sometimes happens that those living a canonically invalid marriage are, for good reasons, convinced that their first marriage was not a proper one but they are unable to prove this conclusively in terms that will satisfy modern legal requirements. Significant in this connection are those cases in which a valid marriage was not consummated but dispensation was withheld on account of inadequate evidence. In so far as the subsequent marriage is a happy one, and the children well cared for, the couple will be firmly convinced that God has blessed their marriage. In these cases there should be no hesitation in giving sacramental absolution. If at the same time limitations are placed on the public reception of communion it should be made clear that this is not discrimination but merely the expression of necessary concern for the peace of the community and the avoidance of scandal.

(b) There may be other cases in which, subjectively, the partners are convinced that their second marriage is blessed by God, whereas the objective reasons supporting their claim that the first marriage was invalid are in some way inadequate or doubtful. Should one withhold absolution if in all other respects the disposition of the partners is good? I believe that there are certainly cases where the giving of absolution is indicated: for instance, when nothing good but quite possibly something harmful might result from an attempt to disturb their conviction.

Consider, for instance, those nominal Christians whom statistics ascribe to a Church or sect, who once contracted a marriage valid in the eyes of canon law but who then discovered it to be a grievous mismatch. Subsequently, and now happily remarried, they ask to join the Catholic Church. Should they be received in good faith, on condition that a return to their first partner is no longer possible?[4] It seems to me that the answer is "yes". I cannot see that this situation is much different from that of Catholics, once mere nominal Christians, who, now married a second time, now truly accept the faith. Provided the rightful demands of a third party for justice, or the good of the community as a whole, do not require it, it is my view that the couple's peace of conscience should not be disturbed and that absolution should not be made conditional upon the fulfilment of subjectively impossible conditions. Living together as "brother and sister" should only be required of a couple when this is anyway what their consciences recommend.

3. Whereas in the case just mentioned the couple's *bona fides* testifies to their belief that their present marriage is a true

one in the eyes of God, this is in some cases accompanied by the painful awareness that they should not have remarried and that their second marriage is not a true one, in spite of its exemplary nature. Nevertheless, they are genuinely convinced that out of responsibility for one another and their children they must live together. They look back on their past with deep sorrow and now try their best to live God's will as they understand it. Not infrequently, such people demonstrate their good faith by admitting their guilt in front of their friends and by advising others about to take a similar step to hold back.

The value of a partner's *bona fides* will depend on whether he is the guilty or the innocent party, and if guilty, whether or not he is conscious of and contrite about his part in the collapse of the first marriage. But guilty or innocent, a precondition is the conviction that a reconciliation cannot be achieved. The distinction between innocent and guilty party is of theological importance in the debate with the Orthodox Churches and their old tradition. Where it is a question of sacramentally proclaiming God's mercy and not of sanctioning a second marriage, the important consideration is an acceptable disposition, by which we understand sorrow for past sins and an earnest resolve to do God's will in the future. In cases where the collapse of a first marriage caused scandal, then extra care must be taken to avoid the giving of further scandal when determining the circumstances in which, now remarried, one or other of the former partners is admitted to communion among people who are aware of their earlier history.

IV
An Important Distinction

To what extent does the pastoral practice I have recommended imply theologically that the Church can dissolve valid and consummated marriages and can authorize remarriage? I don't think it does. In other words, the pastoral solution suggested does not require any change in the Church's teaching. The Church is able to, and in my view should, bless a second but stable marriage rather than a doubtfully valid and hopelessly dead former marriage.[5] In this spirit, the way towards proper legal solutions seems to be open, at least for those who have justified doubts about the validity of their broken marriage. In this type of situation patronizing recommendations that do nothing for those concerned should be avoided. But the pastoral solutions I have suggested do not presuppose these legal reforms, desirable though they may be. I have not recommended that a priest be permitted to allow divorced people to remarry or that he should be able to declare a second marriage legally valid. Given the doctrinal and legal situation, both are unthinkable. My concern is for the credible proclamation of the divine mercy for contrite sinners who in a legally and ecclesiastically regrettable situation are prepared to do the best they can and who sincerely seek God's will. Where there is the honest conviction that doing their best includes ending their present relationship, or an attempt to live as brother and sister, then this is what must happen. But it would be unrealistic to maintain that this is possible or desirable in every case.

In what way is living together in this way, without sacramental recognition of their marriage, an aid to salvation? This is a theological question that can only be answered within the framework of the marriage debate as a whole. But from the purely pastoral viewpoint we can and must help those who live together in such unions to love one another with that respectful, patient and increasingly selfless love that will also give them a clearer idea of the love of God, and that will assist them to practise the Christian life as a whole.

Notes

1. Leo the Great, *Sermo 72, P.L.*, 54, 398.
2. Cf. J. G. Gerhartz, "Exkommuniziert—ein Leben lang?", in *Signum*, 41 (1969), pp. 44-50.
3. Augustine, *De natura et gratia*, c. 43, 50, CSEL, 60, 270; cf. Denz.-Schön., *Ench. Symb.*, n. 1536-9.
4. This point becomes of yet greater importance if one hopes for the reunion of Christendom. Is it conceivable that when union comes the Catholic Church will subject to process of law all Orthodox and Reformed Christians who though happily married now have a broken

marriage behind them and require them to prove either that the first marriage was invalid, or, if they cannot provide such proof, to separate?

5. This inclination towards the *favor juris* was also suggested in the annexe on marriage put forward during the third session of Vatican II at the time when Schema 13 was being debated.

Healing and Hope:
Pastoral Reflections on the
Ministry to Divorced Catholics

John Heagle

I think of myself as a man of hope. This is not the same as saying that I have an optimistic attitude toward life. Optimism can be as blind to pain as it is confident of progress. The hope to which I cling is rooted in the commitment of faith. It is more than a cheerful frame of mind. It is grounded in the experience of sharing brokenness—my own, and that of others—in the search for God's healing.

In the first letter of Peter the followers of Jesus are challenged to give reasons for the hope that lies within them (cf. I Pet. 3:15). As one engaged in pastoral ministry, I believe that this challenge is as important for us today as it was for the early Church. In an age of upheaval it is not always easy to find the reasons for our hope, let alone express them in words. There are times when the search for hope is the only act of trust that we can make. Nevertheless, we continue to carry within us the task of creating a vision for our lives and for the future.

In the reflections which follow, I want to share some of the reasons for the hope that is within me. Specifically, I want to focus on the emerging ministry of separated, divorced, and remarried Catholics as a significant sign of healing and renewal in the contemporary Church. I write from the perspective of pastoral ministry rather than that of systematic theology. I want to respond to the men and women who have experienced the pain of broken relationships. I want to listen sensitively to the voices of those who seek to love again. I also want to celebrate the signs of healing which I see among those who struggle with personal failure. The Spirit is stirring among the brokenhearted. In today's Church they are the reasons God gives us for hope.

The Crisis of Hope

Recently, a young woman came to my office to talk about her broken marriage. She sat down and immediately burst into tears. After a few painful moments she began to share her story.

"Last month I went to see a priest," she said. "My life was falling apart and I needed to know that someone cared. But he told me that since I am divorced he could not help me. He told me that it is my problem now because I have chosen to separate myself from the Church."

She paused, looked at me through tear-stained eyes, and added, "I always thought that if everything else fell apart in my life, I could turn to the Church for support. Now, I'm not so sure."

This young divorcée put into words the feelings of many people in the Church. Many other Catholics are experiencing similar doubts. They are no longer sure about the Church or what they believe. In the fifteen years since the Second Vatican Council, much of the initial enthusiasm for the renewal has faded. Many traditional Catholics are afraid that the Council fathers betrayed the essential elements of faith in an effort to update the Church. They do not view the Council as a "second spring" or as a New Pentecost. They see it as an autumn. They point to the decline in belief and moral practice as evidence for their fears.

On the other hand, there are many progressive Catholics who are also disillusioned. They are convinced that the changes in the Church were too little and too late. As a result, many of them have either withdrawn from the Church or explored alternate forms of human meaning.

Despite the swirl of confusion and the ideological conflict, the majority of Catholics have continued to walk toward the future. But they, too, are less secure about the meaning and implications of their faith.

Most of all, the young woman who came to my office ex-pressed the feelings of thousands of separated, divorced and remarried Catholics who live somewhere at the periphery of the Church's life. She found words for their experience of rejection and alienation. Many of the divorced lose contact with the Church at the time that their marriages fall apart. Others continue to identify themselves with the Church, even though many in the Christian community look upon them as failures.

What can we learn from the crisis of confidence which came in the wake of the Second Vatican Council? What can the alienated and brokenhearted reveal to us about authentic renewal? What do the separated, divorced, and remarried Catho-lics tell us about healing and hope?

The Search for Healing

Disillusionment can become the first step toward hope. This is the first thing we can learn from those who have experienced the pain of broken marriages. When our human expectations are not realized, we are challenged to purify our vision and open our lives to new directions of growth. The story of salvation con-tinues to unfold in the lives of struggling people who, like Abraham, cling to life by "hoping against hope." (Rm. 4:18-20).

The Emmaus story is a striking example of the way in which God stretches our faith beyond our brokenness. Cleopas and his companion walked the Emmaus road with heavy hearts. They carried their fallen expectations with them. Only later, when they were able to look back on their journey, did they realize that their vision was too narrow and their commitment too shallow. Only later did they remember that their hearts were burning when Jesus spoke to them of the necessity of suffering as the pathway to life. At the edge of despair they broke bread with a stranger and found life. In the broken bread they recognized their own frag-mented lives. They looked beyond their brokenness into the eyes of the Lord. In an instant it all became clear. They understood that the power which destroyed their illusions was also the pres-ence which healed their lives.

The Emmaus story is a parable for our times. It captures the journey which every divorced person must make from disillusionment to hope. It is also a description of the contemporary Church. In the creative, but painful years since the Council we have walked far enough and long enough to recognize some of our own illusions. We have learned much about ourselves and our humanity. We have also learned something about the way in which the Spirit renews the Church. We understand more clearly now that we cannot renew the Church simply by changing the structures of authority or the style of leadership. We cannot renew the Church simply because we revise the forms of worship or return to the vernacular language. However important the Council documents are, they can do no more than create a framework within which the Church is called to respond to the future. Renewal is more than a decree, more than a revised rite, more than a proclamation of change. Renewal begins in the recognition of our shared brokenness before God and our need for one another. It moves toward an inward experience of conversion. It is an act of reaching out for healing and wholeness.

Beneath the conflict and upheaval of the last several years, this quiet pattern of conversion and growth has been unfolding in the lives of people. It is significant that the most authentic signs of renewal can be found among those who appear to be the most alienated and disillusioned. The emergence of the divorced Catholic ministry has been a spontaneous flowering of the Spirit of healing. It is the closest thing to a grassroots movement in the Church today.

In recent years divorced Catholics have been able to look toward the Church with renewed confidence. They have heard the compassion of the Gospel as it was articulated in the Pastoral Constitution on the Role of the Church in the Modern World. They have found encouragement in the appearance of parish support groups and the growth of the North American Conference of Separated and Divorced Catholics. They have witnessed the courageous leadership of some American bishops. They have participated in the breakthroughs which occurred at the Call to Action Conference in 1976. They have been encouraged by the recent revocation of the law of excommunication for divorced/remarried Catholics.

These are important signs of compassion and concern. They are reasons for renewed hope in the Church's leadership. But the most significant signs of hope can be found among the separated and divorced Catholics themselves. They have moved beyond pain to participation. They have taken the initiative in building structures of community and reconciliation. In their commitment to the wider community of faith, the separated and divorced are creating a model of ministry for the entire Church. They are, in the words of Henri Nouwen, "the wounded healers" in the contemporary Church.

The Gospel Ideal and Human Brokenness

The experience of separated, divorced and remarried Catholics has taught us that theology has life as its framework and ministry as its focus. Doctrine must take flesh in human hearts before it can become a living faith. It must also take flesh in a communal setting where people of varying backgrounds and experience share the search for meaning. The parish is the primary context in which healing will or will not take place. It is the testing ground of the renewal. It is also the arena in which Catholics wrestle with the significant questions which surround marriage and divorce today.

A short time ago a parishioner approached me after Sunday liturgy and raised one of these questions. "Why is there so much concern about divorced Catholics these days?" she asked. "Doesn't the Church believe in the permanency of marriage anymore?"

Her question was sincere. She was expressing a concern shared by many others in the Church. Part of this concern is related to the issue of priorities in ministry. Some Catholics feel that the Church ought to focus its efforts on preparing young couples for marriage and in helping married couples to deepen their relationships, rather than spending time and energy reaching out to the separated and divorced.

However sincere this opinion might be, I think it misses the point. It is not a question of ministering to the divorced *instead* of those who are preparing for or already sharing married life. Like Jesus, the Church is committed both to forming and to healing the lives of people. In most areas the Church has redoubled its efforts in marriage preparation and enrichment. The ministry to the divorced does not call this important work of the Church into question. As teacher and proclaimer of the Gospel, the Church prepares people to live the ideal of a permanent marriage. As a healing community, it reaches out to those who, for whatever reason, have not been able to realize that ideal.

There is a widespread notion today that divorced people do not believe in the permanency of marriage. In my relationship with people in a pastoral context I have found that this is simply not the case. Most divorced Catholics have a profound respect to the Church's teaching on the indissolubility of marriage. They experience the loss of that permanency in their lives with a deep sense of pain. They are not asking the Church to change its teaching regarding marriage. They are only seeking for healing and the possibility of personal growth. They want to know that their lives in God have not ended and that there is a place for them in the Christian community.

Healing and Hope

Why is there so much concern about divorced Catholics in the Church today? Does the Church still believe in the permanency of marriage?

The concerned people who ask these questions are touching upon an issue that goes deeper than priorities for ministry or the current attitudes toward the separated and divorced. They are asking a question that relates to everyone's struggle for redemption. It is a question about our personal search for God's love and healing.

How can we be disciples of the Lord and still fail? How can we strive to respond to the Gospel ideal and still experience human blindness and brokenness? These are questions not only for the separated and divorced, but for the entire Christian community. The tension between promise and performance is the human experience out of which the Gospels were written. It is a tension that Jesus himself confronted with courage and decisiveness. "While Jesus was at table in Matthew's home, many tax collectors and those known as sinners came to join Jesus and his disciples at dinner. The Pharisees saw this and complained to his disciples. 'What reason can the Teacher have for eating with tax collectors and those who disregard the law?' Overhearing the remark, he said: 'People who are in good health do not need a doctor; sick people do. Go and learn the meaning of the words, "It is mercy I desire and not sacrifice." ' I have come to call, not the self-righteous, but sinners" (Mt. 9:10-13).

Jesus called his disciples to follow him to perfection, but he never ceased to love them in their weakness. He called them to strive for wholeness, but he did not turn his back on their fears or their failures. He understood that our performance seldom measures up to our promise.

Jesus' compassion for human weakness is a model for the pastoral ministry of the Church. He invites all people to accept their dependency on God and their need for healing. He urged his followers to go beyond the moral categories which society and religious institutions tend to create for people.

In today's society we continue to wrestle with the tendency to label others. We group people under headings which lock them into isolated rooms. We speak of deviates and delinquents, of psychotics and sinners. We label people as chemically dependent, culturally disadvantaged, physically handicapped and emotionally unstable. It is a human tendency and perhaps it is even unnecessary for social institutions. The Gospel simply invites those who do the labeling to include themselves in the categories. Jesus challenges the rest of the human community to recognize that they too are handicapped, disadvantaged, unstable, and dependent upon his healing love. The Christian way of life is a commitment to share our brokenness in a healing community and, through the power of the Spirit, to grow toward wholeness. The emergence of the ministry to divorced Catholics is an invitation to the entire Church to embrace the mystery of its humanness. It is a challenge to be a holy people by becoming a healing community.

When Jesus appeared to his disciples after his resurrection they recognized him by his wounds. They knew it was the Lord because even in his risen life he carried the scars of suffering. Jesus is the human face of the Father. He is God's way of being weak with us. God's way of hoping with us, God's way of walking through our darkness. In Jesus, the Father embraces the tension of human life. He overcomes our brokenness and brings us the gift of wholeness. He transforms the paradox of our pilgrimage into a way that leads to life. In Jesus, the Word is made flesh; the covenant is fulfilled; the promise achieves performance.

From prison, John the Baptist sent his disciples to ask Jesus if he really was the saviour. "Are you he who is to come, or are we to wait for someone else" (Mt. 11:3)? Jesus did not have to answer this question with words because he was already answering it with his life. He told the disciples to go back to John and describe to him what they heard and saw: "The blind see again, and the lame walk, lepers are cleansed, and the deaf hear, and the dead are raised to life and the Good News is proclaimed to the poor; and happy is the man who does not lose faith in me" (Mt. 11:4-6).

The Church is the extension of Christ's presence in space and time. The searching men and women of our time may not be able to find the words, but they are asking the Church the same question that John's disciples asked of Jesus: "Are you the community of life, or are we to wait for someone else?"

The Church can attempt to answer this question by words and decrees, by statements and documents. But if the Gospel is to be a living experience of the Lord's presence, we must answer it in the same way Jesus did. We must answer it with our lives. We must be able to say that the alienated and the oppressed are finding healing in our midst. We must be able to say that the compassion of Christ is still with us.

There is increasing evidence that this is taking place in the Church today. There are signs that the prisoners and the outcasts, the lame and the blind, the struggling and the brokenhearted are finding a place of healing in the community of faith. That is reason enough for hope.

Part IV
Sociological Issues

A Demographer Looks at American Families

Paul C. Glick

The title of this paper would be more nearly accurate if it had been changed to "A Social Psychologist Turned Demographer Tries to Understand What Is Happening to Marriage and Living Arrangements in the United States Today." I was a social psychology major under Professor Kimball Young (grandson of Brigham Young) at the University of Wisconsin during the mid-1930's when about the only thing that an undergraduate major could find to do after receiving a B.A. degree was to go to graduate school. My greatest ambition had been to do research on attitudes toward various types of social, economic, and religious behavior to learn more about the extent to which people of a given socioeconomic level who assert liberal or conservative attitudes in regard to one type of behavior tend to hold similar attitudes in regard to other types of behavior.

But at a critical point in my graduate school career I succumbed to an attractive offer to assist Professor Thomas McCormick on a study of the effects of the depression on Wisconsin's birth rates. This research assistantship carried with it a sure-fire source for a Ph.D. thesis, so I accepted it. And, because of having written the thesis, I was offered a position at the Census Bureau. That is why I left the teaching profession after two years and have been studying U.S. population trends since 1939. During all of these intervening years I have been trying to find out all I could about what relationships exist between marriage, fertility, and living arrangements, on the one hand, and socioeconomic level, on the other. Beyond that, I have tried to trace the changes in these relationships and to offer interpretive comment on what appear to be the changing attitudes that underlie the demographic changes.

In August 1974 the Bureau of the Census conducted a ceremony where the thirty-fifth anniversary of my entry on duty with the Bureau was recognized. Just how long that period of time really is can be appreciated better, perhaps, by noting that a person starting employment at the Bureau in 1974 would have to remain there until the year 2009 to equal my length of service at that honorable, but occasionally criticized, Federal agency.

These last 35 years have encompassed a wide range of changes in the U.S. population picture, and so it has been a most interesting period in which to be observing the American scene. In 1939—when I though I was starting a two- or three-year hitch with the Census Bureau—the country was still in the later stages of the Great Depression. So many people with talent were unemployed that we had a larger choice of enumerators, field supervisors, processors, and professional analysts for the 1940 census than for the 1950, 1960, or 1970 census. As we approached censuses after 1940, we used to joke among ourselves that a stiff recession at hiring time would greatly increase our chances of achieving our constant-goal of putting together a first-class team to help us produce another first-class census.

Recent Changes in Marriage and Fertility

The population picture in the late 1930's was gloomy. Many marriages had been delayed, so that the average age at marriage had risen, and a near-record nine per cent of the women 50 years old had never married. Birth rates had lingered at a low level, even without today's wide variety of means for birth control and without today's high degree of acceptance of a small number of children as a desirable family goal. Lifetime childlessness was edging up toward 20 per cent, and many of the children whom some leading demographers thought were merely being postponed were never born; a speculative interpretation is that many of the women who delayed having those other children reached the point where they liked it better without them than they had thought they would.

Then came World War II, with its extensive dislocations of family life particularly among families with husbands—or would-be husbands—of draft age, extending up to around 40 years of age. Marriage and birth rates remained low, and millions of women—married as well as single—were welcomed into the labor force who would never have gone to work outside the home if the male civilian work force had not shrunk so much.

After World War II, the marriage and divorce rates shot up briefly, fell again sharply, and then subsided gradually (Glick, 1974: Chapter III). By the mid-1950's, a relatively familistic period had arrived. Couples were entering marriage at the youngest ages on record, and all but four per cent of those at the height of the childbearing period eventually married. Moreover, the baby boom that had started with the return of World War II service men reached a plateau in the mid-1950's and did not diminish significantly until after 1960. By that time, the rate of entry into first marriage had already been falling and the divorce rate had resumed its historical upward trend.

By the late 1960's and early 1970's, the familistic style of life seemed to be on the wane again. The marriage rate among single persons under 45 years old was as low as it had been at the end of the Depression. Last year, the average age at marriage was close to a year higher than it had been in the mid-1950's, and the proportion of women who remained single until they were 20 to 24 years old had increased by one-third since 1960 (U.S. Bureau of the Census, 1974). The divorce rate had soared to the high level it had reached soon after the end of World War II, and an estimated one out of every three marriages of women 30 years old had been, or would eventually be, dissolved by divorce (Glick and Norton, 1973; Glick, 1973). The birth rate in 1973 was the lowest in the country's history, 15 per 1,000 population. The total fertility rate in 1973, which shows how many children women would have if they continued having children throughout their childbearing years at the same rate as in 1973, stood at a new low level of 1.9

children per woman. This is just one-half as many as in 1957, when the total fertility rate was 3.8 children per woman.

All of this has happened in the last 35 years, with high or low inflection points (depending on the variable) occurring near the middle of this period. It was an exciting period for a demographer to live through, because it was marked by sharp changes which called for careful measurement and perceptive interpretation. It was a period full of headaches for school administrators who had to adjust plant capacity to student load, as well as for manufacturers and distributors of products for babies or teenagers or any other functional age group because of the widely fluctuating demands by age. And it was a period when ideas were changing about the proper age for marriage, about desired family size, and about how serious it is to disrupt a marriage that does not seem to be viable. As ideas changed in one of these fundamental aspects of family life, other ideas came into question. So, we are now going through a period of change in demographic patterns that undoubtedly reflects basic, underlying attitudes toward conformity with traditional behavior, especially as such conformity comes in conflict with the development of the full potentiality of each member of the family.

Some Implications of Recent Changes

During the 12-month period ending in August, 1974, the estimated number of marriages in the United States was about 2,233,000, and the number of divorces was 948,000. For the first time since soon after World War II the marriage total for a 12-month period was significantly smaller (by 68,000) than it had been in the preceding year. However, the divorce total for the 12 months ending in August, 1974, had continued to rise (by 56,000) above the level for the preceding 12 months (U.S. Center for Health Statistics, 1974a).

These current figures are the latest available in a growing series which document a slow down of marriage and a speedup of divorce. Since 1965, the annual number of first marriages has not been keeping pace with the rapid growth in the number of persons in the prime years for first marriage—those who were born soon after World War II. In fact, the number of marriages in recent years would have been even smaller if it had not been for the sharp upturn in remarriages associated with the increase in the number of divorces in this period. According to the latest information available, about four out of every five of those who obtain a divorce will eventually remarry (U.S. Bureau of the Census, 1972a).

From the peak year for births, 1957, to the present the declining birth rate has resulted in part from a decrease in the proportion of children born to women above 30 years of age and has been associated with a decrease in the median age at which women bear their children, from 25 years to 24 years. During this period there has been little change in the interval between marriage and the birth of the first child. At the same time, the proportion of first births that have occurred outside marriage has just about doubled, from 5 per cent in the late 1950's to 11 per cent in 1971.

When married women today are asked how many children they expect to have in their lifetime, those under 25 years old say they believe they will have just about enough for zero population growth (aside from immigration). And answers to this question have been generally consistent over the last few years, with more changes in replies by identical women being in the direction of fewer rather than more children. Although fertility changes during the last 35 years provide ample evidence of the capacity of American couples to change their minds about how many children to have, the general consensus among most demographers is that a repeat of the post-World War II baby boom is most unlikely in the foreseeable future (U.S. Bureau of the Census, 1974a).

Recent Delay in Marriage Among the Young

The average woman at first marriage today is 21 years old. During the approximately 15 years of the post-World War II baby boom, the average woman had been one year younger at marriage, 20 years. Another way of showing the extent of the recent delay in marriage is to point out that a new low level of 28 per cent single was registered for women 20 to 24 years of age in 1960; but the corresponding figure for women in their early twenties in 1974 had jumped up by more than one-third to a level of 40 per cent single (U.S. Bureau of the Census, 1974b). There is no doubt about it. Young women are now postponing marriage longer than their mothers did in the late 1940's and early 1950's. (Corresponding data for men are not presented because their coverage in censuses and surveys has fluctuated as the size and location of men in the Armed Forces has varied widely since 1940.)

A delay in marriage—identified by an increase in the per cent single—has been common to young women (under 25 years old) of all education levels, but census figures show that the increase in singleness was greatest during the 1960's among young women who had not attended college. This finding is probably at least tangentially related to the sharp rise in unwed motherhood among white women during the 1960's; most unwed mothers have never attended college. Young women with a high school education but with no college training continue to be the ones with the smallest per cent single. (The situation among older women is different, as will be shown below.)

Why has this delay in marriage occurred among the young? At least a part of the answer lies in the fact that nearly three times as many women were enrolled in college in 1972 as in 1960 (3.5 million versus 1.2 million), and the college enrollment rate has more than doubled for women in their twenties during those 12 years. Another demographic factor was the "marriage squeeze"; during recent years this phenomenon has taken the form of an *excess of young women* of ages when marriage rates are highest, because women born in a given year during the baby boom after World War II reached their most marriageable age range two or three years before men born in the same year (Carter and Glick, 1970). Still other demographic factors include the sharper increase in the employment of women than men and the amazing decline in the birth rate, both of which signaled expanding roles open to women outside the home. Among the less tangible factors has been the revival of the women's movement. In fact, the excess of marriageable women in the last few years may have contributed as much to the development of that movement as the ideology of the movement has contributed to the increase in singleness.

A detailed analysis of recent marriage trends has suggested that it is too early to predict with confidence that the recent increase in singleness among the young will lead to an eventual decline in lifetime marriage. However, just as cohorts of young women who have postponed childbearing for an unusually long time seldom make up for the child deficit as they grow older, so also young people who are delaying marriage may never make up for the marriage deficit later on. They may try alternatives to marriage and like them.

Early Marriage and High Fertility of Those Approaching Middle Age

Women who are now 35 to 44 years old were born during the Depression years of the 1930's. They have been a most interesting group for demographers to study because of their many unique features: they were born when the birth rate was at the lowest level recorded up to that time (total fertility rate averaging about 2.3 children), with only the rates after 1970 being still lower; they set a record for early marriage (average about 20 years) and for high birth rates (total fertility rate peaking at 3.8 in 1957); and now they have in prospect one of the lowest proportions single on record (likely to fall below 4 per cent before they end their fifties) and one of the lowest proportions who will remain childless throughout life (10 per cent for women regardless of marital status and 6 per cent among those who ever marry). They have shared more fully than the preceding generation—and probably more than the following generation—in the process of marrying and replenishing the population.

These women, now 35 to 44 years of age, are featured here and in the discussion of divorce below because of their uniqueness in another respect. They are old enough to have experienced most of their lifetime marriages, childbirths, and divorces, and yet they are young enough to reflect recent changes in family life patterns. Because of the recent developments with regard to the delay in marriage and the fertility decline among those now in their twenties, it would have been tempting to have featured this younger age group. However, this option was not adopted because not enough time would have elapsed after school attendance for those with four or more years of college to have essentially established their lifetime levels of marriage and childbearing.

As noted above, the marriage history of women now 35 to 44 has culminated in a record low proportion single for women of that age range (now five per cent and likely to drop below four per cent by 1960). But the continuing decline in singleness for women of this age range was not uniformly distributed among the several educational groups. Although the per cent single was *rising* most rapidly among *young* college-educated women (those under 25), the per cent single was *declining* most rapidly among *older* college-educated women (those 35 to 44). Women college graduates 35 to 44 reduced their excess per cent single, as compared with all women in the age group, by a substantial one-fourth during the 1960's. Still, women college graduates with no graduate school training have continued to record a high proportion single, 10 per cent in 1960 and 8 per cent in 1970; and those with graduate school training recorded a *very* high level of 24 per cent single in 1960 but "only" 19 per cent single in 1970 (U.S. Bureau of the Census, 1967 and 1972b).

Similar socioeconomic differentials in the decline in singleness were found when the measurement was in terms of occupation and income. For example, the proportion single among women who were professional workers dropped by about one-third from the high level of 19 per cent in 1960 to 13 per cent in 1970. Moreover, women in the upper income bracket ($7,000 or more in 1960 and $10,000 or more in 1970—about the right difference in income level to adjust for the decreasing value of the dollar) had about a one-fourth decline in the proportion single between 1960 and 1970 (from the very high level of 27 per cent to the still quite high level of 21 per cent). Thus, in summary, the declines in singleness among the women in these upper socioeconomic groups consisted of tendencies for this aspect of their marital pattern to converge with—to become more like—that of women in the lower socioeconomic groups.

Why did this happen? A partial answer must be the relative *scarcity of women* of optimum age to marry during the mid-1950's, a period of affluence when nearly all men in the upper socioeconomic group were marrying. Thus, all but two or three per cent of the men in 1970 in the upper income bracket had married by early middle age; they had been at the height of their period for first marriage during the late 1940's and the 1950's. Another part of the answer must have been the greatly increasing opportunities for young women to work at attractice jobs outside the home even though they were married—a phenomenon that was far less common only a generation before 1960. It had obviously become far easier for a woman to combine a working career and marriage (Davis, 1972).

Why have not still more of the women in the upper socioeconomic groups become married? In 1970, fully 1 in every 5 women around 40 years of age with some graduate school education or with an income of $20,000 or more have not married, as compared with only 1 in every 20 women with no college education (U.S. Bureau of the Census, 1972b). Most of these women were submitted to the maximum pressure to marry during the period 10 to 20 years ago. Probably no one would argue with the interpretation that women with graduate school training have far more options for interesting roles to cultivate—including wife, mother, and/or career woman—than those with less education. But, despite the sharp increase in marriage among "fortyish" upper group women, could it be that a significant proportion of men who are also in the upper socioeconomic group still hesitate to marry a woman who expects to be a partner in an *egalitarian* marriage—or a woman who might be a serious competitor for the role of chief breadwinner or "head of the household?" It seems reasonable to expect a substantial further decline in the force of this factor as the impact of the women's movement is felt increasingly among both men and women. The expected direction of change would seem to be a growing acceptance of the situation in which the wife equals or outranks the husband in such matters—without as much of a disturbing effect on the couple's social relationships as it evidently continues to have today.

Divergence and Convergence of Divorce by Social Level

In 1970, the proportion divorced (and not remarried) continued to be lower among men approaching middle age (35 to 44 years old) than among women of comparable age—3.6 per cent versus 5.5 per cent. This pattern results from the older average age of men at marriage, hence the shorter duration of marriage for the men, and also from the larger proportion of men than women who eventually remarry—about five-sixths versus three-fourths. The difference between men and women in the porportion currently divorced has increased substantially since 1960, when 2.6 per cent of the men and 3.8 per cent of the women were divorced (and not remarried). This divergence between the sexes may have developed because of several factors including the increasing extent to which divorced women tend to outlive divorced men.

Meanwhile, a "democratizing" development in relation to marriage patterns is reflected in the fact that the proportion divorced among men 35 to 44 years of age has tended to converge since 1960 among the educational, occupational, and income groups. Men in the upper status groups continue to have a below-average proportion divorced (but not remarried), however, the gap was smaller in 1970 than it was in 1960. More specifically, the proportion divorced increased during the 1960's by about three-eighths for all men in the age group but by a considerably larger proportion (about one-half to two-thirds) for men with 4 or more years of college, for professional men, and for men in the top income class for which data are available ($10,000 or more in 1960 and $15,000 or more in 1970).

Changes during the 1960's in the proportion divorced among women by social and economic groups were more complex than those for men. For all women 35 to 44, the proportion divorced went up, on the average, by nearly one-half during the 1960's, from 3.8 per cent to 5.5 per cent. But among women who were professional workers or in the uppermost income level—where the per cent divorced among women (unlike men) has been characteristically quite high—the per cent divorced rose by a smaller proportion (under one-third) than among other women. (The per cent divorced for professional women went up from 6.0 per cent in 1960 to 7.8 per cent in 1970; and the per cent divorced for women in the uppermost income group rose from 11.8 per cent to 15.1 per cent.) Thus, for these categories of upper group *women,* the per cent divorced was tending to converge with that for other women by increasing more *slowly* than the average, while for upper group *men* the per cent divorced was tending to converge with that for other men by increasing more *rapidly* than the average.

The pattern is especially complex when changes in the proportion divorced are analyzed for women college graduates 35 to 44 years old. Women who terminated their education with 4 years of college hold the record for the smallest per cent divorced (3.0 per cent in 1960 and 3.9 per cent in 1970). Moreover, they reinforced this position during the 1960's by being the educational group with the *smallest* proportional increase in the per cent divorced (three-tenths). By contrast, women 35 to 44 with one or more years of graduate school have had fewer years since marriage in which to obtain a divorce but still hold the record among educational groups for the largest per cent divorced (4.8 per cent in 1960 and 7.3 per cent in 1970). Moreover, they reinforced this position by having the *largest* proportional increase in the per cent divorced of all educational groups (over one-half). Thus, both women with 4 years of college and those with 5 or more years of college have tended to diverge from the general level of increase in the proportion divorced but in opposite directions.

Why the Upturn in Divorce?

While the number of couples experiencing divorce has been rising, many other changes have also been occurring. Some of these changes might have actually been expected to cause the divorce rate to *decline*. For example, divorce rates are generally lowest among men in the upper socioeconomic groups, and the proportion of men in the upper education, occupation, and income groups has been increasing; yet the proportion divorced has been rising most in these very same groups. One of the many plausible hypotheses for investigation in this context can be posed in the form of a question: Was a larger proportion of men with "divorce proneness" being drawn into the ranks of upper socioeconomic groups in the two decades after World War II? This was a period when those ranks were being augmented by upwardly mobile persons who were rising from the lower socioeconomic groups; persons in the groups from which they were rising have probably always had the highest rates of marital dissolution.

This hypothesis could be examined by studying the relationship between the direction of intergenerational socioeconomic mobility and rates of marriage and divorce. Men who have been upwardly mobile by a substantial amount (defined as men whose achievement is quite perceptibly above that of their fathers) might be shown to have more initial advantage in the marriage market than their brothers with little or no such upward mobility. However, for many the advantage may not have lasted; these upwardly mobile men might have permitted "excessive achievement orientation" or complications resulting from their change of social level to interfere with the promotion of satisfaction in their marriages. Downwardly mobile persons may tend to have even more difficulty in their marital adjustment. This hypothetical relationship may be tested in the next year or so by the present author and Arthur J. Norton as a by-product of the study of "occupational change in a generation" that is being conducted by David L. Featherman and Robert M. Hauser, of the University of Wisconsin, on the basis of data from a Census Bureau survey in 1973.

Socioeconomic changes during the last decade or two that might have been expected to cause a *rise* in the divorce rate are numerous, but the contribution each has made to this rise cannot be readily demonstrated. Illustrations include the increasing proportion of young wives with small families who have succeeded in translating their higher level of education into jobs that make them financially independent of their husband; an increasing proportion of couples whose income has risen to a level at which they can afford the cost of obtaining a divorce to resolve a marriage that is not viable; the increased availability of free legal aid which may have permitted a large number of impoverished families to obtain a divorce; the war in Vietnam which complicated the transition of millions of young men into marriage or made their adjustment in marriage more difficult than it would have otherwise been.

Other changes that may have contributed in varying degrees to the increase in divorce during the last decade have less of an economic orientation. One cluster of such changes includes a greater social acceptance of divorce as a means for resolving marriage difficulties—in particular, the relaxation of attitudes toward divorce by a growing number of religious denominations; the relatively objective study of marriage and family relationships at the high school and college levels; the movement to increase the degree of equality of the sexes which is making some headway toward easing the social adjustment of persons who are not married; and the reform of divorce laws, in particular, the adoption of no-fault divorce.

No-Fault Divorce Laws

An article entitled "Legal Status of Women," prepared at the U.S. Women's Bureau lists 23 States that had adopted "some form" of no-fault divorce by January, 1974—16 of them since 1971 (Rosenberg and Mendelsohn, 1974). The 23 states are Alabama, Arizona, California, Colorado, Connecticut, Florida, Georgia, Hawaii, Idaho, Indiana, Iowa, Kentucky, Maine, Michigan, Missouri, Montana, Nebraska, Nevada, New Hampshire, North Dakota, Oregon, Texas, and Washington. A 24th state, Minnesota, passed a no-fault divorce law in the 1974 legislative session. Moreover, the legislators in nearly all other states are in the process of considering how to incorporate this feature into their divorce laws.

Persons who have examined the divorce laws closely have cautioned, however, that the no-fault movement is not really as far along as the advocates of "true" no-fault divorce would like to see. This view was expressed to me in a letter from Lenore J. Weitzman (University of California at Davis) who, together with two colleagues, is conducting a Federally sponsored study of "The Impact of Divorce Law Reform on the Process of Marital Dissolution: The California Case" (Weitzman, Kay, and Dixon, 1974). According to their calculations, five states have instituted true no-fault divorce by adopting the provisions of the Uniform Act; nine other states have adopted some other form of no-fault divorce. The states which have merely *added* no-fault divorce to their existing grounds for divorce should really not, according to Dr. Weitzman, be considered no-fault divorce states. Under a "true" no-fault divorce law, a couple may terminate its marriage without any expectation of punitive consequences resulting from the action; the main items to be settled are a reasonable division of joint property and arrangements for the maintenance of the children and the maintenance of one spouse on the basis of need. However, in states where no-fault is only one of several grounds for divorce, one spouse may threaten to consider the other "at fault" but settle for a no-fault divorce in the negotiation for a more favorable settlement. For this reason, the number of no-fault divorces in those states may not indicate the true number who obtained divorces without negotiations involving the adversary concept.

Children of Parents Who Have (or Have Not) Been Divorced

Women whose first marriage ended in divorce have been, on the average, about two years younger when they entered marriage than married women of the same age who have not been divorced (U.S. Bureau of the Census, 1973c). However, on the average, about three years elapse between divorce and remarriage. So, if the average divorcee gains a couple of years of married life through early marriage but loses three years of married life through divorce, what is the net effect on her family size? According to 1970 census data for women 35 to 39 years old, the answer varies according to her later marriage experience. First, divorced women 35 to 39 years old who had gone on to marry a man who had not been married before wound up with him and 3.1 children, on the average, or virtually the same number at the census date as that (3.2 children) for couples with both the husband and wife still in their first marriage. Second, those who were still divorced at the census date had borne a smaller number, namely, an average of 2.6 children. And third, among married couples at the census date where both the husband and the wife were divorced after their first marriage, the average number of children was intermediate, 2.9 children ever born (U.S. Bureau of the Census, 1973a).

Another way to show how many children are affected by divorce is to note that 15 per cent of all *children under 18 years of age* in 1970 were living with one or both parents who had been divorced after their first or most recent marriage. Some of these children were born after their divorced parent had remarried, but a larger number were living with a stepparent at the census date. Thus, about two-fifths of the children with a previously divorced parent were born after the remarriage and hence were living with their two natural parents; however, the other three-fifths were living with a stepparent. Besides these children of "ever divorced" parents, another 15 per cent were not living with both (once-married) natural parents. In other words, these figures imply that only about 70 per cent of the children under 18 years of age in 1970 were living with their two natural parents who had been married only once. Among black children the corresponding figure was very low, 45 per cent, but that for white children was also low, 73 per cent (U.S. Bureau of the Census, 1973b).

The proportion of *children of school age* living with both natural parents in their first marriage was even smaller than 70 per cent in 1970. Therefore, the remaining more than 30 per cent of school children were *not* living with a father and a mother who were in a continuous first marriage. This means that such children are no longer rare. Even though children of separated, divorced, or never-married parents still have many problems today, they at least have far less cause to feel unique or exceptionally deprived than similar children of yesterday. Moreover, because the birth rate has been declining for several years, the *average* number of children involved per divorce has declined since the mid-1960's (to 1.22 in 1970 and 1971); however, the *total* number of children involved in divorce was still rising in 1971, when it was 946,000 (U.S. National Center for Health Statistics, 1974b). In a country where many legal grounds for divorce have been established and used, a large number of children will inevitably be involved in separation and/or divorce. But there is no optimum proportion of children who should be thus involved, any more than there is a fixed optimum proportion of couples who should dissolve their marriage by divorce.

What is a Reasonable Amount of Lifetime Marriage (or Divorced)?

Saying that there is no fixed optimum proportion of marriages that really should not remain intact leaves much to be said about the current level of divorce and the prospective level over the next decade or two. For one thing it is now very high, in fact the highest in the world, and seems likely to remain that way. In 1972, the most recent date for which many international figures are available, the divorce rate was the highest in the U.S.A., with a rate of 3.72 per 1,000 population. Other countries with high 1972 levels of divorce were the U.S.S.R. with a rate of 2.64 and Hungary with a rate of 2.32. Cuba had a 1971 rate of 3.23 (United Nations, 1973). More recently, the U.S. divorce rate climbed on up to 4.4 per 1,000 population in 1973 and to 4.5 per 1,000 during the 12 months ending in August, 1974 (U.S. Center for Health Statistics, 1974a).

In the context of our high divorce rate, some questions worthy of exploration can be raised. How many of the divorces are desired by both parties? On the basis of experience in divorce counseling, Emily Brown, current chairman of the Family Action Section of the National Council on Family Relations, estimates that around 4 out of every 10 of the couples obtaining a divorce include one member who did not want it. But that leaves around 6 out of every 10 who did want it. Did the right couples obtain a divorce? Surely some who did so were ill-advised in this respect, whereas others with far more justification for a divorce were inhibited from obtaining one. And yet the situation may be so complex—when all of the pros and cons are considered—that even the wisest of family counselors must have difficulty in rendering objective judgment about the advisability of continuing or ending the marriages of a large proportion of those who come to them for counseling service.

A certain amount of divorce undoubtedly grows out of the fact that the supply of acceptable marriage partners is very often quite limited, and those who would be most ideal partners never meet, or if they do, they may do so at the wrong time or become unavailable to each other at the optimum time for marriage. In other words, marriage partners are typically joined through a process of chance, often involving compromise, and if the compromise element is substantial, there should be no great surprise if the marriage is eventually dissolved by permanent separation or divorce. In view of the haphazard manner in which the important step of marriage is generally undertaken, and in view of the many frailties of human adults, the surprise may be that the proportion of marriages that last—to a happy (or bitter!) end—is as large as it is.

Men at the top of the socioeconomic scale must have the most advantages in marital selection and in the means for achieving a satisfactory adjustment after marriage. Thus, a potential husband with a promising occupational future no doubt arrived at that enviable position usually—but, of course, not always—because of personal characteristics that should also make him an attractive candidate for marriage. This type of man has the widest choice of women for a potential wife—one with maximum appeal and few "hangups." And if the man's work history materializes into occupational success, his chances of keeping his marriage partner satisfied with their marriage arrangement should be accordingly enhanced—other things being equal. In fact, the statistics demonstrate that the most lasting marriages are contracted by men in the upper socioeconomic levels.

Viewed from the vantage point of the potential wife, the line of reasoning is quite similar in some key respects but has important differences. One similar feature is the great amount of competition they face in their search for men who are attractive candidates for marriage. A dissimilar feature is the somewhat different set of personal characteristics which describe an attractive woman as comapred with an attractive man for selection as a marriage partner—under the situation as it has existed for a long time but under a situation that may have already started to make a wide-ranging change.

But if the most attractive men marry the most attractive women, as so often happens, is it any wonder that they turn out to have the highest proportion of continuing marriages? And, by implication, is it any wonder that other persons more often terminate their less-than-ideal matches through separation and divorce? But the situation may not be as bad as it seems, in view of the fact that this discussion relates to a band of persons on or near the diagonal of a distribution showing the marriage appeal of potential husbands cross-classified by the marriage appeal of potential wives.

Thus, a study might be expected to show that, for a given type of men in a given marriage market area, somewhere around the top 20 per cent of men in attractiveness might be considered as reasonably acceptable husbands for the top 20 per cent or so of women, with (sliding) lower quintiles of men being "acceptables" for corresponding lower quintiles of women. As the lowest 20 per cent of potential husbands and wives is approached, those in this group should theoretically be relatively satisfied with their marital partners provided they marry someone within their own range. But are they going to be all that satisfied? And what about those who either by choice or because they lost out in the competition married someone outside their optimal range? It would be logical to expect their marital dissolution rate to be substantial and to account for a disproportionately large share of all divorces. Although dissolution of marriage by divorce is by far the most likely among couples in the lowest economic level, undoubtedly a relatively large proportion of these same couples would still have an above-average divorce rate even if their income levels were augmented considerably.

A key variable in this context is "coping power." Presumably those of upper status have much more of it, on the average, than those who achieve only lower status. Although the development of superior coping mechanisms would ordinarily be expected to result in maintaining a marriage intact, it would also be expected to result from time to time in the firm decision that a marriage is not tolerable and should be dissolved. And yet, the kinds of talent and support that fail to elevate the standing of a person above a low level must tend to leave that person with fewer options within which to achieve satisfactory adjustment either occupationally or maritally. At least the findings for men are generally consistent with this interpretation.

For women, however, the pattern is different, with those who have the most education and the most income being generally less likely to enter marriage or to maintain continuing marriages, on the average, then those with lesser achievement in their educational background and work experience. How long this pattern for women will persist is anyone's guess, but it could last indefinitely among those who genuinely prefer being unmarried. On the other hand, it could change substantially over the next decade or two if modifications of attitudes about what constitute

proper sex roles become modernized through appropriate socialization of the younger generation and resocialization of the older
generations (Bernard, 1972).

Recent Changes in Living Arrangements

Along with the recent decrease in fertility and increases in
separation and divorce have come other developments that have
shrunk the typical cluster of persons who live together as a
household. Very few married couples live in with relatives as they
once did. At the height of the housing shortage after World War
II, fully 9 per cent of all couples were without their own house or
apartment, but now only 1 per cent have to—or choose to—
double up with others. In the 1940's only 1 in every 10 households
was maintained by persons living alone or with a lodger or two,
but now 1 in 5 households is of this type, and 1 in every 6
households consists of one person living entirely alone. As an
overall measure of the shrinking family size, it is instructive to
note that the average household consisted of 5 persons from 1890
to 1910, then 4 persons from 1920 to 1950, and 3 persons since
1960—with the 1974 average dipping fractionally below 3 persons, to 2.97 persons (U.S. Bureau of the Census, 1974b).

This development reflects mainly the longtime decline in
fertility, but now more young adults live in apartments away from
their parental home or in apartments rather than college dor-
mitories, and more elderly persons are financially able—and evi-
dently prefer—to live apart from their adult children. The most
rapid increase in household formation since 1960 has occurred
among young adults with no relatives present, but the numerical
increase has been much larger among elderly persons living
alone. A spectacular 8-fold increase occurred during the 1960's in
the number of household heads who were reported as living apart
from relatives while sharing their living quarters with an unrelated
adult "partner" (roommate or friend) of the opposite sex. One
out of every four of these 143,000 "unmarried couples" in 1970
were women who had a male partner "living in." Among older
men sharing their living quarters with nonrelatives only, one in
every five shared it with a female partner (U.S. Bureau of the

Census, 1964 and 1973b). These older couples must include a substantial proportion of widowed persons who were living in this manner in order to avoid losing survivor benefits through remarriage.

Another "variant family form" is the commune, a type of living arrangement that has not been adequately quantified on a nationwide basis, partly because many of the communes are not welcome in their neighborhood and would rather not be identified in a census of survey.

The shrinking household size and the growing number of small households consisting of single-parent families, unmarried couples, or persons living entirely alone are evidence that large families are no longer regarded with favor by many persons and that new life styles are being tried by who want to learn whether the new ways are more satisfying to them than more conventional patterns. Some of the living arrangements with increasing numbers of adherents are bringing unrelated persons into closer companionship, whereas more of them are providing at least temporary relief from contacts with relatives that were regarded as too close for comfort.

But with four out of every five divorced persons eventually remarrying, the single-parent family has been in large part a temporary arrangement serving as a transition for the parent from one marital partner to another, and between parenthood and step-parenthood. New surveys will be watched for possible evidence that more of those with dissolved marriages will settle down with another unmarried person in a relatively stable union (with or) without a legal "cohabitation contract" that would have to be retracted through a court procedure if the union is to be dissolved later on.

Kin Network Ties and Neighborhood Characteristics

The scattering of adult married and unmarried family members has been accelerated during recent decades through increased migration, which is related to increased amounts of higher education, among many other things. Fewer neighborhoods are now dotted by families of the same surname. Yet a substantial amount of contact is maintained with relatives, even with those who live at a considerable distance. A study under the direction of David M. Heer (on behalf of a committee established by the Family Section of the American Sociological Association) contemplates the collection and analysis of national data on the extent and nature of relationships that keep alive the kin network among persons under 40 years of age and their parents and siblings. The results are expected to quantify variations in types of communication and mutual assistance that are characteristic of "kinpersons" living different distances apart and belonging to different socioeconomic groups. Funds for the support of this project are now being negotiated.

As adults move to localities that are beyond commuting distance of their close relatives, they may (or may not) become closely integrated into their new local neighborhoods. Studies are therefore needed to show the adjustment patterns of families in relation to the type of community in which they live. One study along this line is being planned by the present writer and Larry H. Long, also of the Bureau of the Census, on the basis of computer tapes available from the 1970 census. This source permits the analysis of marital and family characteristics in relation to such variables as duration of residence in the neighborhood (census tract or other small area), the ethnic composition of the neighborhood, the educational and income level of the neighborhood, the rate of turnover of population in the neighborhood, and the age and quality of housing in the neighborhood. Funding for this project may be obtained during the next year.

Concluding Remarks

The foregoing review of certain aspects of American marriage and living arrangements included some facts about what has been happening recently to family life in this country and has called attention to some areas where further research is needed. The accompanying interpretative comments were intended to add understanding to the census and vital facts that were presented. That is about as far as a demographer is expected to go in trying to help people do something about "the situation" in which so many American families find themselves today. Surely there is plenty of room for a division of labor between demographers and others who have a contribution to make in this area, including family lawyers, family counselors, socioeconomists, home economists, psychologists, social workers, religious leaders, and journalists. However, there are undoubtedly some non-demographers who are looking for a cause to promote in this context. My personal opinion is that they might be well-advised to consider some of the following directions in which to exert their efforts:

1. The development of the contents for more practical and effective training at home, in the high schools, and in colleges about how young persons can make a wise selection of their marriage partner and how they can keep their marriage alive and healthy over a long period of time—and about how they can use reasonable criteria to decide whether it is any longer practical to keep their marriage intact (Broderick and Bernard, 1969).

2. Designing a scientifically tested and appealing system for selecting a marriage partner, for bringing together young men and women who would have a much higher probability of establishing an enduring and satisfying marriage than could be expected through the almost universally haphazard system that now exists—at the same time realizing that the rational approach must be supplemented by the strength of emotional appeal (Glick, 1967).

3. Acceptance by the public of the concept of periodic marriage checkups through visits to highly expert marriage counselors (when a sufficient supply becomes available), with these visits occurring in a manner analogous to periodic physical checkups that are voluntarily made, and with the visits considered urgent when a seemingly dangerous marital condition is developing.

4. Continuing modernization of marriage and divorce laws, which would tend to encourage couples to take much more seriously their entry into marriage but not qute so seriously as some couples do the hazards of ending a marriage that is no longer worthy of continuation.

5. Development of child care facilities staffed by highly professional personnel, so that more mothers can feel free to maximize the alternatives available for the use of their time while their children are growing up—provided that careful attention is

given in choosing the ways in which the additional free time is used (Campbell, 1973; Low and Spindler, 1968).

6. Finally, programs to increase the appeal of experiencing a good marriage, including the continued collection and dissemination of knowledge about how to cultivate such a marriage—so that more emphasis can be placed on building up the positive side of married life, in a period when so many stimuli that reach the public have the effect of making nonmarriage appear to be much more desirable (Mace and Mace, 1974).

Certainly demographers cannot be counted upon—in their capacity as practicing demographers—to promote such causes as these to improve family relations in the modern world, but they can help to promote such causes indirectly by providing imaginative factual information about the types of circumstances which tend to be associated with enduring marriages and about other types of circumstances that tend to be associated with a substantial amount of seemingly inevitable marital dissolution.

A New Marital Form:
The Marriage of Uncertain Duration

Robert S. Weiss

The most striking characteristic of American family life today is the great frequency with which it is disrupted by divorce. The number of divorces is now nearly half the number of marriages: in the twelve months ending November, 1977, about 2,200,000 marriages took place and about 1,100,000 divorces.[1] Earlier estimates that between thirty-five percent and forty percent of new marriages will eventually end in divorce now appear to be too conservative.[2] It should be kept in mind, too, that these figures deal only with formal divorce and so understate the degree of serious familial disruption. If we consider not just divorce but any voluntary separation in which partners move to different households without intent of future rejoining, it appears that well over half the marriages now being formed will sustain a significant break.[3]

The rate of divorce in the United States has been increasing in a rather uneven fashion for as long as we have records. But after a post-war peak in 1945, it was temporarily stable through the decade of the fifties. In 1960 it resumed its increase, at first slowly, then quite rapidly. In 1975 the rate of increase suddenly slowed, and since 1976 the divorce rate has again been stable.

Despite the present stability of the divorce rate, the rate appears to be high enough to justify the assertion that we have developed a new marital form, a marriage that is about as likely to end in divorce as not: a marriage of uncertain duration. Before the upsurge in the divorce rate a marriage could be counted on to persist until one or the other partner died. Although divorce was not unknown, in most states it was extremely difficult to obtain. Divorce would only be granted to a husband or wife who could demonstrate that the other party to the marriage had committed a fault which the legislators of that particular state had previously judged to be sufficiently serious to warrant the marriage's dissolution. If the husband and wife decided together, before going to court, that they would cooperate in obtaining the divorce, the judge might deny the petition for divorce on grounds of collusion. And even more of a barrier to divorce than legal restrictions, in the society of twenty-five years ago, was the social unacceptability of divorce. To obtain a divorce was to bring scandal to one's family. Those who had divorced were seen as odd and somewhat shady by respectable members of the community. A widely shared belief that marriage was to be endured, no matter what, prevented the unhappily married from even contemplating a visit to a lawyer.

Now all this has changed. Although marriage may be entered into as hopefully as ever, separation and divorce are widely accepted as events that might happen to anyone. Most states have changed the statutes governing divorce to make it possible for divorce to be granted even where fault has not been demonstrated, so long as a judge can be satisfied that the marriage has suffered irretrievable breakdown. Even more important than change in statute law has been change in judicial treatment of divorce petitions. Now petitions for divorce are almost uniformly granted. It would be astonishing, now, to hear a judge express outrage on discovering that there was pre-trial agreement between husband and wife regarding the complaint to be made. Judges no longer recognize any mandate to protect marriages against the men and women within them. And at the same time the separated and divorced are no longer a pariah folk with whom the respectable feel uncomfortable. Separation may still be faintly discrediting, but it is seen now more often as a variety of misfortune than as a consequence of delinquency. We now accept that individuals who choose to end their marriages need not be expressing a character flaw.

A number of changes in our social life have contributed to this changed definition of the nature of marriage. Keniston finds an explanation for the increase in the divorce rate in the reduction in the number of bonds that tie husband, wife, and children together. When father worked long hours on the farm or in the factory and mother stayed home to care for the many children, neither father nor mother could function without the other. The marriage might be unhappy, but it would not end.[4] Yet this appraisal, though it may explain the steady rise in the American divorce rate since the country's earliest days, cannot explain the dramatic rise that began about 1960.

Something happened in the early sixties to the American understanding of familial responsibilities. One possibility is that the early sixties witnessed a very general movement to celebrate the rights of the individual in opposition to the rights of institutions. Certainly, there was at this time an upsurge in attacks on the legitimacy of institutions. Politicians had always been held to be suspect, but only in the early sixties did large numbers of Americans begin to question government itself.[5] It was in the sixties, too, that university students learned to criticize not only specific administrators but administration itself and to organize "free universities" as an alternative and a protest. Big business began to be portrayed as dehumanizing, and executive positions as traps rather than opportunities.

At a time when any corporate group might be seen as blocking the desires of its members rather than channeling them or expressing them or responding to them, it would be surprising if marriage were not also subjected to the same criticism. The idea developed through the sixties that what really mattered in life was making the most of one's own potential. Service to others was performed by combatting repressive institutions and insuring the availability of opportunity everywhere. This ethic of self-realization was not necessarily hedonistic in character. Indeed, it might lead to choice of a life that was stressful and ungratifying. But to refuse to be one's self, to choose instead for safety, to accept a good job one did not really want, to stay in a marriage which, while not actively unhappy, was stultifying, would be to fail in one's duty to one's self. It would be more than simply compromise; it would be cowardice.

The Women's Movement adopted this theme of self-realization. The Women's Movement said that the housewife's role as self-abnegation; that women, too, ought to be able to grow, to become whatever they could. Partly as a consequence of this insistence, partly as a consequence of anti-discrimination laws whose initial intent had been only to end discrimination by race, women have begun to achieve increased opportunity within the labor force.

Although we still have far to go before we can claim sexual equality within the labor force, the distance we have already come has greatly increased the practicality of a woman's going it alone. And while it remains true that many long-married women are totally unprepared when overtaken by marital separation it is much easier than it once was for a woman to get training and a job. And in response to these greater opportunities in the labor force, together with new definitions of the right of the self when in contest with the demands of marriage, some women have reconsidered earlier decisions to devote themselves to family life and have embarked on new careers, on occasion ending or interrupting a marriage in the process.

The increased rate of separation and divorce has become self-reenforcing. It is much more difficult to stigmatize as pathological or irresponsible those seeking divorce when they become a sizable portion of the population. Twenty-five years ago Edmund Bergler could write in a book titled *Divorce Won't Help* that separation and divorce were consequences of neurotic conflict. While vestiges of this view may still be expressed, increased frequency of separation and divorce makes it evident that separation and divorce occur to many different kinds of people in many different kinds of marriages. There has been modification of objections to the separated and divorced on moral grounds. A recent evidence of this is the changed stance of the Catholic Church toward its separated and divorced members; no longer are they required to consider themselves still married in the eyes of the Church, whatever their secular status.

It is my impression, on the basis of crisis-focused work with a small number of divorcing couples and on the basis of interviews with a more extensive number of single parents, that the increased acceptability of separation and divorce has had an effect on the treatment of marital conflict by the partners them-selves. Now partners in marriage are less tolerant of discomfort, less willing to compromise their interests or to relinquish their hopes, in order to adapt to their marriages. Twenty years ago a woman could say, as one did on discovering her husband had fathered a child by another woman, "Marriage is for better or for worse. I guess this one, now, is for worse. But that's the way it is." Today marriage appears to be for worse only up to a point, and a point well within reach.

The increased acceptability of divorce also encouraged legis-lators to modify state laws so that it no longer is necessary for a couple bent on divorce to concoct a story of mental or physical cruelty or to relate in court mistreatment that unhappily actually occurred. Nor did legislators find it desirable that couples with adequate income could obtain a migratory divorce by sending the wife to establish token residence in Nevada or Alabama or Mexico while other couples, who could not afford the trip, stayed married. In general, legislators and perhaps even more so the judges who administer the laws, have come to see as the greater evil requiring couples to remain in marriages the couples feel to be hostile to their well-being. And so the greater acceptability of divorce has led to divorce becoming easier to obtain. And this, in turn, has led to more frequent recourse to divorce.

Twenty-five years ago the presence of children was a strong deterrent to the voluntary dissolution of a marriage. For a given length of marriage, the divorce rate among parents was only about sixty percent the divorce rate among the childless. But beginning in the sixties the increase in the divorce rate among parents has been even more rapid than the increase in the overall divorce rate.[6]

Twenty-five years ago parents might have told themselves and others that no matter how bad their marriages were, they would stay together for the sake of their children. Staying together for the sake of the children was a position supported by the widespread belief that a broken home was a catastrophe for a child: a certain cause of distress and a likely cause of delin-quency. But now there is a contrary belief based, with more confidence than the evidence warrants, on questionnaire studies of college students,[7] to the effect that children do better if their parents divorce than if their parents continue in an unhappy marriage. I have spoken with couples on the brink of separation who finally decided to separate for the sake of the children, because the children seemed to be suffering in the embattled home, because one parent thought it important to protect the children from the other, or simply because the parents felt that their children would suffer in the future if they themselves remained unhappy.

Evidence regarding the comparative well-being of children of divorced parents is, in fact, equivocal. A recent national survey conducted by the Foundation for Child Development suggests that children whose parents have separated or divorced are about as likely to be troubled themselves as are children whose parents describe their marriages as unhappy.[8] The question of whether children are better off if their unhappily married parents separate is a complex one, dependent on many factors, including the ability of the parents to provide a supportive setting for the children despite the parents' difficulties. Despite the complexity of the issue, many parents now accept the simplistic dictum, "Better a happy home with one parent than an unhappy home with two."

There is still another factor that should be noted in connection with our high divorce rate, and that is the importance to us of marriage. It is extremely difficult for us in America, given the way we organize our lives, to tolerate an unsatisfactory marriage. Survey studies repeatedly show that satisfaction with home life is central to satisfaction with life as a totality. The University of Michigan's Survey of the Quality of American Life found satisfaction with family life and satisfaction with marriage to be the most important determinants of overall satisfaction with life.[9] Individuals whose marriages have failed them are peculiarly vulnerable to depression and self-doubt.[10]

We Americans tend to be distant from our kin in space if not in feeling, and the considerateness we display toward our friends includes an unwillingness to burden them with our troubles. Our primary sources of sympathy and support are our spouses. We are, in consequence, both bruised and bereft when our spouses turn from allies to critics. In addition, because our feelings about ourselves are so accessible to influence from our immediate environments, we take to heart the negative appraisals we hear in our marital quarrels. We are deeply affected by the reflections of ourselves we see in the way we are talked to and treated by our spouses. And so our marriages have much to do not only with our moods but also with our notions of who we are.

With marital support so important, a spouse's slight can easily be felt to be a grievous injury and what might appear to an oursider to be an unimportant misunderstanding can give rise to feelings of intolerable misuse. Often enough we counterattack in order to protect ourselves. This form of reaction may, perhaps, be especially marked among Americans. We earn our own self-respect to the extent that we refuse to accept undeserved injury from another, and instead stand up for ourselves whatever the cost of self-defense. And so marital quarrels lead easily to threats of separation because neither husband nor wife is willing to sustain the narcissistic damage that would stem from apology.

Survey data suggests that marriages that encounter unusual stress are more likely to experience internal disharmony and so are more likely to move along the pathway to separation and divorce. The imposed stress can be of any sort, but often enough is economic. An unemployed husband and a depleted bank account can both be shown to be casually related to marital separation.[11] So, we might surmise, might be a chronically ill child, unsatisfactory housing conditions, and shift work.

It is tempting, when reviewing the reasons for our high level of separation and divorce, to see ourselves as commenting on a social ill. Yet not so long ago the difficulty of obtaining a divorce might well have been viewed as the more significant problem. Not quite fifty years ago several distinguished writers, both European and American, contributed to a volume in which, with startling uniformity, they held that an ending of restrictive divorce laws was necessary to a better society.[12] We should not forget that divorce furnishes a remedy for those unhappy situations that might in an earlier time have permanently blighted the lives of trapped husbands or wives. Women are no longer condemned to life with a brutal husband. A loveless marriage is no longer required to continue.

But if our current situation is a solution to one set of problems, there is no gainsaying that it is a source of another. Marital separation is a regularly traumatic event.[13] Individuals discover that even though they may be relieved that they are free of an oppressive marriage, they are bereft of a relationship that, despite its discomforts, provided them with an anchor for identity and a defense against loneliness. The parent who loses custody of the children and who had, during the marriage, an ordinary level of parental investment in them, is apt to be severely depressed by separation from them. The parent who retains custody of the children is apt to discover that parenting alone is an unremittingly demanding enterprise. And the childless as well as those with children are apt to discover that separation and divorce disrupt their linkages with others, that the friendships they made when married lose their validity, that for a time they are socially marginal.

The increased frequency of marital separation does not reduce its traumatic impact. Increased frequency does serve to lessen the sense of stigmatization that once accompanied marital separation, and has resulted in certain improvements in the treatment of the separated and divorced by institutions: for example, it is now much easier for a divorced woman to obtain credit than was true only five or ten years ago. But the increased frequency of marital separation has not reduced the emotional and social upset it produces. Marital separation in this respect resembles an auto accident: that it has happened to others does not make it hurt any the less.

If this is the case for the couple themselves, it is even more the case for the children. For while husband and wife ordinarily can anticipate eventually entering a new marriage whose felicity may compensate for the pain of having ended the old one, the children must live with the mutual distancing and often mutual animosity of the only parents they will ever have. Adolescent children whose parents have divorced regularly complain of the difficulties of maintaining relationships with two contesting parents, and of the tendency of parents to try to make allies of them or to use them as messengers or as spies. These children have had to learn to see their parents as people with lives of their own, and in addition as people troubled by ambivalences, moods, and irrational angers, and while all this may provided the adolescents with an early wisdom, it has also cost them energy they might otherwise have devoted to their own development. Again and again these adolescents say that they will not take their parents as models for their own adult lives.

It is not only those children whose own parents' marriages have ended who are affected by the high rate of separation and divorce. Many schools, especially those in apartment districts, have classrooms in which from a quarter to a half of the children are from single-parent households. The other children must give thought to their own situation: will their parents' marriages continue? They, too, must wonder about the reliability of marital commitments.

By the time children reach college age they are wary of marriage. Often they want love and serious commitment, but they are afraid that marriage may be the first step to divorce. Many young people at our best colleges have implemented an idea of Margaret Mead's for a two-tier marriage system. Dr. Mead's proposal, described by her in a *Redbook* article and on national television, was that we should have two different kinds of marriage. One kind would be easy to enter and easy to leave. Individuals in it would be prohibited from having children. The other kind would be difficult to enter and even more difficult to leave. But couples who established this second form of marriage would be permitted to have children. Our young people seem to have adopted this system except that they enter the first form of marriage, which they call "living together," without any ceremony whatsoever. Then they have the usual ceremony when they enter the second form of marriage, "real marriage."

This system has as one consequence that individuals' first divorces are not registered because their first marriages are not. And so the system, if it became widespread, would effectively reduce our divorce rate. But it is not evident how much of a solution the system offers to other problems. The distress attendant on the ending of a committed non-marriage is nearly the same as the distress that accompanies the ending of a marriage. There may not be the same degree of social dislocation, but feelings of loss are as intense. And there is likely to be less support from friends and kin. One woman told me that at about the same time that she ended a six-year relationship with the man with whom she lived, her sister ended a two-year marriage. Her parents shrugged off the ending of her relationship with the comment, "How good it was that you did not marry." Her sister received all her parents' sympathy.

There does not seem much reason to believe that postponing "real marriage" so that it more or less coincides with parenthood provides greater assurance that the children of the marriage will not at some point have to cope with the separation of their parents. It may even be that putting "real marriage" off until parenthood costs young people a chance to get used to marriage at a time when they do not yet have to respond to the additional demands of parenthood. Marriage is a relationship quite different from living together. In marriage, but not in living together, people have to learn to function in the social roles of husband and wife, have to become accustomed to auxiliary membership in the family of the other spouse, and have to accept the social understandings implied by the phrase, "next-of-kin." Living together only partially prepares for marriage. If a couple are certain of their commitment to each other, they might do better to marry and learn to live as a married couple, rather than simply live together until they are ready to have children.

If one response among young people to a recognition that marriage today is of uncertain duration is to put off marriage entirely, another is to accept marriage, hope for the best, and nevertheless be prepared for the marriage ending. Not only is it the case that increased employment opportunity for women has contributed to the development of our new marital form, but it is also the case that recognition of this form has made it almost imperative that women develop skills that will enable them to support themselves if need be. At one time it was an unquestioned assumption in American society that women throughout their lives were dependent on a male relative for financial support and moral direction. The phases of a woman's life could be marked by which male relative she was dependent on: the father gave the woman away to her husband at the woman's marriage, and on the husband's death, the woman became dependent on a mature son, or failing this, a husband's brother. Now, increasingly, it is understood that women go off on their own before marriage, and that even in marriage they retain the capacity to manage on their own if need be. A woman's career has become for her a kind of hedge, insurance that she can survive without dependency if her marriage should end. Even young women who do not describe themselves as bent on careers nevertheless want to develop marketable skills so that if they have to support themselves, they can.

Another response to the recognition that marriage today is of uncertain duration is the drafting of pre-marital contracts in which not only are the rights and obligations of each partner in the marriage specified, but also specified are how property will be divided in the event of divorce and what then will be the husband's and the wife's rights and obligations in relation to the children. Such pre-marital contracts are as yet unusual, and perhaps, so long as each new marriage is made in the spirit of, "This time for keeps," they will continue to be so. Yet, they are now occasionally discussed in the popular press, and may yet become a recognized, if infrequently adopted, practice.

Young people recognize that marriages today are of uncertain duration. That their marriages may end by divorce is a threat they must live with, in some ways like the possibility of cancer: something that happens to lots of people, but that one hopes won't happen to oneself. None find attractive the idea that a marriage may be less than lifelong.

We cannot, as a society, return to the understanding of marriage we once held. But we may be able to reduce the damage so regularly produced by the early endings of our marriages. What may be the most pressing need is protection of children's well-being despite the separation of their parents. Work now being done demonstrates convincingly that children are intensely upset by parental separation.[14] Most children seem able in time to resume their developmental progress, but ordinarily only after a difficult period.

We are beginning to be able to identify which children are a special risk when parents separate. Particularly likely to be upset by parental separation may be children who have been taken unawares by the separation, children who were already doing badly with friends or at school, children whose parents even after separation keep the children's lives in a state of turmoil, children whose parents after separation are totally preoccupied with their own concerns, and children who, because of the parents' separation, lose contact with a parent to whom they had been very much attached.

Parents can, to an extent, reduce their childeren's risk of continuing distress. They can provide their children with adequate preparation for a forthcoming separation, seek counseling themselves to help minimize quarrels within the home, resolve not to display dramatically their anger with the other parent, and resolve to apportion some part of their time and energies to helping their children deal with the separation. An educational program for separating parents might be a useful service for their children.

We might consider modification of our present custody and visitation arrangements to make them more responsive to the emotional needs of children. The arrangement that is most usual at present, "Custody to the mother and reasonable visitation to the father," fails to work for many mothers and fathers and for most children. For mothers it implies the assumption of sole responsibility for the children, with the father relegated to the role of intermittent disrupter of her routine. It makes her the parent in charge of daily chores, the parent ultimately answerable for the children's care, while the father becomes the parent in charge of outings and happenings. For the father, the arrangement means that at weekly or bi-weekly intervals he must struggle to reestablish genuine communication with his children and, shortly after achieving this, must relinquish it until the next time. It gives rise to repetitive loss and pain. And so the system sponsors resentment in the mother and frustration and anger in the father. The tensions between the parents exacerbate the children's conflicts of loyalty. In addition, the arrangement forces the children to see their father as having become more distant from them, inaccessible except for his visits. He becomes a figure of diminished authority, perhaps a romantic figure, perhaps a sad one, but no longer much of a parent.

Certainly we can devise a better system than this for structuring the post-marital relationship of parents and children. One possibility is that responsibility for decisions regarding the children's schooling and summer camp and orthodonture and Church attendance. In addition the parents would decide together how the children's time would be divided and whose home would provide the children's bedrooms. It could be objected that divorced parents never agree, but all divorced parents managed somehow to arrive at decisions while their marriages were deteriorating, and it should not be more difficult to arrive at decisions in the ordinarily more stable post-marital situation. The provision of mediation, perhaps through a social agency, might be necessary to back up this sort of shared custody. Such a system, in which both parents retain normal parental responsibilities for their children, should go far toward relieving mothers of a sense of unshared responsibility, supporting fathers' continued investment in the children and providing reassurance to the children that both their parents continue to function as parents.

Both parents should be aware of the importance of their remaining accessible to the children. In the usual case, in which both parents have been emotionally essential to their children, and especially if their children are small, parents should strive to live as near to each other as they can and to keep both their homes open at all times to their children. When parents have participated equally in the children's upbringing, and have encouraged the children to accept both as providers of nurturance and security, then each is under even more severe obligation to remain accessible to the children after separation. A marriage in which parenting has been shared implies a separation and divorce in which children continue to have full access to both parents.

In an influential book, Goldstein, Freud, and Solnit responded to some of the problems of "Custody to Mother, Reasonable Visitation to Father," by recommending that custody should not be limited by the requirement that the non-custodial parent be permitted to visit the children.[15] Rather, they said, the custodial parent should be able to decide whether there would be visitation. Their aim in this recommendation was to strengthen the position of the custodial parent. It may be argued, in opposition to the proposal, that it is neither wise nor just to so neglect the right of non-custodial parents to keep in touch with their children. But quite apart from what might be the rights of non-custodial parents, from the standpoint of the children's stake in continuing relationships with both parents, the Goldstein, *et al.*, recommendation is mistaken. Insofar as it would encourage the custodial parent to limit the children's access to the non-custodial parent, and insofar as it would attack the investment in the children of the non-custodial parent, the recommendation goes exactly counter to the children's interests.

The recognition that both parents remain important to their children after the parents' separation implies that marital separation does not provide the parents with the freedom to begin again as though the marriage had never occurred. Marital separation may free husbands and wives from obligations to each other, but not from obligations to their children. It is as yet an unmet task for our society to work out how separated parents can best discharge these obligations. Our present approach will not do. But the suggestions I have made might be a beginning.

Notes

1. See *The Monthly Vital Statistics Report, Vol. 26,* No. 11, "Births, marriages, divorces, and deaths for November, 1977," National Center for Health Statistics, 1978.

2. See Hugh Carter and Paul Glick, *Marriage and Divorce,* Second Edition. (Cambridge, Massachusetts: Harvard University Press, 1976.) Carter and Glick assumed a continuation of 1975 rates. Current rates are about five percent higher. Even taking current rates into account, the Carter and Glick estimate appears conservative.

3. See Robert S. Weiss, *Marital Separation.* (New York: Basic Books, 1975,) chapter two.

4. Kenneth Keniston and the Carnegie Council on Children, *All Our Children: The American Family Under Pressure,* (New York: Harcourt-Brace Jovanovich, 1977.) pp. 20-21.

5. "Trend data available from the Center for Political Studies have shown a dramatic deterioration of public trust in the rectitude, competence, and responsiveness of the national government which was underway as early as 1964 and has continued downward through the recent writing (1973)." Angus Campbell, Philip E. Converse, and Willard L. Rodgers, *The Quality of American Life: Perceptions, Evaluations, and Satisfactions,* (New York: Russell Sage Foundation, 1976.) p. 30. Other

surveys have reported decreasing confidence in organized medicine, the police, business, and, with few exceptions, all other organized bodies.

6. See Alexander Plateris, *Children of Divorced Couples*, Public Health Service Publication, Series 21, No. 18, National Center for Health Statistics, 1970, p. 2.

7. For example, see Judson T. Landis, "A comparison of children from divorced and non-divorced unhappy marriages," *Family Life Coordinator*, July, 1962, Vol 2, pp. 61-65.

8. Nicholas Zill, "Divorce, marital happiness and the mental health of children: findings from the Foundation for Child Development National Survey of Children," a working paper prepared for the National Institute of Mental Health Workshop on Divorce and Children, Bethesda, Maryland, Feburary 7-8, 1978. (New York: Foundation for Child Development, 1978.)

9. Angus Campbell, *et al.*, *op cit.*, p. 85.

19. See Myrna M. Weissman and Eugene S. Paykel, *The Depressed Woman: A Study in Social Relationships*, (University of Chicago Press, 1974) chapter 7, pp. 87-102.

11. See Andrew Cherlin, "Economics, social roles, and marital separation," paper presented at the Meetings of the American Sociological Association, 1976.

12. Bertrand Russell, Fanny Hurst, H. G. Wells, Theodore Dreiser, Warwick Deeping, Rebecca West, Andre Maurois and Lion Fuchtwanger, *Divorce as I See It*, (London: Noel Douglas, 1930).

13. See, for further material on this point, my *Marital Separation, op cit.*

14. See Judith Wallerstein and Joan B. Kelly, "Children and Divorce," in *Basic Handbook of Child Psychiatry*, (New York: Basic Books, 1976).

15. Joseph Goldstein, Anna Freud and Albert Solnit, *Beyond the Best Interests of the Child*, (New York: Free Press, 1973).

The Family Today

John L. Thomas, S.J.

As we celebrate our nation's Bicentennial, it is appropriate and somewhat sobering to recall that in 1776 only a few colonial families were living along the immediate western boundaries of the eastern seaboard settlements. Yet, in little over a century the American frontier had ceased to exist. Our vast country had been settled from coast to coast. This amazing development was largely the result of a steady influx of immigrants. Decade after decade throughout the nineteenth and first quarter of the twentieth century, they came by the hundreds of thousands, sturdy of heart and eager of hand, pushing ever westward the stubborn frontier, flooding and developing industrial centers of the East and Great Lakes Regions, clearing the forests and plowing the plains of the North and Middle-West. Although Europe furnished the majority of immigrants who influenced the dominant culture during the country's early formative years, nearly all races and nations of the world have contributed to our present population. Truly, "America is a nation of nations."

Despite the great diversity of Old World backgrounds and New World experiences, contemporary American families are becoming increasingly alike in such external characteristics as size, structure, and the general patterning of activities throughout the life-cycle. Among other things, this trend reflects the adjustments required by an industrialized urban environment. American families now operate in a technologically advanced, highly complex, and competitive open-class social system. As a whole, they tend to be geographically and socially mobile. Compared to the rest of the world, they enjoy considerable affluence. During

227

the past several decades, in particular, they have become fully exposed to the uniformities promoted by modern, facile means of travel, universal education, and mass communications media. Having to adjust to roughly similar social pressures and conditions, they tend to adopt fairly similar family patterns.[1]

Yet these external similarities may conceal more than they reveal, since a family system, like all social institutions, includes values as well as structures. From its very foundation, our nation has contained a number of sizeable religious minority groups displaying considerable diversity in their beliefs, values, normative standards, and approved moral practices relating to sex, love, marriage, and parenthood. More recently, particularly following World War II but having their ideological roots much deeper in the past, a number of novel sexual and marital "styles" have been receiving vociferous advocacy in some sectors of the population. These "styles" include trial marriage, group or communal marriage, co-marital sex, mate swapping or "swinging," "open" marriage, and various other forms of innovative living and cohabiting.[2]

Unfortunately, there is little reliable information available either on the true incidence of such arrangements or on the characteristics of couples attracted to them. Although books and articles on "alternatives to marriage" or "beyond monogamy" currently receive good press, it is difficult to assess their overall import for the future of the American family. At a minimum, the toleration or apathy with which their public advocacy is greeted suggests a rather radical shift in the general climate of opinion relating to traditional Western ideals of monogamy and chastity. Whether these ideals can long be maintained under such permissive public conditions appears highly questionable. Experience shows that social ideals can remain operative or persist even as ideals only to the extent that they are embodied in concrete normative relationships and enjoy widespread public support.[3]

Whatever the future of the American family may be, and prediction in this regard is extremely hazardous, we can summarize the present situation briefly as follows. Although Americans are heterogeneous in national backgrounds, recency of immigration, social class, regional environment, and religious beliefs, they are beginning to share a number of views and attitudes relating to marriage and the family. Thus, selection of a mate should be free; marriage should be based on mutual love; ideally, the marital bond should be permanent, though legal provision should be made for separation and divorce; parenthood should be responsible and therefore restricted; newlyweds should establish a household apart from their parents; grown children should be self-supporting; and solidarity of kinship should be founded on affection rather than on formally defined obligations. Some residual ethnic and regional differences in the form of distinctive family customs, marital and parental role-patterns, or national prejudices still persist. Discrimination and exploitation continue to deprive a sizeable number of the requisite social and economic bases for stable family living, as in the case of lower-class blacks, migrant workers, and some others; but, apart from these, the trend toward external uniformity is evident.[4]

The Situation of the Catholic Minority

As we have noted, these external similarities may conceal sharp differences in beliefs and values. Members of the Catholic minority, in particular, cherish a distinctive set of beliefs regarding the meaning of life, the sacramental quality of the marital bond, the purposes of the marriage vocation, and the normative moral values pertinent to the use of sex. Since they constitute an identifiable cultural sub-group and must consequently rely chiefly on their own resources in striving to actualize their distinctive marriage and family values, we may safely predict that they will encounter some distinctive problems as they continue to move toward fuller integration with American society.

Stated briefly, a minority can retain its religious minority identity either by isolating itself from the alien influence of the dominant culture, as some groups such as the Mennonites are striving to do, or by selective integration. American Catholics have always opted for the latter solution, but until the last few decades the major portion of them remained relatively isolated, owing to their ethnic and regional urban concentration, immigrant and culturally alien origins, and related socio-economic status.[5]

This incidental form of isolation is rapidly ceasing to exist, with the result that Catholics are beginning to experience the full impact of their increasingly secularized social environment. Under these conditions of pluralism and rapid change, modern Catholic couples can be expected to retain their distinctive family values only on the condition that they clearly understand the religious foundations of their values, are adequately motivated, and enjoy some measure of group support from their coreligionists.[6] Because selective integration, as the term is used here, requires careful discernment in adopting behavioral patterns and practices that are consonant with the effective attainment of their values, the development of appropriate critical acumen and discriminating moral judgment must henceforth claim top priority in the religious formation of minority group members. This clearly implies a considerable change in the Church's traditional system of religious indoctrination, which up to the present has largely been concerned with only the routinized transmission of basic doctrinal formula, ritual etiquette, and a more or less standardized series of moral imperatives.[7]

Keeping in mind their historical background, religiously distinct minority status, and relatively high mobility, what are the major problems that Catholic families now face? In general, evidence that the modern American family's adjustment to its industrialized urban environment is not proceeding satisfactorily appears in the roughly one million marriages annually broken by divorce or separation, in the precipitous fall in the birth rate, in the apparent steady increase of all types of juvenile delinquency, and in the numerous indications of widespread pre-marital and extra-marital promiscuity resulting annually in an estimated 800,000 out-of-wedlock pregnancies.[8] As a matter of fact, a profound malaise prevades the national climate of opinion in regard to sex, marriage, and the family. This reflects a vague though fairly generalized awareness of an impending unresolved moral crisis.

It would indeed be superficial to view the present state of uncertainty and confusion in this regard as little more than perplexed concern with the personal maladjustments or transitory social imbalances resulting from lags or delays in adopting traditional ways of thinking and doing to the shifting requirements of our technologically advancing urban environment. Rather, it is becoming increasingly clear that we have finally succeeded in rejecting past "medieval," "Puritan," or "Jansenist" attitudes, assumptions, and norms only to discover that we lack a commonly acknowledged set of beliefs and values on the basis of which we can formulate acceptable new goals and standards. When there is no agreement on basic beliefs and values, there is likely to be little agreement on practical programs of action. Particularly under conditions of democracy, conflicting moral ideals and ideologies tend to neutralize each other in the public forum since the concerted effort needed for shared thinking and acting is paralyzed by the divergence of opinions.

In the practical order, this means that rapidly changing, complex, pluralistic societies like our own, by placing the burden of choice wholly on the individual, make heavy demands on their members. At a minimum, responsible decision-making requires some understanding of pertinent facts, relevant value premises, available alternatives, and practical consequences. Our current national malaise relating to sex, marriage, and the family should serve to remind us that failure to provide people with these prerequisites of responsible decision-making can prove just as destructive of authentic freedom as the arbitrary imposition of external restraints on its exercise.

Catholic families are necessarily exposed to all the social features generating these difficulties, but because they cherish a distinctive set of marriage and family values, they are bound to experience their impact somewhat differently from others. In this regard we may assume that since the family is designed to promote the happiness and development of the couple, together with the adequate socialization of their offspring, as these basic functions are currently defined by the Christian community, anything that inhibits or impedes the satisfactory fulfillment of these functions will constitute a source of disorganization.

Special Problem-Areas

What features of contemporary society are most relevant in this regard? Let us begin with one of the more obvious. Out-group marriages pose a perennial threat to the survival of any cultural or religious minority. Yet, for a number of reasons, it seems safe to predict that the rate of mixed marriages will continue to increase. Not only are many of the formerly inhibiting factors such as ethnic solidarity, high urban concentration, and lower social-class status of Catholics gradually disappearing, but there is considerable evidence that contemporary young people are not strongly disposed to accept religious restraints in matters they regard as subject primarily to their personal decision and concern.[9] Even those who identify themselves as Christians, or, at least, as earnest seekers after truth, are little inclined to acknowledge the need for legal codes or formal authoritative structures. Further change in the Canon Law affecting mixed marriages may be forthcoming, yet the major problem such marriages involve are not legal but distressingly human. The intimacy normally associated with marital companionship and parenthood is not easily reconciled with marked differences in beliefs, values, and normative practices acquired through long years of learning and conditioning. This observation applies to all marriages, though its special relevance for mixed marriages should be clear.

Another feature of contemporary society that is bound to affect Catholic families increasingly in the future is the widespread acceptance of divorce and separation.[10] The shift to a conjugal-type family has placed a heavy strain on marital unity, for the restricted family circle now remains the only acceptable social vehicle providing for the expression of affection and for the potentially explosive emotional interaction resulting from stresses and frustrating strains generated outside the family but finding no outlet there, where they have arisen. Add to this situation the popular philosophy that each individual has the right to seek complete personal fulfillment regardless of previous commitments, present responsibilities, or future consequences; the promotion or toleration of early cross-sex relationships leading to precocious emotional involvement, sexual experience, and premarital pregnancy; the limitation of family size and the consequent shortening of the period during which women must be preoccupied with the immediate needs associated with bearing and rearing children; the resultant increased freedom of married women to enter the work force, enjoy wider social contacts, and achieve greater independence; the recent discovery and extensive acceptance of contraceptive techniques that effectively separate sexual relations from procreation and which, together with family limitation, give rise to a new awareness of women's capacity to enjoy sexual relations; and it should be evident that the maintenance of marital fidelity and stability will constitute an increasingly difficult challenge.

A further problem-area that the modern family must deal with relates to population control. The drastic reduction in the family's procreative function, progressively rendered imperative by the recent continued rise in both *the absolute increase* of the world's population and the *rate of increase,* necessarily involves a number of basic structural and value changes that seriously challenge essential elements in traditional family patterns and makes the future of these systems highly problematic. This is a qualitatively different situation from any the family has faced in the past. The changing American context of responsible family planning in relation to contemporary population problems, for example, is indicated by the following estimate. Under current conditions, that is, 5 percent of women remaining single, 96 percent surviving to the mean age of childbearing, and the sex ratio at birth remaining about 105 males to 100 females, married couples need to have only about 2.2 children for purposes of replacement. All births in excess of this number represent a population increase, and since the population base is large, even a small percentage increase constitutes a large number of people.

It should be noted that the central issue in regard to this problem is not the matter of population control or lack of natural resources, but, rather, the far-reaching individual and societal implications of this limitation of reproduction considered as an essential component of the future human condition.[11] In other words, given the eventual imperative need for a generalized drastic curtailment of procreation, what types of personality structure, sexual relationships, and marriage and family patterns will be functionally feasible? What types are most likely to emerge? Frankly, we have no way of knowing for sure. In the present state of the social sciences, we must rest content with more or less educated guesses. Nevertheless, what we do know for certain is that we must now deal with a substantially new situation and that this entails, at a minimum, a comprehensive reappraisal and reformulation of long-standing conceptions of human sexuality, of the purposes and properties of marriage, and of the meaning of human fulfillment. In the practical order, it also entails a judicious redefinition and restructuring of masculine and feminine roles in marriage, society, and throughout the life-cycle.

Another area of major concern relates to young people and the structure of modern society. Because successful participation in our complex, technologically advanced society requires a lengthy period of increasingly specialized formal preparation, modern young people must spend a good portion of their youthful years attending various types of educational institutions. This lengthened period of youthful dependency not only greatly increases the material and psychic costs of parenting, but places biologically mature young men and women in the difficult situation of trying to avoid deep emotional involvements and sexual intimacy while spending years of study and leisure together in a relatively closed academic sub-culture where they are excluded from responsible participation in the adult community.[12] Neither society nor the churches have yet developed any workable programs for dealing with this extremely critical situation. Apparently because of the peculiar aberrations relating to Christian conceptions of modesty and chastity that became current in Western culture several centuries ago, most contemporary parents, teachers, and religious leaders seem incapable of understanding, or at least of acknowledging, the obvious biological, psychological, and social implications of sexual development in their growing children—perhaps even in themselves. Hence it is small wonder that some troubled teenagers regard their elders with a mixture of pity and contempt. Hypocrisy, even when unconscious or disguised as pious ignorance, is not one of the qualities of leadership.

Finally, owing to an impressive combination of changes— increased longevity, greatly reduced family size, earlier age at marriage, and the restriction of childbearing to the initial years of marriage—the relative portion of the average woman's total life span now devoted to bearing and rearing children has been greatly diminished. Given current rates of life expectancy, at 40, she still has more than half her life-span ahead of her. This situation has given rise to a number of presently unanswered questions.[13] Are women to combine marriage and a job outside the home? They presently make up roughly 40 percent of the labor force. Are young women to be trained for a career in the same manner as young men? At present they receive over 40 percent of the college degrees granted, and if recent trends continue, they will soon equal or surpass young men in this respect. Since advance in one's career frequently involves an individual in geographical mobility, how feasible are two-career marriages? Modern couples enjoy a much longer marriage expectancy and a longer period of the "empty nest"—at the turn of the century, over half of all marriages were broken by the death of one of the partners before the last child was "launched." How can couples develop and maintain the kind of enduring companionship needed, particularly since their work experience usually involves them in separate "worlds," and the scope of their shared concern with children has been notably diminished? Now that the use of sex is largely separated from procreation and serves primarily as a relational function, while its significance for women has shifted from the obligation of rendering the "debt" to the right of equal enjoyment, what changes in values, attitudes, and norms are required to assure not only its restriction to marriage but also its function as a mutually supportive, unifying, unique expression of "coupleness" in marriage?

Family Education and Action

If the foregoing facts and observations are substantially correct, we may safely conclude that the American Catholic community will encounter special difficulties in providing the understanding, motivation, and support that are required for the effective maintenance and transmission of its marriage and family values. In particular, its members must acquire a clear understanding of the religious foundations of these values; that is, they must understand how these values are related to the superordinate system or complex of distinctively Catholic beliefs which gives these values their normative significance and makes them matter of ultimate concern. Today, perhaps as never before, these values are being challenged in both theory and practice. Under such conditions, they can continue to "make sense," to attract lasting commitment, and to provide the essential moral guidelines for making discerning choices when adjusting to change, only if the faithful are accustomed to view them within their comprehensive, integral, creedal context as a matter of course.

Several additional factors underlining this need for a more discerning religious training on the part of all come readily to mind. Owing to increased education and social mobility, as well as to the "normative ambiguity" and "credibility gap" resulting from recent developments and controversies within the Church, the upcoming generation of American Catholics are no longer likely to accept their family values solely on the basis of authority or tradition. At the same time, the powerful supernatural, juridical, social, and psychological sanctions that formerly operated to encourage conformity and inhibit deviance have been seriously eroded. Whether we consider the balanced Christian "sense of sin" normally acquired in early home and school training, or the more general respect for authority structures and authority itself, we can easily document a notable attrition in these areas, particularly among adolescents and young adults but also as a pervasive component of the total climate of opinion affecting all members of society.[14] This anomic or normless orientation of contemporary American thoughtways is bound to result in a considerable "withdrawal of affect" from Catholic family values, together with a marked diminution of needed mutual encouragement and support even on the part of minority group members.[15]

Although secularizing trends undoubtedly vary in strength from diocese to diocese and have a different impact on different social classes within each diocese, no perceptive observer of the contemporary scene can deny that they have serious implications for practical programs of action relating to marriage and the family. Stated in summary fashion this means that in designing a feasible pastoral approach to the challenging new issues we face in regard to sex, love, marriage, and the family, we can no longer assume that the faithful fully understand the total Christian context of relevant beliefs within which acceptable solutions must be formulated. In the practical order, this implies that we take as our starting point what might be called the essential religious vocation of Christians that they receive at baptism and which calls them to union with Christ in his mission of building up the Kingdom through operative charity, that is, through progressive love of God and neighbor.

The marriage vocation, like all other Christian vocations, involves a further and more specific determination of this essential religious vocation. In other words, it defines the essential relevant relationships through which and within which conjugal partners are to manifest their operative love of God and neighbor. Although these essential relationships are ultimately founded on the dual sexual character of the human species as God created it, and they consequently involve some basic "givens," their specific determinations will depend on the socio-cultural situations within which the family operates, as well as upon the religious context of beliefs within which they are interpreted and attributed Christian meaning and value.

This means that as a voluntary total sharing of the whole of life, marriage is both "covenant" or "contract" and "community." As a mysterious two-in-one-flesh, potentially procreative unity involving a unique sacramental givenness, it is community, and this constitutes its unchangeable aspect. As a union of love and life involving what is culturally conditioned and freely chosen, it is covenant or contract, and this is its voluntary, dynamic aspect. Among different family systems, as well as among individual marriages, primary concern may be placed on either covenant or community, on what each partner chooses to give or what is "given" in the nature of things; but both are involved in every marriage.

Owing to this dynamic, voluntary, "covenant" aspect of marriage, we should regard the marriage contract primarily as a learner's permit. Marriage involves "givens" in terms of unity and potential parenthood, but the Christian quality of a given marriage will depend on the continued willingness of the partners to grow in mutual understanding, respect, trust, tenderness, and love. Only on this voluntary, carefully nurtured, dynamic foundation will they be able to extend their concern to children and the wider community. Perhaps because conjugal love is initially so normal and so needed, it is too readily taken for granted. But marriage is a way of life, and all living implies growth. Partners can grow together or grow apart. They can help each other actualize their individual potentials as unique images of God or inhibit and smother them. Finally, marriage is not only an "I" and a "thou," but a "we" relationship; two persons proceeding hand in hand, looking in the same direction and mutually supporting each other as they move toward the fulfillment of their highly personal yet inextricably inter-related goals.

Notes

1. Yankelovich, Skelly, and White, Inc., 1975 *The General Mills American Family Report: A Study of the American Family and Money,* (Minneapolis: General Mills, Inc., Paul C. Glick, 1975), "A Demographer Looks at American Families," *Journal of Marriage and the Family,* 37:15-26.

2. N. and G. O'Neil, 1972 *Open Marriage,* (New York; M. Evans and Co.; Smith J. and Smith L., 1974), *Beyond Monogamy,* (Baltimore; Johns Hopkins Press).

3. James L. Gibbs, 1964, "Marital Instability among the Kpelle: Toward a Theory of Epainogamy," *Readings on the Family and Society,* ed. by William J. Goode, (Englewood Cliffs, N.J.: Prentice-Hall, Inc.), 196-203.; William J. Goode, 1964, "The Meanings of Class Differentials in the Divorce Rate," ibid, 204-206; S. F. Nadel, 1968, "Social Control; Internal Variety and Constraints," *Modern Systems Research for the Behavioral Scientist,* ed. by Walter Buckley, (Chicago; Aldine Publishing Co.), 401-408; John L. Thomas, *The American Catholic Family,* (Prentice-Hall, Inc.), 327-372.

4. U.S. Bureau of the Census, 1975, "Some Recent Changes in American Families," Series P-23, No. 52, (Washington, D.C.: U.S. Government Printing Office).

5. Thomas, 1956, *The American Catholic Family* passim.

6. Thomas, 1958, *The Catholic Viewpoint on Marriage and the Family,* (Garden City, N.Y.; Hanover Press).

7. Thomas, 1963, *Religion and the American People*, (Westminister, Md.: The Newman Press).

8. June Sklar and Beth Berjov, 1975, "The American Birth Rate: Evidence of a Coming Rise", *Science,* 189:693-700.

9. Larry L. Bumpass and James A. Sweet, 1972, "Differentials in Marital Stability: 1970," *American Sociological Review,* 37:754-766;

John Mulhern, 1968, "Interfaith Marriage and Adult Religious Practice," *Sociological Analysis,* 30:23-31; Thomas, 1956, *The American Catholic Family,* 148-69.

10. Paul C. Glick and Arthur J. Norton, 1971, "Frequency, Duration and Probability of Marriage and Divorce," *Journal of Marriage and the Family,"* 33:307-317; 1973, "Perspectives on the Recent Upturn in Divorce and Remarriage," *Demography,* 10:301-314.

11. Thomas, 1958, *Marriage and Rhythm,* (Westminister, Md.: The Newman Press), 26-55; "Family Sex, and Marriage in a Contraceptive Culture," *Theological Studies,* 35:134-153.

12. J. Richard Udry, 1974, "Premarital Sexual Behavior," *The Social Context of Marriage,* 3rd ed., (New York: J.B. Lippincott Co.), 102-130.

13. Jesse Bernard, 1975, *Women, Wives, Mothers: Values and Options.* (Aldine Publishing Co.).

14. Philip Reiff, 1966, *The Triumph of the Therapeutic,* (New York: Harper and Row).

15. Thomas, 1970, "The Catholic Tradition for Responsibility in Sexual Ethics," *Sexual Ethics,* ed. by John Charles Wynn, (New York: Association Press), 131-151; "The Road Ahead," *Sexual Ethics and Christian Responsibility,* ed. by Mary S. Calderone, (Association Press), 132-151.

Part V
Documentation

The Problem of Second Marriages

AN INTERIM PASTORAL STATEMENT
BY THE STUDY COMMITTEE
COMMISSIONED BY
THE BOARD OF DIRECTORS
OF
THE CATHOLIC THEOLOGICAL SOCIETY OF AMERICA
REPORT OF AUGUST 1972

Introduction

The Church's mission where the institution and the sacrament of marriage are concerned is to aid individuals and the community to live marriage according to the teaching of Christ. This aid must include constant proclamation of the meaning of marriage "in Christ" and its indissolubility, preparation for permanent marriage and support for existing marriages. It must also include some form of pastoral care for those involved in unions which have failed. This statement will consider two general areas of pastoral concern: 1) the problem of entering second marriages; 2) the problem of participation in the full life of the Church by those already involved in them.

Problem of Second Marriage

It would be rash to assert that every first marriage that has failed was invalid from the beginning, but there are serious reasons today that were either not present or not recognized in the past to question the validity of many of them. One reason that is deservedly being given attention today by the human sciences and theology is the incapacity of some individuals for the type of commitment marriage calls for. This condition, sometimes called "psychological impotence," is being increasingly recognized by church tribunals. And there is good reason to recognize it not only as a defect that would disqualify a person for any marriage, but like physical impotence, one that can be relative to a particular marriage partner.

This incapacity is especially evident in many teenage marriages. The much higher divorce rate currently associated with teenage marriages forces one to question whether many young people are sufficiently mature to make a marriage commitment. The question of maturity has been an important factor in ecclesiastical legislation regarding the age requirement both for perpetual vows and for sacred orders. Is the difference between the religious commitment and the marriage commitment so great that the latter calls for less maturity? Is there not reason to think that it may take at least as mature a person to see beyond the natural attractiveness of marriage and properly assess the long range problems of this commitment? Such maturity cannot indeed be identified with any particular chronological age, but neither can it be entirely dissociated from age.

In connection with this problem of marital commitment attention should be called to the shift in emphasis that has taken place in Catholic thought on the nature of marriage. Before Vatican II the emphasis was on marriage as a contract. Marital consent was aimed at the act of sexual intercourse, and primarily at the procreative aspect of this act. Since Vatican II the Church sees marriage and marital consent oriented not simply to a particular act but to a total community of life and love. In demanding a basic capacity for marital community as a requirement for valid consent, the tribunals have already moved in this direction. But even more is possible. For in cases where this kind of community has never developed we believe that there is reason to question the validity of the original consent even apart from the more basic issue of capacity. It may not always be easy to judge these cases, but the current emphasis on this type of commitment would seem to demand that they be given consideration.

In addition, we cannot ignore the impact the American attitude toward marriage and divorce must have on those who live in this country. In our culture today there is a desire for loving union, but the growing divorce rate clearly indicates a lack of interest in continuing it if it does not work out. There is a recognition of permanence in the marital commitment, and a desire for it, but considerably less acceptance of absolute indissolubility. According to present church law, simple error regarding indissolubility will not invalidate a marriage consent, but one wonders how realistic it is to speak in terms of simple error in a culture where this type of thinking prevails. We believe that even in Catholic marriages, and in spite of the official teaching of the Church, the intention of those entering the marriage may often be at least implicitly conditioned. (Reason for concern about this is indicated also by the fact that the rate of marital breakup for Catholics approximates the general divorce rate.)

All of these considerations, where they are applicable, raise serious questions about the validity of a marriage that has failed. On the other hand, they may not always, or even often, add up to the moral certainty a tribunal requires.[1] This means that in current law and much tribunal practice nothing can be done for problem marriages, at least in the legal forum, since apart from such certainty a marriage tribunal may not declare a marriage null. In many instances, therefore, these men and women are not being treated as free to enter another union.

As long as the first marriage is not declared invalid, it is understandable in the present conditions that the Church would hesitate to celebrate a second union. But can these people be reasonably obliged in conscience not to enter a second union? There is question here of a very basic right, the right to marry. Can the Church forbid a person to marry unless it is certain that he does not have this right? In our judgment the absolute prohibition of a second union in cases of doubt is not a necessary public protection of Christian marriage.[2]

In the light of these considerations it is the judgment of this committee that a marriage case is not automatically closed by a negative decision in the legal forum. Regard for the limitations of the law as well as respect for conscience demand that the local Christian community provide further professional assistance on a more personal level to help couples form their consciences regarding their freedom to marry. While the criteria that should guide such conscience decisions can hardly be spelled out precisely or exhaustively, the following may be helpful in determining whether a true Christian marriage ever came into existence: 1) fidelity or its absence from the beginning of the union; 2) absence of every conjugal or familial characteristic; 3) brevity of common life; 4) tolerance or intolerance of common life.

If after such professional consultation a couple decide in conscience that they are justified in entering a second union, the Christian community and its designated representatives should refrain from a judgment of their decision, neither disapproving nor penalizing the couple in any way. Since there are numerous reasons for questioning the validity of first marriages that break down irrevocably, reasons which may not provide the moral certainty demanded by a tribunal, we believe that it is reasonable to admit that a person's marital status before God may not correspond to his status before the law. To accept this is to recognize the limitations of any human community, even one established by God, in determining true marital status. While the community will not officially celebrate these second unions, it will, however, respect the good consciences of those who enter them and help them with whatever pastoral guidance or assistance is necessary.

This is not to say that an individual couple will always be right in their judgment about their freedom to marry. It is not to say either that every couple will be in good faith or that there will be no moral fault in their decision to marry again. There may well be cases in which there is little or no reason to doubt the validity of the first marriage. There will surely be many cases where, if the person is honest, he will accept the conclusion of the tribunal and the advice of his counselors, and judge that he is not free to enter a second marriage. The point we wish to make here is that the Church should develop a pastoral practice that recognizes the limits of human efforts, especially in the legal forum, to determine a believer's marital status.

Second Marriages and Participation in the Life of the Church

A second problem concerns the reception of the sacraments and participation in the life of the Church by those who have already entered second marriages. At the present time, because of a long-standing theological position, these people are judged unworthy of receiving the sacraments, especially sacramental absolution and the Eucharist, and are frequently subjected to certain social sanctions. This has been true even where the second marriage is obviously stable and the couple are living up to all their other religious obligations. The Church, while acknowledging that it may be wrong in many cases for these couples to separate because of obligations to the children and even to each other, has nevertheless continued to refuse them the sacraments unless they would agree to live as brother and sister. Since the willingness to accept such an arrangement and the possibility of living up to it have been understandably rare, most of those presently living in invalid marriages have been deprived of integral participation in the life of the Christian community.

It is the judgment of this committee that, whatever may have been its theological justification or benefits in the past, there is serious reason to modify this practice. From the many reasons we have already cited for questioning the validity of marriages that have broken down, and the powerlessness of any human community to judge so many of these cases with certainty, one can reasonably conclude that there are Catholics whose marital status in the eyes of God does not correspond to their legal status. Also, there are unions, e.g., where children are involved, where it may be morally wrong to terminate the relationship. Many will not understand how it will be possible for them to sustain this relationship without marital union. We do not think these people should be excluded from the sacraments or participation in the life of the Church. If a couple decide after appropriate consultation, reflection and prayer that they are worthy to receive the sacraments, their judgment should be respected. If the consultation and the judgment that takes shape around it are to be responsible, they must center on the quality of the present union, its fidelity and stability, the state of conscience of the couple, the quality of their Catholic lives in other respects, their acceptance by the community.

Some might object that this solution would be a source of scandal. It would arise from the fact that these people are accepted into full participation in the life of the Church without any change in their present status. But we believe that if the reasons we have given are properly explained to the Catholic people, fear of scandal is unjustified. Morever, when these couples are leading otherwise responsible and religious lives, their standing in the community is usually very good.

Theology of Marriage

Our experience in preparing this statement has convinced us that any attempt to provide a pastoral response to these urgent problems raises fundamental questions about the theology of marriage. For instance, the criteria for determining the existence of an indissoluble marriage call for a judgment regarding the sacramentality of the marriage. The method of arriving at this determination has traditionally paralleled that used for establishing consummation, namely a single discrete physical act (apart from the marriage consent), in this case the valid reception of baptism. The relation of that isolated act to a person's subsequent life was not taken into consideration. Advances in the fields of ecclesiology, ecumenism and sacramental theology have convinced us that such a procedure represents an inadequate understanding of the sacrament of baptism, and therefore of the sacrament of marriage. The act of baptism can only be properly understood as part of a life-long process of commitment which is constantly being renewed. The evidence of one's total life as a Christian must be taken into account in evaluating the sacramentality of a marriage. However difficult this norm may be to apply, we must work toward transcending an evaluative norm which in fact embodies an inadequate baptismal theology.

Questions are also raised regarding the nature of the marriage covenant, the meaning of consummation, the role of the Church in regulating marriage, indissolubility, the power of the Church to dissolve marriages. It is our belief that the theological community has an obligation to the people of God to address itself to such questions as these in greater depth than it has. It is our belief also that the investigation of these questions cannot be carried out in isolation from other branches of theology or from the human sciences. We recommend therefore that the Catholic Theological Society of America set up a committee to study these questions. Without such a study one can hardly expect a growing and harmonious convergence of the Church's public witness (doctrine, law, practice) with the inner life of individuals and their judgments of conscience.

COMMITTEE ON THE PROBLEM OF SECOND MARRIAGES

John R. Connery, S.J., *Chairman*
Joseph E. Kerns
Richard A. McCormick, S.J.
Brendan McGrath, O.S.B.
James T. McHugh
John L. Thomas, S.J.
George B. Wilson, S.J.

Notes

1. The tribunal system has been helpful in determining the true marital status of couples whose marriages have failed. Like any legal system, however, it is not without its limitations. The most a tribunal has ever attempted by way of a negative judgment is to pronounce that proof of invalidity is lacking (*non constat de nullitate*). There is admittedly a wide gap between such a judgment and one that would pronounce a first marriage certainly valid. In fact, a tribunal judgment of itself says no more than that proof of nullity is lacking, and it can coexist with actual nullity in a first marriage. The ability of a court then to determine true marital status is quite limited.

2. One might wish to argue that such a presumption is necessary to support first marriages, and that without it many first marriages would not survive. Because of the case with which one could be freed of the obligation, many couples facing a marriage problem would not make the effort necessary for survival. This objection fails to take into account the moral obligation those who enter a marriage covenant have to make it succeed. The possibility of entering a second marriage does not remove this obligation, nor the responsibility for a failure.

Resolutions on Family from the Detroit Call to Action Conference

Delegates to the U.S. bishops' bicentennial justice conference in Detroit in October 1976, made three basic recommendations to the bishops for improving family life: development of a comprehensive pastoral plan for family ministry; increased emphasis on the family's social role; and an improve ministry to separated, divorced and remarried Catholics. Calling for a "catechesis of marriage, sexuality and family" that will "create a favorable impression of marriage and an appropriate understanding of sexuality," the delegeates said they also see a "need to broaden our concept and practice of family ministry to families of diverse lifestyles." They urged that the "entire Catholic community" regularly and systematically participate in developing clear church positions on family-related issues through such mechanisms as pastoral councils. Pledging themselves to promote the reconciliation of separated, divorced and remarried Catholics with the community of faith, they urged the bishops to study the question of the reception of the sacraments by divorced Catholics and to seek an end to the automatic excommunication of divorced U.S. Catholics who remarry. The following resolutions were approved by the assembly.

Recommendation:
Support for Family Values

Christ, our Savior, both beautifully and forcefully spoke of the permanence and indissolubility of marriage. In response to his teaching and to assist the whole Catholic community to reaffirm its support of the beauty, dignity and sacramentality of marriage and the family and to increase its awareness that Christian marriage is to be a great sign of Christ's love for the church, we recommend:

1. That this assembly affirm: a) that committed, life-long marriage is a part of God's plan; b) that when husbands and wives love each other, they serve God; c) that children are an expression of the creative fruitfulness of human life and love; d) that to live in peace and security is the right and duty of every family, beginning in service to its members; e) that each family, as one among many families in the world, finds fulfillment in service to others; f) that within the common bonds of faith, each family has the right, and is encouraged to express its religious values within the context of its cultural heritage and to share it with others; g) that within the Christian family commitment marriage and family life should also enhance the freedom of men and women to fulfill their personal potential and participate fully in the life of their world; and h) that there is a powerful witness in loving families in which parents have been separated by divorce, death or economic crisis and in which a single parent and children cooperate in nurturing and supporting one another.

2. That the whole church, through the example of the lives of its members and through action undertaken in cooperation with other religious and civic groups, pledges itself to combat those contemporary social, economic and cultural forces which threaten all families.

There is a special need within the church that theologians collaborate in developing further the theology of matrimony. Recognizing the special needs of married couples and families, we strongly believe that a catechesis of marraige, sexuality and family based on contemporary and sound theology and the lived experience of the married should be implemented on every level of the church's life. This educational process should involve the church in educational programs for effective parenthood. This catechesis should create a favorable impression of marriage and an appropriate understanding of sexuality.

3. That the church, with the leadership of the bishops, develop a comprehensive pastoral plan for family ministry based upon a continuing process of dialogue between families and competent authorities.

Recognizing the value of the traditional nuclear family, we

see a need to broaden our concept and practice of family ministry to families of diverse lifestyles, including, but not limited to, single-parent families, childless couples, widowed and separated people.

In developing such a plan particular concern should be shown for:

a. The racial, ethnic and cultural diversity of the Catholic community;

b. The need for family-centered worship and religious education, both in the home and in the parish; we further recommend that Sunday be truly the Lord's day by establishing that day as a family day for all the members of the parish. In addition to the liturgy, the day shall include educational, recreational, and paraliturgical celebrations;

c. Pastoral programs which encourage formation of family groups for prayer, worship, sacramental preparation, marriage enrichment, family life education and mutual support, either within parishes or across parish boundaries;

d. The need for consideration of the family in Catholic programs of social service at all levels;

e. The need to develop an overall vision of social legislation that will strengthen marriage and foster family life, including legislation to protect the rights of parents to the moral guidance of their children;

f. The need to utilize the resources of other private and public agencies in the community if the needs of all families are to be served;

g. The need to formulate diocesan policies that would not only stress marriage as a sacramental vocation within the church but also apply some of the same safeguards and principles of preparation utilized in readying candidates for holy orders;

h. The need for providing information, counselling and support for families who have members who are part of a "sexual minority."

We recommend, further, that the bishops declare in the near future a family year.

4. That the bishops in conjunction with existing Catholic

marriage and family life movements provide a national structure to formulate and implement a pastoral plan for integrated family ministry. This structure should involve:

a. Establishment of a standing committee of the National Conference of Catholic Bishops with responsibility for marriage and family life. Furthermore, we strongly recommend the enlargement and support of the National Family Life Office by July 1, 1977.

b. Prompt establishment and support for diocesan family life offices with appropriate diocesan, vicariate, deanery and parish committees. To further this goal, we urge that every diocese name at least a family life liaison officer by September 1, 1977.

c. Recognition of the special competency of permanent deacons and lay people, especially married couples, in family ministry by seeking them out and assuring them roles of leadership and authority.

d. Appropriate training for all those involved in leadership positions in family ministry.

e. A just allocation of church resources, on every level, for family ministry programs and a review of all present church budgets in order to bring about an equitable distribution of personnel and finances for supporting these programs.

Recommendation: Family and Society

In order to assist the Catholic family to fulfill its responsibility to assist other families and participate in the redemption and transformation of society through an awareness of the constitutive gospel dimension of action on behalf of social justice, we recommend:

1. That all programs dealing in family life, at all levels in the church, address in a special way the specific education of families in making them aware of the needs of others in their neighborhood, their local communities, or in the world community. These family life efforts will work with other social justice agencies to create environments and develop programs which encourage families to get involved in an action and reflection process in the

service of others and the attainment of justice.

2. That ministry to strong marriages, as well as those in difficulty, be recognized as part of the social justice dimension of family life and that organizations and movements which specialize in marriage and family life include and/or develop programs dealing with the social justice dimension of family life and provide materials, models, resources and skills to enable families to open themselves to the injustices in the world, to reach out to those in need, and to provide channels through which they can contribute to the solution of such problems of injustice.

3. That the entire Catholic community regularly and systematically participate in developing a clear position on public policy and legislation. This public policy and legislation most specifically should promote societal conditions based on human rights and social justice which allow all families and individuals to function as free human beings. Further, public policy and legislation should protect the rights of families to participate in decision making regarding, but not limited to, education, total health care, and moral guidance of their members.

In order to help families arrive at positions of personal involvement and organized political action, the National Conference of Catholic Bishops and each diocese should work out mechanisms for organizing families into coalitions on family-related issues. To achieve these ends, we recommend the establishment of pastoral councils on the national, regional, diocesan, district, parish and neighborhood levels. State Catholic Conferences and the United States Catholic Conference, in implementing programs for political responsibility and social action, should consult with these councils and give priority attention to developing positions on issues of public policy which affect family life. Where possible, there should be ecumenical participation.

4. That families, as part of a pastoral social justice program related to media, and aided by parish and diocesan family life commissions, in cooperation with diocesan communications offices, the United States Catholic Conference Department of Communication, UNDA-USA (Catholic Association of Broadcasters and allied communicators) and the Catholic Press Associ-

ation and other religious and civic organizations and coalitions,

— Initiate or support efforts to *evaluate* the impact on family life of present and developing social communications media.
— And suggest positive actions for family utilization of and involvement in media.

That families, especially with the structures mentioned above and other organizations and coalitions dedicated to better broadcasting:

— Work to *promote* the human and aesthetic quality of network and local programming and policies in order to counteract dehumanizing values of consumerism and materialism;
— Work for the further limitation of programming depicting excessive violence and irresponsible sex:

    a. Through government regulatory agencies;
    b. Through local station accountability and ascertainment procedures;
    c. Through influencing program sponsors.

That families work again through the above mentioned structures to *support* programming which reinforces family values.

Recomendation: The Church and Divorced Catholics

We pledge ourselves to a serious effort to reconcile separated, divorced and remarried Catholics within our community of faith. Toward that end we recommend:

1. That dioceses and parishes extend pastoral care to separated, divorced and divorced/remarried Catholics by the development and implementation of effective programs of ministry, education, and group support.

2. That the people of God in the local Catholic communities put an immediate end to practices which brand separated, divorced, and divorced/remarried Catholics as failures or discriminate against them or their children in parish or diocesan

activities; further, that educational programs be developed and funded aimed at eliminating discriminatory attitudes which underlie these practices.

3. That the church leaders publicly address the request of the divorced who have remarried to receive, under certain conditions, the sacraments of the church. We ask this because many Catholic people do not understand that many divorced who have remarried are not necessarily excluded from the eucharist. We ask the bishops to develop more consistent, equitable, effective and more pastorally oriented procedures for dealing with annulment and dissolution of marriages throughout all the dioceses of the United States of America.

4. That the church invest in serious study of the causes of marital breakdown with particular attention to the impact of cultural conditions on marriage and family life. These studies, conducted in dialogue with married as well as separated, divorced, and divorced/remarried Catholics, would help shape realistic policies for strengthening family life.

5. That the bishops of the United States take the action required to repeal the penalty of automatic excommunication decreed by the Third Council of Baltimore for Catholics who "dare to remarry after divorce."

Bishops Vote to Repeal Excommunication

Bishop Cletus O'Donnell

The U.S. Catholic bishops voted in May, 1977 to lift the penalty of excommunication imposed on divorced Catholics who have remarried. Bishop Cletus O'Donnell of Madison, Wis., chairman of the National Conference of Catholic Bishops Committee for Canonical Affairs, issued a statement explaining the implications of the bishops' action. "We wish to help divorced and remarried Catholics without seeming to weaken the unbreakable bond of marriage covenant entered into freely in Christ," O'Donnell said. Divorced Catholics who have remarried should see in this action "a genuine invitation from the church community," he added. This step is "not a total solution," according to the bishop. But it is a "promise of help and support"; above all it is a "gesture of love and reconciliation from the other members of the church." The text of O'Donnell's statement follows:

All Catholics should be concerned, compassionate and loving toward their sisters and brothers in the faith who have suffered the tragedy of marital failure.

How are we to manifest Christian love toward those who are in invalid marital unions, without compromising or diluting Catholic teaching about Christian marriage? This is a critical, continuing problem. We wish to help divorced and remarried Catholics without seeming to weaken the unbreakable bond of marriage covenant entered into freely in Christ.

The decision of the Catholic bishops of the United States to seek to remove one burden from the shoulders of divorced and remarried Catholics—the church penalty of excommunication—must therefore be prefaced by a clear explanation.

To understand this decision, some explanation of church penalties is necessary. Most violations of church law and certainly most moral transgressions are not punished by church law. The latter is very different from civil law in which every regulation carries with it a penalty for violators.

Sometimes, however, church law does add the sanction of a penalty, because of the extreme seriousness of the violation or sinful action or perhaps because the abuse in question is or may become widespread. The added sanction does not make the transgression any more serious, nor does the absence of a sanction indicate that the act is not a sinful violation. In 1884 the bishops of the Third Plenary Council of Baltimore judged that remarriage after divorce, prohibited then as it is now, should have the added sanction of excommunication.

Excommunication is the most severe of church penalties. It means separation from the community of the faithful, prohibition of reception of sacraments, loss of any share in the public prayers of the church, prohibition of the holding of church offices and the exercise of church jurisdiction, etc. So severe is this penalty that it is never imposed simply as a punishment or for retribution. It is always an invitation to repentance and reconciliation with God and the church.

After study and reflection, the bishops of the United States have concluded that the removal of this particular excommunication, which is not in effect in other countries, can foster healing and reconciliation for many Catholics remarried after divorce. Apart from a national council, the bishops cannot take this action without prior permission of the Holy Father. Their decision is therefore subject to confirmation or ratification by him.

The positive dimensions of this decision are very real. It welcomes back to the community of believers in Christ all who may have been separated by excommunication. It offers them a share in all the public prayers of the church community. It restores their right to take part in church services. It removes certain canonical restrictions upon their participation in church life. It is a promise of help and support in the resolution of the burden of family life. Perhaps above all, it is a gesture of love and reconciliation from the other members of the church.

However, this important step is not a total solution to the problems of these people. It would be false and unfair to them to suggest otherwise. The church cannot recognize as valid and sacramental those second marriages after divorce, unless there has been a determination by a church tribunal on behalf of the church community that the persons involved are free to marry in Christ the Lord.

The general church law is to limit the full active participation of the remarried in church life. And the lifting of the burden of excommunication does not of itself permit those who have remarried after divorce to receive the sacraments of penance and the holy eucharist. This last and most difficult question—return to full eucharistic communion—can be resolved only in a limited number of instances, depending on the particular circumstances.

Those who have remarried and may have incurred the church penalty of excommunication should see in this decision to remove the penalty a genuine invitation from the church community. It is up to them to take the next step by approaching parish priests and diocesan tribunals to see whether their return to full eucharistic communion is possible.

The priests, religious and lay people who work in diocesan tribunals have made extraordinary efforts in the last few years to study and solve these problems. Clearer and simpler procedures together with a more profound understanding of the marriage covenant, have helped achieve an equitable solution of very many difficult personal problems. No one should hesitate to seek such assistance from parish priests and diocesan tribunals.

This decision, to remove the penalty of excommunication for remarriage after divorce, will not answer all questions by any means. It is only a single step but it offers encouragement and hope to disaffected or alienated Catholics.

Pastoral counseling, resolution of problems of conscience, evaluation of first marriages by diocesan tribunals, all are needed. For the future, thorough preparation for marriage and support for marriage and family life by the whole community of the church are the only genuine solutions.

Select Bibliography on Divorce and Remarriage in the Catholic Church Today

Robert T. Kennedy, J.U.D.
John T. Finnegan, J.C.D.

CHRISTIAN MARRIAGE

Books

Farley, *A Study in the Ethics of Commitment* (Dissertation Order #74-10, 674) Xerox University Microfilms, P.O. Box 1346 300 North Zeeb Rd., Ann Arbor, Michigan, 48106.

Gerke, *Christian Marriage: A Permanent Sacrament* (C.U.A. Studies in Theology #161 — Washington, 1965).

Haughey, *Should Anyone Say Forever?* (New York: Doubleday 1975).

Mueller, *The Inseparability of the Marriage Contract and the Sacrament According to 17th Century Authors* (Rome, 1958).

Schillebeeckx, *Marriage: Human Reality and Saving Mystery* (New York: Sheed and Ward, 1965). Cf. Part II "Marriage in the History of the Church".

Schleck, *The Sacrament of Matrimony* (Milwaukee, 1964).

Articles

Ashdowne, "A Study of the Sacramentality of Marriage: When is a Marriage Really Present? Future Dimension", *Studia Canonica* vol. 9 no. 2 (1975) pp. 287-304.

Croghan, "Is baptism the decisive factor?" 118 *America* (1968), pp. 222 ff.

DiSiano, "On theSacramental Reality of Christian Marriage", 24 *American Benedictine Review* (1973), pp. 493-509.

Dominian, "From Law to Love: An Evolving Theology of Marriage", *The Australasian Catholic Record*, January 1976, pp. 3-16. Also published in the *Catholic Mind*, May 1976.

Haring, "Fostering the Nobility of Marriage and the Family" in Commentary on Vatican II—ed. by Vorgrimler, 5 (1969), pp. 225-245. Since Haring was so influential in the drafting of *Gaudium et Spes*, arts. 47-52, this article is highly informative.

Kelly, "The Church's Understanding of Marriage", *Studia Canonica*, vol. 9 no. 2 (1975), pp. 277-287.

Kerns, "Triangular Marriage", *Communio* Fall 1974, pp. 275-284.

Kilmartin, "When is a Marriage a Sacrament?", 34 *Theological Studies* (1973), pp. 275-286.

LaDue, "Conjugal Love and the Juridical Structure of Christian Marriage", 34 *The Jurist* (1974), pp. 36-67. A very important article.

————," The Sacramentality of Marriage", *CLSA Proceedings* 6 (1974), pp. 25-35.

Lesage, "The Consortium Vitae Conjugalis: Nature and Applications", 6 *Studia Canonica* (1972), pp. 99-113. A remarkable article that has received wide circulation and comment.

McDonald, "Theological Development of Marriage as a Sacrament" 4 *Resonance*, pp. 87-117.

Mackin, "Consummation of Contract or Covenant?", *The Jurist* 32 (1972), pp. 213-223; 330-354.

Murtagh, "The Juridical Importance of Amor Conjugalis", 33 *The Jurist* (1973), pp. 377-383.

————, "The Consortium Vitae and some implications of the Jurisprudence on Verum Semen", *Studia Canonica*, vol. 8 no. 1 (1974), pp. 123-134.

O'Callaghan, "Marriage as a Sacrament", 55 *Concilium* (1970), pp. 101-110.

Palmer, "Christian Marriage: Contract or Covenant?" *Theological Studies*, (1972), pp. 617-665.

————, "Needed A Theology of Marriage", *Communio* Fall 1974, pp. 243-260. The articles, especially the first, have made the author quite famous.

Rahner, "Marriage as a Sacrament", 10 *Theological Investigations*, pp. 199-221.

Wicks, "Sacraments"—American Catechism—*Chicago Studies*, vol 12 no. 3 (1973), pp. 349-356.

. . .For an interesting exchange of letters on marriage as a sacrament, cf., "No Sacrament, No Marriage", in *The Furrow*, April 1975, pp. 230-233; June 1975, pp. 358-361.

THE ENDS OF MARRIAGE

Books and Recent Magisterial Statements

Cornely, *The Purpose of Christian Marriage* (C.U.A. 1950)

Doms, *The Meaning of Marriage* (London: 1939)

Ford and Kelly, *Contemporary Modern Theology*—vol 2 1964—Part I—"Ends of Marriage", pp. 1-165.

Griese, *The Marriage Contract and the Procreation of Offspring* (C.U.A. 1946).

Noonan, *Contraception* (Harvard Univ. Press, 1966), pp. 307-533.

Pope Paul VI, "On Human Life" (Humanae Vitae)—U.S.C.C. Publications, 1968.

_____, "Declaration on Certain Questions Concerning Sexual Ethics", Congregation for the Doctrine of the Faith, Dec. 29, 1975 (U.S.C.C. Publications, 1976).

_____, "Allocution to the Roman Rota on the Stability of Marriage", cf. *Origins,* March 18, 1976 (vol. 5 no. 39).

National Conference of Catholic Bishops Statement, "Pastoral Letter on Moral Values", Nov. 11, 1976. Cf. *Origins,* Nov. 25, 1976 (vol 6 no. 23). Also published in pamphlet form by U.S.C.C. Publications-1977.N.B. in section, "The Family" where the Bishops speaking about contraception, ". . .urge those who dissent from this teaching of the Church to a prayerful and studied reconsideration of their position".

Articles

Ahern, "The Marital Rights to children: A Tentative Re-examination", *Studia Canonica* 8 no. 1 (1974), pp. 91-108.

Conway, "The Recent Papal Allocution: The Ends of Marriage", 19 *Irish Theological Quarterly* (1952), pp. 75-79.

Connell, "The Catholic Doctrine on the Ends of Marriage", 1 *CTSA Proceedings* (1946), pp. 34-55.

Ennis, "The Ends of Marriage", 37 *The Clergy Review* (1952),   pp. 270-281.

Ford, "Marriage: Its Meaning and Purposes", 3 *Theological Studies* (1942), pp. 333-374.

LaDue, "The Ends of Marriage", 29 *The Jurist* (1969), pp. 424-427.

Levis, "Ends of Marriage", 9 *New Catholic Encyclopedia* (1967), pp. 267-270.

Lochet, "Ends of Marriage", 1 *Theology Digest* (1953), pp. 21-26.

Lonergan, "Finality, Love, Marriage", 4 *Theological Studies* (1943), pp. 477-510.

O'Callaghan, "Purposes of Marriage", 108 *Irish Ecclesiastical Record* (1967), pp. 266-272.

Regan, "Catholic Approach to Marriage", 21 *Irish Theological Quarterly* (1954), pp. 188-192; 258-264.

Vidal, "The Object of Consensus" in *The Future of Christian Marriage*—Concilium Series (Herder and Herder 1973), pp. 88-97.

Zaphiris, "The Morality of Contraception: An Eastern Orthodox Position", *Journal of Ecumenical Studies,* vol. 11 no. 4 (1974), pp. 677-690.

NB. The literature surrounding the "Humanae Vitae" issue was generally not included here. The pro and con of that debate comprises an extensive bibliography of its own.

THE INDISSOLUBILITY OF MARRIAGE

Books

Doherty, *Divorce and Remarriage* (St. Meinrad, Ind.: Abbey Press, 1974). For a review of this book and of Kelleher's, *Divorce and Remarriage,* cf., "Some thoughts on Divorce", P. J. Fitzpatrick, *New Blackfriars,* July 1976, pp. 292-303.

The issue of *Living Light* (vol. 13 no. 4), Winter 1976 has a special feature entitled, "Ministry to Separated, Divorced and Remarried Catholics", pp. 545-611. It might be worthwhile to mention this at this point in our course development.

Articles

Ambrozic, "Indissolubility: Law or Ideal?", *Studia Canonica* 6 (1972), pp. 269-288.

Bevilaqua, "The History of the Indissolubility of Marriage", 22 (*CTSA Proceedings*—1967), pp. 253-308.

Bosco, "Explosive new interpretations of Divorce and Remarriage", 54 *Marriage* (1972), pp. 2-9.

Boulanger, "L'indissolubilite du mariage, porquoi?", *Studia Canonica* vol. 8 no. 2 (1974), pp. 363-378.

Brown, "The Natural Law, the marriage bond and divorce", 15 *The Jurist* (1955), pp. 21-51.

Burre, "Perpetuity in the Marriage Bond", 14 *The Jurist* (1954), pp. 47-59.

Crouzel, "Remarriage after Divorce in the Primitive Church: Apropos of a recent book", 38 *Irish Theological Quarterly* (1971), pp. 21-41.

The "recent book" referred by Crouzel is, *Divorce and Remarriage,* by Victor J. Pospishil (Herder: 1967). Pospishil replies to the criticism of Crouzel in *Irish Theological Quarterly*, 38 (1971), pp. 338-347.

Curran, "Divorce: Catholic Theory and Practice in the United States" 168 *American Ecclesiastical Review* (1974), 3-34; 75-95. Reprinted in *New Perspectives in Moral Theology* (Fides 1974), pp. 212-276. A superb article but needs to be read critically.

_____, "Divorce: From a Perspective of Moral Theology", *Origins* vol. 4 no. 21 (Nov. 14, 1974), pp. 329-335. Also published in *CLSA Proceedings* 6 (1974), pp. 1-24.

Demmer, "The Irrevocable Decision: thoughts on the theology of vocation", *Communio* (1974), pp. 293-308.

DeRanitz, "Should the Roman Church Recognize Divorce?", *Listening* 6 (1971), pp. 60-70.

Doherty, "Consummation and the Indissolubility of Marriage" in *Absolutes in Moral Theology*, ed. C. Curran (Corpus Books)-1969-pp. 211-231.

_____, "Divorce and Remarriage: Catholics and Credibility", *CTSA Proceedings* 30 (1975), pp. 121-128.

Fellhauer, "The Exclusion of Indissolubility: Old Principles and New Jurisprudence", *Studia Canonica* vol. 9 no. 1 (1975), pp. 105-134.

Finnegan, "When is a Marriage Indissolubile?: Some Contemporary Reflections on the Ratified and Consummated Marriage", *The Jurist* 28 (1968), pp. 309-329.

Harrington, "Jesus' Attitudes Toward Divorce", 37 *Irish Theological Quarterly* (1970), pp. 199-209.

_____, "The New Testament and Divorce", 39 *Irish Theological Quarterly* (1972), pp. 178-187.

Hurley, "Christ and Divorce", 35 *Irish Theological Quarterly* (1969), pp. 58-72.

Jossua, "The Fidelity of Love and the Indissolubility of Christian Marriage", 56 *Clergy Review* (1971), pp. 172-181.

Kuntz, "Is Marriage Indissolubile?", *Journal of Ecumenical Studies* 7 (1970), pp. 333-337.

Lehmann, "Indissolubility of Marriage and the Pastoral Care of the Divorced who Remarry", *Communio* (Fall 1974), pp. 219-242. A superb article integrating the scriptural, theological, canonical and pastoral. Well worth reading.

Maloney, "Catholicism, Orthodoxy and Divorce", 7 *Diakonia* (1972), pp. 297-300.

Manning, "Divorce and Remarriage", 3 *Louvain Studies* (1971), pp. 243-258.

McCormick, "Notes on Moral Theology", 32 *Theological Studies* (1971) pp. 107-122; 33 *Theological Studies* (1972), pp. 91-100; 36 *Theological Studies* (1975), pp. 100-117.

McEniery, "Divorce at the Council of Trent", 167 *Australasian Catholic*

Record (1970), pp. 188-201.

Mills, "The Council of Trent and the Permanence of Marriage", *Resonance* (Spring 1967), pp. 35-47.

Noonan, "Indissolubility of Marriage and Natural Law", *American Journal of Jurisprudence* (1969), pp. 79-94.

O'Callaghan, "How far is Christian Marriage Indissolubile??", *Irish Theological Quarterly* (1973), pp. 162-173.

O'Shea, "Marriage and Divorce: The Biblical Evidence", 57 *Australasian Catholic Record* (1970), pp. 89-109.

Ryan, "The Indissolubility of Marriage in Natural Law", *Irish Theological Quarterly* 30 (1963), pp. 293-310; 31 (1964), pp. 62-70.

_____, "Survey of Periodicals: Indissolubility of Marriage", *The Furrow*, 24 (1973), pp. 150-159; 214-224; 272-284; 365-374; 524-539.
An outstanding summary of the "indissolubility question". Well worth reading and highly recommended.

Thompson, "A Catholic View of Divorce", *Journal of Ecumenical Studies* 6 (1969), pp. 53-67.

van der Poel, "Marriage and Family as an expression of 'communio' in the Church", *The Jurist* (1976:½), pp. 59-88.

Vawter, "Biblical Theology and Divorce", 22 *CTSA Proceedings* (1967), pp. 223-243.

THE INDISSOLUBILITY OF MARRIAGE AND THE CHURCH'S POWER TO DISSOLVE

Books

Bassett, ed., *The Bond of Marriage* (Notre Dame: 1968)

Kelleher, *Divorce and Remarriage for Catholics?* (Doubleday: 1973)

Meyendorff, *Marriage: An Orthodox Perspective*(St. Vladmir's Seminary Press, 1975).

Monserrat-Torrents, *The Abandoned Spouse* —trans. by G. MacEoin (Bruce: 1969).

Noonan, *The Power to Dissolve* (Harvard: 1972).

Pospishil, *Divorce and Remarriage* (Herder and Herder, 1967).

Steininger, *Divorce* (Sheed and Ward, 1969).

The Future of Marriage as an Institution —Concilium Series (1970).

The Future of Marriage —Concilium Series (1973).

Wrenn, *Divorce and Remarriage in the Catholic Church* (Newman: 1973). Winner of the Catholic Book Award in 1974.

Liberty and Justice for All —The Atlanta Hearing— "The Family" August 7-9, 1975 (Washington: U.S.C.C. Press, 1976).
Some excellent articles here on the contemporary experience of marriage, and the challenge this poses to Church people.

Articles

Bassett, "Divorce and Remarriage: The Pastoral Search for a Pastoral Reconciliation", 162 *American Ecclesiastical Review* (1970), pp. 20-36; 92-105.

Byron, "The Brother or Sister is not bound: Another Look at the New Testament Teaching on the Indissolubility of Marriage", 52 *New Blackfriars* (1971), pp. 514-521.

———, "General Theology of Marriage in the New Testament and in I Cor. 7, 1-15", 49 *Australasian Catholic Record* (1972), pp. 1-10.

———, "I Cor. 7, 10-15: A Basis for Future Catholic Discipline on Marriage and Divorce", *Theological Studies* 34 (1973), pp. 429-445.

Boivin, "On Dissolving Indissolubility", *New Blackfriars* 56 (November 1975), pp. 493-499.

Catterall, "Divorce and Remarriage", *Clergy Review* 52 (1967), pp. 887-892.

Curtin, "The Dilemma of Second Marriages", *America* 129 (1973), pp. 88-91.

Dupre(s), "Till Death Do Us Part", *America,* February 17, 1968. This entire issue is dedicated to the divorce question and is well done.

Gerhartz, "Can the Church Dissolve Sacramental Marriages?", *Theology Digest* 21 (1973), pp. 28-32.

Hertel, "Save the Bond or Save the Person", *America,* February 17, 1968.

Huizing, "The Indissolubility of Marriage and Church Order", *Concilium* 38 (1968), pp. 45-57.

Kuntz, "The Petrine Privilege: A Study of Some Recent Cases", *The Jurist* 28 (1968), pp. 486-496.

Leguerrier, "Recent Practice of the Holy See in Regard to Dissolution of Marriages Between Non-Baptized persons Without Conversion", *The Jurist* 25 (1965), pp. 458-465.

Maloney, "Oeconomia: A Corrective to Law", *Catholic Lawyer* 17 (1971), pp. 90-109.

McNevin, "The Indissolubility of Marriage as Effected by Consummation", *Resonance* 4 (1967), pp. 16-34.

Noonan, "Papal Dissolution of Marriage: Fiction and Function", *CLSA Proceedings* 1 (1969), pp. 89-95.

O'Connor, "The Indissolubility of a Ratified Marriage", *Ephermerides Theologicae Lovaniensis* 13 (1936), 692-722.
    A landmark article which triggered the modern development. Truly classic.

O'Callaghan, "Divorce and Remarriage", *Irish Ecclesiastical Record* 109 (1968), pp. 185-190.

Theology Digest 19 (Spring 1971). Entire Issue.

Walker, "The Invalid Convalidation: A Neglected 'Caput Nullitatis' ", *Studia Canonica* vol. 9 no. 2 (1975), pp. 325-336.

THE MATRIMONIAL TRIBUNAL

Abate, *The Dissolution of the Matrimonial Bond in Ecclesiastical Juris-prudence* (Rome: Desclee, 1962).

Amoto, et al., "Use of Objective and Projective Personality Test Data in the Determination of Nullity of Marriages: A New Method", 7 *CLSA Proceedings* (1975), pp. 106-128.

Burns, "Moral Certitude", 7 *CLSA Proceedings* (1975), pp. 38-47. For further reflections on this issue, cf., Lavin, "Canonical Equity applied to Moral Certainty and to the Worth of Expert Testimony", *The Jurist* (1975/2-3), pp. 316-322.

American Procedural Norms (Washington: USCC Publications, 1970). Also cf., "Procedural Norms for the United States"—ltr. of the Consilium Pro Publicis Ecclesiae Neqotiis of May 22, 1974 in *The Jurist* (1974/3-4), pp. 417-418; *Catholic Mind,* Oct. 1970.

Arella, "Approaches to Tribunal Practices", *The Jurist,* 31 (1971), pp. 489-505.

———, "Case for the Marriage Court", *America,* October 21, 1972. For a reaction to this article, cf., *America,* Nov. 4, 1972, p. 350.

Broussard, "Notes on Gathering Evidence in Formal Trials", *Studia Canonica* (vol. 8 no. 1), 1974, pp. 163-166.

Canon Law Society of Great Britain and Ireland Study Paper, "The Church's Matrimonial Jurisprudence: A Statement on the Current Position", October 1975. Published by Canon Law Society Trust, London. *This is required reading.*

Burns, "Do the Marriage Courts Creak?", *Origins* (vol. 3 no. 19), November 1, 1973. Also published in, 5 *CLSA Proceedings* (1973), pp. 138-147.

Cunningham, "Recent Rotal Decisions and Todays Marriage Theology: Nothing has Changed, or has it?", *Origins,* Oct. 28, 1976 (vol. 6 no. 19). Also, published in, 8 *CLSA Proceedings* (1976).

Dooley, "Marriage Annulments", *The Furrow,* April 1975, pp. 211-219. The author takes a dim view in the development of Marriage juris-prudence.

Dissolution of the Marriage Bond in the Favor of the Faith—A Declaration of the S. C. of the Doctrine of the Faith, Dec. 6, 1973. Published in *The Jurist* (1974/3-4), pp. 418-423.

The NCCB has circulated a document dtd., February 28, 1977, entitled: "Commentary on Instruction and Norms for the Resolution of Marriages in Favor of the Faith". (Available from JTF)

Finnegan, "The Current Jurisprudence Concerning the Psychopathic Personality", *The Jurist,* 27 (1967), pp. 440-453.

———, "The Capacity to Marry", *The Jurist,* 29 (1969), pp. 141-156.

———, "Marriage Law", *Chicago Studies* (Fall 1976), pp. 281-304. *This is required reading.*

Hudson, et al., *Handbook for Marriage Nullity Cases,* (Ottawa: St. Paul

268 MINISTERING TO THE DIVORCED CATHOLIC

University Press—2nd edition—1976). *This is a required text.*

Kelleher, "The Problem of the Intolerable Marriage", *America,* Sept. 14, 1968. On the occasion of the 50th Anniversary of *America,* the editors stated that this was the most controversial article in their history and received the most reader reaction. For a reaction to this controversial article, cf., Marion Reinhardt, "Updating Marriage Tribunals", *America,* November 9, 1968.

_____, "Annulments and Dissolutions of Particular Marriages", *Dunwoodie Review* 12 (1972), pp. 135-144.

Kenny, "Homosexuality and Nullity: Developing Jurisprudence", *The Catholic Lawyer* 17 (1971), pp. 110-122.

Lasage, "Pour une renovation de la procedure matrimoniale", *Studia Canonica* 7 (1973), pp. 253-280.

Morrisey, "Preparing Ourselves for the New Legislation", *The Jurist* 33 (1973), no. 343-357.

Nace, *The Right to Accuse a Marriage of Invalidity* (Washington: Catholic University Press, 1961).

O'Brien, "Are Marriage Courts Obsolete?", *Homiletic and Pastoral Review* (1971).

Pijnappels, "The Sufficiency of Evidence in Formal Trials", *Studia Canonica* vol. 8 no. 1 (1974), pp. 167-182.

O'Donnell, "Sunt Incapaces Matrimonii Contrahendi", *The Australasian Catholic Record,* January 1976, pp. 27-43.
   Don't be fooled by the latin title of the article. It is written in english and is well done.

Pope Paul VI, "Causas Matrimoniales", March 28, 1971. Cf. *The Jurist* 31 (1971), pp. 668, 672. This is also published in *Origins,* vol. 1 no. 5, June 22, 1971.
   For an interpretive study, cf. "Le motu proprio, 'Causas Matrimoniales' " 5 (1971), pp. 213-226.
   For a comparison with the *American Procedural Norms* (APN), cf., " 'Causas Matrimoniales' and the APN: A Comparison", and also, " 'Causas Matrimoniales' and the APN: A Survey", LaDue and Green, 5 *CLSA Proceedings* (1973), pp. 112-125.
   For a furthur in depth study and comparison here, cf., Green, "The American Procedural Norms: An Assessment", *Studia Canonica,* vol 8 no. 2 (1974), pp. 317-348.
   In regard to "Procedures" (called "De Processibus" and is Book IV of the present Code of Canon Law), the Commission for the Revision of the Code of Canon Law released to the world Episcopacy in early 1977 a proposed revision of "Procedures" or "Process". It is entitled: *Schema Canonum De Mode Procedendi Pro Tutela Iurium Seu De Progressibus.* As noted at the conclusion of Practicum #8 (*infra.*) there is no provision in the above proposal for the continuation of the APN.

Provost, "Church Tribunals and the Sacrament of Matrimony", *Chicago*

Studies (Fall 1972), pp. 319-328. A good article.

————, "Marriage: Change in Pastoral Care and in Canonical Practice", *Louvain Studies* (Fall 1974), pp. 179-189. Also worth reading.

Sanson, "Jurisprudence for Marriage: Based on Doctrine", *Studia Canonica* vol. 10 no. 1 (1976), pp. 5-36. This is a good article, and along with LaDue's article on p. 3 of this bibliography/outline, "Conjugal Love and the Juridical Structure. . . ."; and Cunningham's article cited on p. 31; and *Handbook for Marriage Nullity*, pp. 1-28, you have a good summary of the impact of Vatican II theology of marriage on the jurisprudence of the Church.

Salter, "Canon Law Divorce and Annulment of the Roman Catholic Church at the Parish Level", *Journal of Marriage and Family* (J- (January 1969), pp. 51-60. One disturbing fact discovered in this survey is that the most serious injustice in the entire annulment procedure is the failure of recourse that people (parishoners) have when the local clergy show disinterest in their petition for annulment.

Wrenn, *Annulments* (Harford: CLSA—2nd edition, 1972). A classic. By the end of 1976 more than 35,000 copies of this work have been sold.

————, "The American Procedural Norms", *American Ecclesiastical Review* (November 1971), pp. 175-186.

The Matrimonial Tribunal—Some Specialized Readings

Ahern, "Psychological Incapacity for Marriage", *Studia Canonica,* vol 7 no. 2 (1973), pp. 227-252. A good article.

Bauer, "Relative Incapacity to Establish Christian Conjugal Union", 6 *CLSA Proceedings* (1974), pp. 36-44. Dr. Bauer is a psychiatrist who works closely with the Brooklyn Tribunal.

Brown, "Incomplete Consent of Lack of Commitment: Authentic Grounds for Nullity?", *Studia Canonica* (vol. 9 no. 2), 1975, pp. 242-266. A companion piece to this excellent article is, "Total Simulation: A Second Look", *Studia Canonica,* vol. 10 no. 1 (1976), pp. 235-250.

Msgr. Ralph Brown of London is an excellent canonist and a name to remember.

Cleckley, *The Mask of Sanity,* (St. Louis: C. V. Mosby Co., 1964). This book is a great help to canonists working in the field of "forensic psychiatry".

Conway, "Psychiatric Immaturity and its Implications for the Marriage Contract", *The Australasian Catholic Record* 50 (1973), pp. 152-162.

Daley, "The Distinction between Lack of Due Discretion, and the Inability to fulfill the Obligations of Marriage", *Studia Canonica,* vol. 9 no. 1 (1975), pp. 153-166.

A fine article. I heard this paper delivered at the annual meeting of

Canon Law Society of Great Britain and Ireland, Ilkley (Yorkshire), England, May 10-13, 1975.

Dolciamore, "Interpersonal Relationships and Their Effect on the Validity of Marriages", 5 *CLSA Proceedings* (1973), pp. 84-100. Also published in *Origins,* vol. 3 no. 18 (Oct. 25, 1973), under the title of: "Annulments: The Psychology in Marriage".

Keating, *The Bearing of Mental Impairment on the Validity of Marriage* (Rome: Gregorian University Press, 1964). A classic doctoral thesis that developed the nexus between law and the behavioral sciences in determining the validity of marriage. Most likely every Marriage Tribunal in the world has a copy of this magisterial work.

———, "Marriage and the Psychopathic Personality", *Chicago Studies,* (Spring 1964), p. 19 ff.

———, "The Province of Law and the Province of Forensic Psychiatry in Marriage Nullity Trials", *Studia Canonica,* vol. 4 no. 1 (1970),pp. 5-24. Fr. Keating is a priest of the Archdiocese of Chicago.

Lesage, "The Consortium Vitae Conjugalis: Nature and Applications", 6 *Studia Canonica* (1972), pp. 99-113. This article was previously cited on p. 3 but fits in here as well. Some articles previously cited on p. 3 that are important here are: LaDue, "Conjugal Love. . . ."; Murtagh, "The Juridical Importance of Amor Conjugalis", and his other article, "The Consortium Vitae. . . ."

Lesage and Morrisey, *Documentation of Marriage Nullity Cases* (Ottawa: St. Paul University Press, 1973). A magisterial compilation of major Tribunal decisions on marriage (in several languages) from 1965-1973. Members of the Canadian Canon Law Society were notified in March 1977 that the sections of this work needing translation have now been put into english by Edward Hudson (vii–195 pp). Available through the Canadian Canon Law Society, 223 Main St., Ottawa, Canada. K1S 1C4.

McMahon, "The Rolo of Psychiatric and Psychological Experts in Nullity Cases", *Studia Canonica,* vol. 9 no. 1 (1975), pp. 63-74.

Morrisey, "Defective Consent: Toward A New Church Law", *Origins,* vol. 4 no. 21 (Nov. 14, 1974). Also published in, 6 *CLSA Proceedings* (1974), pp. 71-82 under the title of, "Proposed Legislation on Defective Marital Consent".

———, "The Incapacity of Entering into Marriage", *Studia Canonica* vol. 8 no. 1 (1974), pp. 5-22.

Matrimonial Jurisprudence—as of now 4 vols., 1968-1971; 1972; 1973; 1974. Published by the Canon Law Society of America. For another work on important Marriage Tribunal decisions, cf., *The Tribunal Reporter,* ed., Adam Maida (Huntington, Ind.: Our Sunday Visitor Press, 1970). NB.—The famous Anné Decision of the Roman Rota on Feb. 25, 1969 was an appeal from the Tribunal of Montreal, Canada. The original Montreal Decision is published in this work under the (pseudonym) title: "Fortin-Boisvert—Grounds: Lesbianism", pp. 457-473. To understand the implications and importance of the *Coram Anné* Decision it is helpful to place it in context by reading this summation of the original case in Montreal.

Murtagh, "The Jurisprudential Approach to Consortium Vitae", *Studia Canonica*, vol. 9 no. 2 (1975), pp. 309-324. Should be read in conjunction with his other articles cited on p. 3. He is a fine canonist, and is a priest of the Diocese of Portsmouth, England. A Rotal Decision, *Coran Raad* of April 14, 1975 was very negative in its analysis of contemporary jurisprudence in various parts of the world, especially the U.S.A. A Rotal Decision, *Coram Anné* of March 11, 1975, was, as might be expected, much more open to contemporary developments. Cyril Murtagh compares these two Rotal Decisions skillfully in, *Newsletter*—Canon Law Society of Great Britain and Ireland, No. 29 (June 1976), Appendix VIII, pp. 57-63. Anné's Decision, just cited, is translated in the same *Newsletter*, Appendix IX, pp. 64-75.

Russon, "Assessment of Personality Disorder in Marriage", *Studia Canonica*, vol. 9 no. 1 (1975), pp. 57-62.

Schumacher, "Interpersonal Communication in Marriage", *Studia Canonica* (vol. 9 no. 1), 1975, pp. 5-36.

This is a competent study of another famous Rotal Decision, *Coram Serrano*, dtd. April 5, 1973. For a translation of this important Decision, cf., *Newsletter*—Canon Law Society of Great Britain and Ireland, dtd. June 1975, Appendix III. For a superb Commentary on the "Coram Serrano Decision", cf. the article by Martin Lavin in Sept. 1975 issue of *Newsletter,* Appendix VIII.

For those interested in reading the issues of *Newsletter* which have been cited through this bibliography/outline I would be happy to make this possible.

————, "The Importance of Interpersonal Relations in Marriage", *Studia Canonica*, vol. 10 no. 1 (1976), pp. 75-112.

Seal, "Marriage: Psychiatric Incapacity", *The Australasian Catholic Record* 50 (1973), pp. 140-151.

THE INTERNAL FORUM SOLUTION TO THE CANONICALLY INVALID MARRIAGE

Allard, The Invalidly Married and Admission to the Sacraments", 56 *Clergy Review* (1971), pp. 34-41.

Carey, "The Good Faith Solution", 29 *The Jurist* (1969), pp. 428-438.

Carr, "The Invalidly Married and the Sacraments", *Homiletic and Pastoral Review* 71 (1971), pp. 316-318; 72 (1972), pp. 67-71; 71-74.

Catoir, "What to do when the Courts don't work", *America* (1971), pp.

272 MINISTERING TO THE DIVORCED CATHOLIC

254-257. A fine article.
CLSA Report of the Committee on Alternatives to Tribunal Procedures, cf. *CLSA Proceedings* 7 (1975), pp. 162-177. Also published in *Origins* (vol. 5 no. 18), dtd., Oct. 23, 1975 under the title of, "Pastoral Proposal for Divorced Catholics".
Coleman, "Pastoral Theology and Divorce", *American Ecclesiastical Review*, vol. 169 no. 4 (April 1975), pp. 256-269.
CTSA Committee Statement, "The Church and the Second Marriage", *CTSA Proceedings* 27 (1972), pp. 233-240. Also published in *America* (1972), pp. 258-260, and in *Origins*, (vol. 2 no. 16), dtd., October 12, 1972.
Dickey, *Divorced Catholics: An Imperative for Social Ministry* (Washington: National Conference of Catholic Charities, November 1, 1974).
Farley, Margaret, "Society and Ethics: Divorce and Remarriage", *CTSA Proceedings* vol. 30 (1975), pp. 111-120.
Farley, Leo and Reich, "Toward and Immediate Internal Forum Solution for Deserving Couples in Canonically Insoluble Marriage Cases", *The Jurist* 30 (1970), pp. 45074.
Finnegan, "Spiritual Direction for the Catholic Divorced and Remarried", *Chicago Studies* 13 (1974), pp. 54-64. Also published in, *CLSA Proceedings* (1973), pp. 70-83.
_____, "The Pastoral Care of Marriage", *Origins* (vol. 5 no. 10), August 28, 1975.
Haring, "Pastoral Work Among Divorced and Invalidly Married", *Concilium* 55 (1970), pp. 123-130.
Heffernan, "Divorce and Remarriage in the Contemporary United States", *Communio* Fall 1974, pp. 285-292.
Haring, "Internal Forum Solutions to Insoluble Marriage Cases", *The Jurist* 30 (1970), pp. 21-30.
Huizing, "Law, Conscience and Marriage", *The Jurist* 30 (1970), pp. 15-20.
Kelly, "The Invalidly Married and Admission to the Sacraments", 55 *Clergy Review* (1970), pp. 123-141. A good and thoughtful presentation.
Kosnik, "The Pastoral Care of Those Involved in Canonically Invalid Marriages", 30 *The Jurist* (1970), pp. 31-44.
Lehmann, "Indissolubility of Marriage and the Pastoral Care of the Divorced who remarry", Communio (Fall 1974), pp. 238-250. This article was previously cited and is well worth reading.
Living Light, Winter 1976—Special Feature, "Ministry to Separated, Divorced, and Remarried Persons". There are some excellent articles here on the pastoral care of divorced families. Well worth consulting.
Lobo, "The Invalidly Married", *Clergy Monthly* (1971), pp. 155-160.
McAndrew, "Pastoral Ministry to the Invalidly Married", *Homiletic and Pastoral Review*, vol. 73 (1973), pp. 26-30.

McCormick, "Indissolubility and the Right to the Eucharist: Separate Issues or One?", 7 *CLSA Proceedings* (1975), pp. 26-37. A superb treatment of the issues and should be read.

Nessel, "The Catholic Divorced: A Catholic Approach", *Homiletic and Pastoral Review* 73 (1973), pp. 10-14.

Origins—vol. 2–cf. pp. 130, 176, 188, 220, 251, 254-256, 320 in regard to the "Good Conscience Solution" . . . (to be distinguished from the Internal Forum Solution. Cf. *Chicago Studies* (Fall 1976) "Marriage Law" and the treatment of the IFS). "Good Conscience Procedures" were very much in the news in 1972 after the Bishop of Baton Rouge publicly encouraged them. For further info here, cf., *NCR*, Sept. 1, 1972; *ad correspondence,* "Good Conscince Cases", Sept. 16, 1972; *Catholic Mind* 70 (1972), pp. 5-8; *Social Justice* 65 (1972), pp. 200 ff.

Orsy, "Intolerable Marriage Situations: Conflict between Internal and External Forum", *The Jurist* 30 (1970), pp. 1-14.

Peter, "Divorce and Remarriage", *Communio* (Fall 1974), pp. 361.374.

Peters, et al., "Cohabitation in the Marital State of Mind", *Homiletic and Pastoral Review,* April 1966. One of the most important articles written on these issues since Vatican II, and certainly *the article* that inaugurated the contemporary Catholic concern for divorced persons.

Provost, "Divorced and Remarried Catholics", *Chicago Studies,* vol. 14 no. 2 (1975), pp. 218-224.

Rue and Shanahan, The Divorced Catholic (New York: Paulist Press, 1972). A good popular work. Chapter 11 of Alvin Toffler's *Future Shock* speaks of the impact on marriage and family life caused by contemporary life and mores.

Ryan, "Survey of Periodicals. . . .", *op. cit.* (cf. p. 12). Of special note are the last two cited which deal with the pastoral care of the divorced and the ensuing pastoral dilemmas.

Sattler, "Divorce and Remarriage in the Church", *American Ecclesiastical Review* 165 (1973), pp. 553-573.

True and Young, "Divorce and Remarriage", *Commonweal,* November 22, 1974, pp. 185-190; and "Divorce: Pastoral Concern", *Origins* (vol. 4 no. 4), dtd., June 20, 1974, pp. 49, 51-59.

Weisner, "Divorce: Remarriage and the Sacraments", *Catholic Mind* 69 (1971), pp. 34-38.

Whalen, "Divorced Catholics: A Proposal", *America,* Dec. 7, 1974, pp. 363-365. Also cf. the editorial in the same issue of *America,* p. 362. This article served as a basis of discussion on "Divorce and Reconciliation with the Church" at the NFPC House of Delegates Meeting, St. Petersburg, Fla., March 10-13, 1975. For the conclusions of the meeting re this topic and others, cf., *Origins* (vol. 4 no. 40), dtd. March 27, 1975. (pp. 629-631 for the NFPC Statement on Divorce and Remarriage)

Notes on the Contributors

GEORGE W. MacRAE, S.J., Ph.D. is Charles Chauncey Stillman Professor of Roman Catholic Theological Studies, Harvard Divinity School, Cambridge, Mass.

CHARLES E. CURRAN, S.T.D. is Professor of Theology at the Catholic University of America, and former president of the Catholic Theological Society of America.

RICHARD A. McCORMICK, S.J., S.T.D. is Rose F. Kennedy Professor of Ethics at the Kennedy Center for the Study of Human Reproduction and Bioethics, Georgetown University.

ANTHONY J. McDEVITT, J.C.D. is Officialis of the Tribunal, Diocese of Mobile, Alabama.

JOHN T. FINNEGAN, J.C.D. is Professor of the Canon Law of Marriage, Pope John XXIII National Seminary, Weston, Mass., and Weston School of Theology, Cambridge, Mass.

LEWIS J. PATSAVOS is Professor of Oriental Canon Law at Holy Cross Greek Orthodox School of Theology, Brookline, Mass.

JOHN L. THOMAS, S.J., Ph.D. is Research Professor at the Jesuit Center for Social Studies of Georgetown University, Washington, D.C.

PAUL C. GLICK, Ph.D. is Senior Demographer, Population Division, Bureau of the Census, U.S. Department of Commerce, Washington, D.C.

ROBERT S. WEISS, Ph.D. teaches sociology at the University of Massachusetts, Boston, and is research associate on the staff of the Laboratory for Community Psychiatry, Harvard Medical School, Boston, Mass.

JOHN HEAGLE is pastor of St. Patrick's Church, Eau Claire, Wisconsin, and Chairman of the Peace and Justice Commission, Diocese of LaCross, Wisconsin.

BERNARD HÄRING, S.T.D., C.SS.R. teaches theology at Fordham University, Bronx, New York.

KARL LEHMANN, S.T.D. is a member of the editorial board of *Internationale katholische Zeitschrift*.

THOMAS GREEN, J.C.D. is Professor of Canon Law, Catholic University of America.